Pushing Against Darkness

*Editorials on Morality and Ethics, Christianity, Islam,
Nature, Political Affairs, News Media, Globalism Policies,
National Cover-Ups, Military, United Nations, Israel,
and Miscellaneous Commentaries*

Michael H. Imhof

U.S. Navy SEAL Commander (Ret.)

Copyright © 2021 Michael H. Imhof
Copyright © 2021 ASPECT Books
ISBN-13: 978-1-4796-1345-8 (Paperback)
ISBN-13: 978-1-4796-1346-5 (ePub)
Library of Congress Control Number: 2021900194

The website references in this book have been shortened using a URL shortener and redirect service called 1ref.us, which TEACH Services manages. If you find that a reference no longer works, please contact us and let us know which one is not working so that we can correct it. Any personal website addresses that the author included are managed by the author. TEACH Services is not responsible for the accuracy or permanency of any links.

Published by

ASPECT Books
www.ASPECTBooks.com

Endorsements
PUSHING AGAINST DARKNESS

"In the battle of good versus evil, Commander Imhof takes a thorough look at the history of current issues that flood the world and specifically the United States. The author maintains **a frank perspective, while still reminding readers that the love and forgiveness of God prevails.**"

—Timothy Hullquist/Consultant

"This book by Commander Michael Imhof **sets the stage for understanding what is happening in the world around us.** Through my own interest, I read this book slowly and deliberately because there was so much **eye-opening information.** *Pushing Against Darkness* is a brilliant way of Michael saying to the reader 'I care about you, so let me uncover the truth and foundation/origin about these present day events, so you can see how they will open the door for developing your tomorrow and future to come.' **Absolutely everyone can glean from this book as a guide to understand what is in store for us as we plan for tomorrow's world.**"

—Patricia Plummer, President/Founder of Heart of Prayer Ministries, Inc., marketplace nonprofit ministry to business, government, and school leaders

"Ever hear, '*What on Earth is happening these Days?*' **From the Word of God, Commander Michael Imhof explains the good, plus this growing evil surrounding us.** This book shows the LORD's plan how to be saved. Salvation is not by our deeds; it is only by the free gift of the LORD's Grace. This is the only way and truth to spend eternity in Heaven living with God and those believers who by faith repented and asked Jesus to forgive their sins."

—John A. Sterba, M.D., Ph.D., FACEP/Missionary, Saved by Grace Ministry, Inc./Commander, Medical Corps, USNR (Hon. Dis.)

"As a U.S. Navy SEAL, Mike at times and at great personal risk, demonstrated a deep love for this country by providing actionable intelligence to his superiors so that they could make the right decisions going forward. Now retired, he continues to fight a "spiritual battle" for his beloved America by providing readers intelligence and warnings concerning politics, globalism, Israel, the military and much more with his years of newspaper submissions contained within the covers of this book. **Highly**

Recommended for those who have a love for country and the pursuit of righteousness!"

—Chris Coppler/ Sergeant Major, U.S. Army (ret.)

"I found in my reading that I quickly began to see the strategies of the dark kingdom as its agenda influences the heart of man. It's one kingdom (darkness) striving to circumvent the overall agenda of the other (light/ life). We need not be ignorant to the schemes of the adversary and his forces ability to influence our fellow citizens here on earth. The kingdom of heaven suffers violence and the violent (pro-active) take it by force. Let us not find ourselves as pawns in a dark kingdom. <u>After being exposed to the information presented in this book how can we sit back and not engage.</u> **It's high time we acknowledge our adversary and stand with the kingdom of our God and King. May we be found engaging in the conflict by praying, taking a stand, and speaking out!"**

—Mark Berney/Sr. Pastor

"If you are looking for a book to give you **factual knowledge with view-points established in Christian Conservatism**, and that can be used in outlines to engage in successful debates with leftist progressives, then **this is a must read.**

Michael has the intestinal fortitude to explain and state truths that most leftists and liberals would consider to be politically incorrect in exist-ing times. He cites hard historical evidence that has been forgotten, or intentionally, not taught by our schools and universities.

He has a great understanding of the Islamic system of authority and the history behind it. His explanation of why almost all Arab nations are ruled by dictators is eye opening.

On the Second Amendment, he discusses the main reason the Founders, especially President Thomas Jefferson, thought that the 'right to keep and bear arms is, as a last resort, to protect themselves against tyranny in government.' He correlates this to the 20th Century brutal and ruthless communist and socialist dictators that killed millions of their own people after disarmament of their populations.

These are just a few of his enlightening and historical facts that reminds the reader that America is changing not for the better. 'Evil is being cel-ebrated as good, and good as evil in America today.' Michael Imhof's book asks one **reverberating simple question to every reader** which every respectable God fearing American should be demanding an answer to, **'Why is morally wrong being celebrated in America?'"**

—Nick Ficarello/Chief of Police (ret.)

"I like facts, and Michael tackles issues factually. I enjoy the zeal that Michael has for reaching people as an ambassador for Christ. Michael breaks down the topics, and explains them from a Christian standpoint. His proclaimed Biblical principles in these articles are refreshing! **May this man touch your heart like he has mine! Highly Recommended!**"

—Joe Skonecki/ Mechanical Engineer/DOD Afghanistan Contractor (former)/State Trooper (former)

"***Pushing Against Darkness*** <u>grabs your attention from the very first paragraph</u> and takes the reader on a spiritual rollercoaster ride that leads to God.

Michael Imhof expels myth, misconception, and misdirection by Satan through man leading us to believe that evil is good, and good is evil.

Through Michael's excellent writing skills he masterfully exposes the battle between good and evil happening all around us, and how you can overcome it.

I **highly recommend *Pushing Against Darkness*** for anyone seeking real answers."

—Robert Saviola/Conservative Radio Talk Show Host

"Our Founding Fathers based much of our Constitution on their belief in God. Former Navy Commander and retired Navy SEAL, Michael Imhof, **captures the patriotic spirit of our Founding Fathers in his book**, *Pushing Against Darkness*. Commander Imhof's well-written book also provides a path to spiritual fulfillment. **Take a walk with him out of darkness, and toward the light.**"

—Chet Truskowski/Executive (ret.)/Chairman of Board (former)/ Bishop's Advisory Development Board Diocese Member

"Michael Imhof is a **dedicated** Christian who addresses issues that need to be confronted. It's clear that he loves this great nation, and is passionate against its misguided direction. Although his views may not be popular with leftist thinking, he demonstrates boldness in standing up for truth in the face of opposition. I most **Highly Recommend** this book for its insightful, educative, and direct approach on matters that concern us as individuals, and as a nation. **People should immensely enjoy this book**."

—*Loyce Webb/Sr. Pastor*

"When first meeting Commander Michael Imhof he quickly related that he was in Afghanistan when God told him to leave and go back to America and save souls. He did this and has been on a mission to save as many souls as possible through his writings and preaching. This book, a compilation of his published editorials, gives us an opportunity to read a brief, concise **biblical perspective on many topics of great importance**. The **power of these writings is the truth it conveys**, that **compels the reader to confidence** in the love of Jesus Christ as the savior of all and the surety of heaven and hell. I have had the chance to hear Commander Imhof speak, and while listening I can only thank God that this man was on the battlefield protecting my freedom and leading others to strength in Christ. Godly men are desperately needed in military service. The mission he is on now is more vital as it will lead those he reaches to eternity with God."

—*Kathy Weppner/Radio Talk Show Host*

Acknowledgements and Dedication

Special thanks to Patricia Plummer and Colleen Biffert for administrative review and support.

Freely use comments from these individual editorials to support your positional arguments or endeavors as appropriate.

Dedicated to all the Christian martyrs who have given their lives for the gospel of Jesus Christ. They gave their all in pushing against the darkness.

"Righteousness exalteth a nation: but sin is a reproach to any people."
Proverbs 14:34

"Woe unto them that call **evil good**, and **good evil**; that put darkness
for light, and light for darkness; that put bitter for sweet,
and sweet for bitter!"
Isaiah 5:20

"To give **light** to them that sit in **darkness** and in the shadow of death,
to guide our feet into the way of peace."
Luke 1:79

Table of Contents

Foreword

A common theme in humanity is good versus evil. Genesis chapter one of the Bible reveals that in the beginning God created, and it was good. Yes, it was good in the beginning, but what happened after that? Sin came forth, and life changed for the human species and Planet Earth. When sin entered the picture, then came evil. Good versus evil is a major theme in our society today, and each battles for the soul of man and the soul of a nation.

In observation of those struggles, I've written editorials over the years that I submitted to various newspapers, addressing areas on morality and ethics, Christianity, Islam, the natural world, political affairs, news media, globalism policies, national cover-ups, military, United Nations, Israel, and miscellaneous commentaries. Many people enjoy reading blogs; thus, I've presented in this book a consolidation of many interesting submissions on varied subjects with personal and distinct opinions.

These are common subjects for all born into humanity. They're integrated into our lives, everyday living, and the way that we see the world. Our perceptions of these subjects are typically shaped by parental influences, personal experiences, what we read, and what we see. These perceptions then help us form opinions and the way we see the world and act in it.

All people have opinions. It's common to the human species and all societies. It doesn't mean all opinions are right, but it's the way one sees the world. Sometimes opinions may be influenced, or swayed, and changed in some cases. Opinions then affect our behaviors. They affect our behaviors positively or negatively and strongly affect our decisions and how we function in life.

That's where this book comes in. Over the years, these editorials were written and submitted to different newspapers over time for printing in the opinion page section of the newspapers. Why would one want to take the time and do this?

First, based on my Judeo-Christian values, I wanted to push against the darkness, evil, and injustice of this world. Second, newspapers provided the means for me to get information out to a wide audience. I realized what one reads has an effect on one's perceptions of life. Thus, newspapers provided a forum for these editorials to go forth. At the very least, I wanted to get people to ponder and think about what was being written and presented for their consideration.

Did it mean that all would agree with my submissions? Certainly not, but if I could influence some positively toward good, then the effort would have been worth it.

Further, while much church leadership and many Christians are not keenly interested in government or politics, I am. In 2 Samuel, chapter 21, of the Bible, David went to God about a famine that had been in the land for three years. "Why, God?" God revealed to David that it was something that Saul set in motion from what he did to the Gibeonites years earlier. Saul represented government and the nation reaped the results of those government decisions. There are numerous other examples I could also give in support. My point is that what government does has a direct effect on a nation from both the physical and spiritual realms. That's why it's exceptionally important that we have righteous leadership. Righteousness exalts a nation.

Michael H. Imhof
Commander, U.S. Navy (ret.)

Introduction

Morality and ethics, Christianity, Islam, the natural world, political affairs, news media, globalism policies, national cover-ups, military, United Nations, Israel, and miscellaneous commentaries are subjects that often stir emotions. I've listed numerous editorial submissions under these categories that cover a broad range of subjects and issues in life. As I say this, and as you read the following pages, you'll find that my editorial perspectives are commonly rooted in my Judeo-Christian beliefs and values.

For me, my reference for truth in life is the Bible. This forms my foundational belief system. One who has the same belief system will typically enjoy the editorial verbiage. Contrarily, if one does not have this belief system, then one may strongly oppose these editorials. Even so, I hope it will make people ponder what's being submitted.

The editorials are written in simplicity, and the points should be easily understood by all who read them. They were written over a span of approximately twenty years, and most were printed in various newspapers. Some of the editorials, being opinion, cannot necessarily be proven, especially some editorials in the political section. Thus, readers must make their own conclusions as to the veracity of the submissions in their own consciences and minds.

In reality, much could be written and developed on the many varied subjects, but the newspapers limit the number of words that they allow. As such, much must be said in a concentrated amount of space. I've tried to do that. One will find some of the submissions applicable to any time period or year. Others will be applicable to the time period they were written in and submitted for print.

There's a part of me that always wants to know the truth and oppose injustice. I don't want to build my house on lies, and I don't want to see the American people deceived by unscrupulous elements from society or government. You'll see this come out in many of the editorials.

This, I know—God loves you so much. Know this is true. He only wants the best for you and wants to do good things in your life. As you read the editorials, glean what you will, and apply to your life where applicable. In some cases, some editorials may make for some entertainment reading, but in other cases, they may speak to your inner man for change. Embrace what God would have you to receive, and then apply it for good.

MORALITY

Chapter 1

Morality and Ethics

Note: This chapter has 34 separate newspaper editorials and are not presented in a specific order of when written.

America on Trial for Murder

On January 22, it will have been twenty-nine years since the *Roe vs. Wade* Supreme Court ruling that allowed legalized abortion in America. Even so, I think it would be interesting to visit a court higher than the Supreme Court. Let's visit the throne room of God, where America is on trial for murder.

God is now reviewing the evidence. Nearly forty million babies have been slain since the infamous *Roe vs. Wade* ruling in 1973.

God: "What does America have to say about this?"

America: "Well, God, the Supreme Court said that it was legal."

God: *"Did the Supreme Court take into account My biblical Word that one should not murder?"*

America: "God, really, a fetus is just a fetus."

God: *"My Word says that life begins in the womb."*

America: "We don't see it that way."

God: *"Then you're saying that you don't respect My Word, for I call it murder."*

Aborted children are now coming into the throne room to provide their comments.

Aborted children: "God, America never gave us a chance. We wanted to live, but we were defenseless. America literally tore us into pieces, and we felt such horrible pain."

God: *"America, why would you murder all these children and put them through such excruciating pain?"*

America: "We really didn't think we were doing that."

God: *"You're now lying because evidence showed that these children experienced tremendous pain. You became apathetic and overlooked it because of your selfishness and materialism."*

America: "God, really, it's the fault of our leaders. After all, they passed legislation to make all these abortions legal."

God: *"Didn't you elect these people to lead on your behalf? Many of you were so apathetic that you didn't even vote. You must always remember that I gave you the privilege of ruling yourselves since your inception. What did you do with that privilege?"*

America: "God, aren't You getting a bit harsh?"

God: *"No, I'm not being harsh at all. You should have voted for godly leaders and prayed for them. I don't buy into this attitude of separation of church and state. You see, that's a lot of bunk and a big mistake in your thinking. Godly leadership would never have allowed passage of Roe vs. Wade in the first place."*

Satan now comes into the throne room to provide his comments.

Satan: "God, since You do not change, You must find America guilty of murder. I used selfishness and materialism to appeal to her indifference, and she bought into it. This appears to be an easy case in my eyes. America deserves judgment.

God: *"You know My Word well. You remember that the innocent shed blood of Abel cried out from the ground to me when Cain murdered him."*

Satan: "That's right, God, and I know that the innocent blood of all these children does the same. Remove your protection from America, and

I'll make her wish she was never created as a nation. She won't know what hit her."

The church is now coming into the throne room to provide her comments.

God: *"How could you allow this to take place in America?"*

Church: "Well, God, we didn't want this to take place, and some of us did pray."

God: *"I said if My people would humble themselves and pray and seek My face and turn from their wicked ways, then I would hear from heaven, forgive their sin, and heal their land. Are you calling Me a liar?"*

Church: "Maybe we were too apathetic and not in enough unity."

God: *"You dropped the ball."*

All the participants are now in the throne room for the decision.

God: *"America, you're guilty of murder. What else do you have to say?"*

America: "Can we appeal to Your mercy?"

God: *"Church, do you have anything else to say?*

Church: "God, forgive us."

God: *"I'll be watching both of you. I want to see repentance, and I want to see it now. You know I've brought judgment against insolent and deviant nations in the past. Show Me you mean business and turn from your wicked ways."*

In conclusion, what will America do? Will she overturn *Roe vs. Wade?* Will she seek godly leadership? What will the church do? Will she earnestly pray for this nation and become more unified in purpose?

These questions and many more will be answered in the near future. Let's say you'll all be participants and witnesses to the answers.

***

A Nation without Moral Absolutes

Slavery and abortion have a common link. The 1973 Supreme Court declared in Roe versus Wade that the unborn child is not a person. The 1857 Supreme Court declared in the Dred Scott case that a slave is not a person. In both the *Roe versus Wade* and Dred Scott cases, nine men in black robes made decisions adversely affecting the lives of millions. A government without moral absolutes makes abhorrent decisions of this nature. One decision was made for selfish, economic reasons, and the other decision was made for selfish, personal convenience.

Without moral absolutes, there can be no "certain justice." Everything in government and law is determined by those who have power. Ultimately, justice becomes what people in power say it is. That said, evil is inherent in human nature, and no amount of legal maneuvering can eliminate its influence.

> *Ultimately, justice becomes what people in power say it is.*

People with Christian values must be in leadership if a republic is to succeed. Without this being the case, the republic will slowly crack, and ultimately, fall into decadence. It's common to refer to democracy as a government of laws and not men, but that's not true. Character and personal values of those in power influence their decisions and determine the direction of that nation.

People typically elect people who share their values; thus, leadership reflects the state of the people. Since Christianity has moral absolutes, it can be concluded that America, on the whole, is not a righteous nation based on prominent unjust and immoral laws. As such, we as Christians must continue to pray for America.[1]

***

Bible Establishes Moral Absolutes

There has been pressure from the White House for the Boy Scouts to allow gays into its organization. I think this pressure is wrong. I'll explain why. It's a lesson that our government and populace have repeatedly failed to learn.

By allowing gays into the Boy Scouts, basically, it acknowledges that the gay lifestyle is totally acceptable. People are becoming more "desensitized" to immoral standards as being the norm. After the gay lifestyle becomes more acceptable in our society, then some other immoral standard will be peddled as being totally acceptable. Gradually, step-by-step, our society is being taken down the road of decadence.

Much of this process can be initially traced back to when they took prayer out of the schools in the early 1960s. In 1973, *Roe v. Wade* came along and still remains. Tolerance and compromise of moral standards have been in evidence since.

---

[1]Resource reference: Ivy Scarborough, *Into the Night—The Crisis of Western Civilization*, Jackson, TN: Issachar Press, 2011.

There are moral absolutes. This is not what our government, nor does much of the populace desire to hear today. The anti-Christ spirit behind this attitude would contend that there are no moral absolutes. Why, because we, as people, have decreed it so. This humanistic and secular mind-set opposes the concept of moral absolutes. That's also why, in essence, the Ten Commandments are not in public buildings anymore.

The Word of God (Bible) establishes moral absolutes. I've got a word for our government and populace. Truth is absolute and will always prove its course. You can believe me now, or you can believe me later, but you will believe me.

***

End Partial-Birth Abortions

Since the tragic *Roe vs. Wade* Supreme Court ruling in 1973, there have been nearly forty million children killed due to legalized abortion in America. Even though it's medically proven that heartbeat and brain waves occur just forty-one days after conception, many in America have become ambivalent to abortion. It's clear that indifference to the subject has created a complacency among many people in this nation regarding the sanctity of life. This should not be so.

I did an article on this subject last year but must return to this matter once more since the Partial-Birth Abortion Ban Act is now again before Congress. To put it bluntly, partial-birth abortion equates to infanticide. Color the picture as you may, but truth is truth. No need to hide behind fictitious lies. Partial-birth abortions typically occur from four and one-half months to nine months into the pregnancy.

Congress has passed the Partial-Birth Abortion Ban Act twice, only to have it vetoed by President Clinton on both occasions. Interestingly, more than twenty states have successfully passed a ban on partial-birth abortion, but unfortunately, many of these have been struck down by misguided federal judges. What's missing here? Passage of this bill ensures children will not have to endure this inhumane and terrible treatment. People will do more for animals than for unprotected children such as these.

Yes, babies feel pain during partial-birth abortions. According to congressional testimony by the nation's leading anesthesiologists, including the president of the American Society of Anesthesiologists, the anesthesia given to the mother has little or no effect on the baby.

Here's another one for you. Dr. Martin Haskell, who has performed more than 1,000 partial-birth abortions, said that he performs them "routinely" for non-medical reasons and that 80 percent are "purely elective." Medical experts agree it's not necessary to kill a baby that has been almost entirely delivered to preserve the life or health of the mother.

This brings us to another item that's occurring, in conjunction with abortions, in our highly advanced and civilized nation. Many people are not aware of the fetal trafficking of body parts that has been ongoing. Basically, the abortion clinic "donates" aborted baby parts to a wholesaler. The wholesaler processes the parts for shipment to the end-user, such as a hospital or research facility. The wholesaler pays the abortion clinic a "site fee" and then charges the end-user a "delivery fee."

Excuse me, although "profitable" for some, this practice is depraved. First, abortion is wrong. Second, trafficking of body parts compounds this error in judgment. One can easily conclude trafficking of body parts helps to "legitimize" abortion in the minds of some parents. Some mothers, undecided and agonizing over the issue of having their babies, may be convinced that aborting their children will help society through research. Trafficking of body parts should be stopped. It's inherently wrong.

***

Abortion Is Wrong, Has Consequences

Life starts in the womb. Although the Bible clearly states this, many willingly choose to ignore a preponderance of evidence that corroborates this. Numerous children are born prematurely and live to become healthy adults. Personally, my brother had twin boys born at about seven months, and they've grown to be healthy young men.

John Kelly and Thomas Verny wrote "The Secret Life of the Unborn Child" in 1980. In reference to this book and ongoing research, unborn babies react to what happens around them. They hear, taste, feel, and learn in the womb. Babies are even keenly aware of the mother's emotions. Some adults have had actual memories of birth trauma, induced labor, or breech birth. Others have had dreams concerning womb experiences.

The womb should be a safe place for babies, and yet, our policies have made it a terror zone for many infants who are aborted. These little babies cannot protect themselves. *Roe vs. Wade* should be repealed. To put it bluntly, abortion is homicide. Abortion is immoral, and it brings shame in many ways. Not only does it bring shame to a nation, it brings shame to the individuals involved.

Men and women who choose abortion will often suffer consequences throughout their ongoing years. Truth and reason are tainted as the conscience becomes dulled and hardened. Guilt and shame remain hidden or unresolved throughout their lives. If this is you, please know that God forgives and wants to compassionately heal you from this trauma.

***

Abortion Is a Scourge

Abortion of the unborn is the scourge of America. More than sixty million abortions have taken place since the *Roe versus Wade* decision, according to the National Right to Life Committee.

God had a plan for each of those children. I wonder how many would have been doctors, teachers, plumbers, carpenters, nurses, policemen, firemen, soldiers, and so forth. We'll never know, and we're not the better for it.

The global elitists, Democrats, and liberals want to make unforgiving light of yearbook pages from decades ago for targeted individuals, yet fully remain insensitive to the rights of the unborn. Many premature babies are born who live worthwhile lives. It's not just a fetus; it's a life.

It's not just a fetus; it's a life.

Scientific evidence reveals that unborn babies feel pain. "The neural pathways are present for pain to be experienced quite early by unborn babies," explains Steven Calvin, M.D., perinatologist, chair of the Program in Human Rights Medicine, University of Minnesota, where he teaches obstetrics.

With the advent of sonograms and live-action ultrasound images, neonatologists and nurses are able to see unborn babies at twenty weeks gestation react physically to outside stimuli such as sound, light, and touch. Surgeons entering the womb to perform corrective procedures on tiny unborn babies have seen those babies flinch, jerk, and recoil from sharp objects and incisions. These are signs of life.

It's time to overturn *Roe versus Wade*. Pray against this infanticide because it's morally wrong. God isn't pleased.

***

Roe Versus Wade Should Be Repealed

I visited the Yad Vashem Holocaust Museum near Jerusalem in 2007. I left that visit in an exceptionally somber mood, as I had been touched by the depravity of mankind. The feelings still linger within my heart, and equally, so do the feelings I have for the more than fifty million aborted children in America since *Roe vs. Wade*.

King Herod decreed that the young children would be killed in Bethlehem. American policy has allowed for the execution of millions of unprotected children since 1973. The wise men did not return to Herod with the news he wanted. Where are the wise men today in America when it concerns abortion? Where are the wise men that will do the right thing?

In the land of Canaan, child sacrifice to the gods Baal or Molech was practiced. Today, in America, it's a flourishing practice to the god of Self. Morally and spiritually speaking, it's "wrong." It's "wrong."

Has one ever wondered why the practice of partial-birth abortion has been supported in light of its abominable procedures? Here's the answer—it's a very profitable business. Partial-birth abortion is the key method that provides intact fetal bodies from which they can sell organs for research. Selling fetal parts is quite a lucrative business, and the longer the gestation period, the better for business.

Shame on you, America, you emulate pagan countries of old with your infanticide child sacrifices. Where has your moral fiber gone?

Roe vs. Wade should be repealed "now."

***

Where Are Babies' Rights?

Birth control options include barrier methods, such as male and female condoms and contraceptive sponges, and hormonal methods, such as birth control pills, vaginal rings, and implantable rods. Others are intrauterine devices, abstinence, withdrawal, and rhythm methods. The list seems extensive unless you want to choose abortion like millions have done.

There have been more than sixty million abortions in America since *Roe v. Wade*, according to the National Right to Life Committee. Thus, it must be a popular means of birth control. It appears the cards are all in favor of the woman's "right to choose." Given certain circumstances, that right includes abortion after full gestation. But does the baby have any choices?

It's been scientifically proven (and is backed by the Bible) that life starts in the womb. So why is abortion such a popular means of birth control given all the other options? Selfishness and inconvenience are common answers.

It's puzzling that so many global elitists, Democrats, liberals, and RINOs clamor for the protection of illegal immigrant children at the border but refuse to give unborn babies any considerations or right to life. They want the news cameras to focus on illegal immigrant children at the border and to picture them as defenseless creatures—while totally rejecting photos of dismembered babies from commonplace abortions.

The silent cries of defenseless babies are real. There are better means of birth control. The babies should have rights, too.

***

The Adoption Option Is Best

Adoption provides an excellent alternative to abortion. There are similarities and differences in comparison of both decisions. Bethany Christian Services, a not-for-profit agency, has printed material available for those who are confronted with this important decision.

Based on some of their material, some of the similarities between the two decisions include:

- Earlier goals and plans can still be pursued.
- Life can be lived independently.
- One will not have to parent prematurely.
- One will be free from the financial burdens of parenting.
- There's freedom to choose if a long-term relationship with the baby's father is desired.
- Education or career can be resumed.

That's pretty much where the similarities end. The "differences" between adoption and abortion are significantly pronounced. Compare the following analogies:

- Pregnancy ends with giving of life or death.
- One may feel positive about one's choice, while guilt and shame may accompany the other decision.
- Memory will remain of giving birth or the taking of a life.

- One will have plenty of time to plan one's and the baby's future, while the other choice has finality with no reversal.
- One can have continued contact with one's child, while in the other case, one will never have that opportunity.

Adoption has many good features. First and foremost, if one is not ready to become a parent, one can still give one's baby the gift of life through adoption. With Bethany Christian Services and other agencies, one can plan for the baby's future by selecting a stable, loving family to care for the baby. After birth, one can see the baby, name the baby, and spend time with the baby. If one chooses, one can get updates on the child's progress, or have ongoing visits throughout the child's life, while one continues education or career goals. There are screened couples out there who want to become parents if given a chance.

Typically, adoptive families must meet standards that are shared with the donor. Adoptive agencies commonly complete a thorough assessment of potential adoptive families. Prior to finalizing an adoption, Bethany will make home visits to ensure the child's well-being. In an open adoption, one will see how well the child is cared for and loved.

In Bethany's case, one does not need an attorney, and there are no costs for the assistance provided through the adoption process. Legal details are handled. In addition, if desired, Bethany will continue to be available after the child's adoption is finalized.

I'm sure there are many questions that go through one's mind when confronted with a decision of this nature. As there are questions, there are also different options that must be scrutinized in the decision-making process. I, for one, believe adoption provides a preferable alternative to the trauma and heartbreak of abortion.

Bethany Christian Services has seventy-one offices in thirty states. One may contact them to learn more about the subject I've just discussed by calling 1-800-613-3188 or visiting www.bethany.org. Their pregnancy crisis line is one 1-800–BETHANY. In addition, the Indianapolis number is (317) 578-5000. There may be updates in procedures since this was previously written.

***

Planned Parenthood Destructive to Society

Affiliates of the Planned Parenthood Federation of America (PPFA) operate 900 health centers nationwide that serve five million Americans annually. Its international service division, Family Planning International Assistance, works in sixteen countries.

The political arm of the PPFA is the Planned Parenthood Action Fund. Together, they exert a substantial influence on the American and world populace and political arena.

The PPFA espouses that every individual has the fundamental right to decide when or whether to have a child. Yet, one needs to examine the roots of the PPFA to see why this organization promotes the issues with the slant they do. As such, let's briefly examine its background and see how it came into being.

Margaret Sanger, born Margaret Higgins on September 14, 1879, in Corning, New York, was to be instrumental in the formation of the PPFA. She later married William Sanger and grew up to be a radical activist. Key events in her life are documented as follows:

- In 1914 she published *The Woman Rebel*, a feminist monthly that advocated birth control. She was indicted for sending "obscene" materials through the mail.
- In 1916 she opened a clinic in Brooklyn, N.Y., was arrested, and served thirty days for distributing information on contraceptives.
- In 1921 she founded the American Birth Control League (which became the PPFA in 1942).
- In 1929 she formed the National Committee on Federal Legislation for Birth Control to lobby for birth control legislation that granted physicians the right to disseminate contraceptives.

The PPFA certainly has a positive name and conveys a family-oriented image, but in reality, is not an organization devoted to true family values. Closely examine its positions and pursuits on abortion, promiscuity, and religion. Closely examine its literature.

A strong advocate of abortion rights, this organization also undermines the moral values of teens. Its literature teaches children to masturbate; endorses premarital fornication; approves of homosexuality; encourages sexual experimentation, and scorns Christian values and prohibitions.

In *The Woman Rebel*, Margaret Sanger admitted that, "Birth control appeals to the advanced radical because it is calculated to undermine the authority of the Christian churches. I look forward to seeing humanity free someday of the tyranny of Christianity no less than Capitalism."

Dr. Alan Guttmacher, who succeeded Margaret Sanger as president of the PPFA, once stated, "We are merely walking down the path that Mrs. Sanger carved out for us."

The PPFA is clearly a visible and forceful advocate for reproductive rights. Some may argue that, in the beginning, Margaret Sanger saw birth control as part of a socialist reordering of society. Some may argue her crusade was to prevent the multiplication of the inflicted or to assure happy marriages. Some may argue that it was a woman's issue all the time where women had the right to control their own destinies.

Even so, this organization, which substantially benefits from government contracts and grants, continues to undermine the moral values of America in its advertisements, literature, and programs. Disinformation is gainfully used in its lucrative birth control, sex education, and abortion programs to achieve its purposes. Breakdown in morality is not constructive, but ultimately, destructive to the individual and society.

***

Planned Parenthood Should Be Defunded

Planned Parenthood is a nonprofit organization that markets itself as a provider of reproductive, maternal, and child health services. More than half a billion dollars of taxpayer money goes to Planned Parenthood every year. Some of that money has been fraudulently obtained through overbilling federal and state government Medicaid programs for services rendered. In addition, Planned Parenthood is also given substantial money from public grants.

Undercover journalists with the Center for Medical Progress released eight shocking investigative videos in July and August showing morally repulsive and horrific behavior by Planned Parenthood executives toward unborn children and their mothers. Selling of aborted body parts including lungs, hearts, livers, extremities, and heads by Planned Parenthood affiliates is morally wrong, period.

It's a common perception that mammograms are provided by Planned Parenthood. The fact is, although President Obama has propagated the mammogram myth, mammograms are not performed by any Planned Parenthood clinic. Another misperception is that Planned Parenthood helps women to have safe and healthy pregnancies, but percentages are very low regarding prenatal services.

Planned Parenthood should be defunded. It does not provide true reproductive health care. It's the nation's largest abortion provider and makes billions of dollars from the practice. It does not provide meaningful cancer, primary, or prenatal health care. Planned Parenthood is not trustworthy, nor is it safe for women and young teens. Further, it is not a wise investment in public health.

I recommend that you call your congressman to support the defunding of this organization. It should have been defunded a long time ago.

***

Government Leading in Wrong Direction

The Founders would be shocked at the amount of government interference and intrusion that permeates life in America today. Guaranteed, they would completely disagree with the government's overreach into the Christian churches. Our nation was created by people whose main purpose was to worship freely, living clean and moral lives without government intervention or enforcement of policies contrary to their faith. Churches and Christian schools with biblical standards are now consistently being challenged by the government and society.

The rights of Christians are being trampled in a modern attempt to purge Judeo-Christian values from the American culture. This is totally foreign to the original roots of America. Historian Peter Marshall makes some remarkable comments about the Pilgrim settlement: "This was the only place on the face of the earth where free Christian people were creating their own government, electing their own civil leadership – the only time in history, as a matter of fact, when a nation, from scratch, was based on God's Word."

Biblical knowledge was prevalent and often quoted in colonial everyday life. School instruction used Scripture verses, and moral living was commonplace. Sin was discouraged and seen as unacceptable behavior in the culture as a whole. Understanding the foundation of America puts recent decisions by our Supreme Court into an alarming perspective. Principles of morality and truth have given away to "anything goes" and "the end justifies the means." Many of these rulings are framed in terms as good for the whole, but in reality, they are centered in foolishness.

***

Supreme Court Tyranny Prevails

Non-elected left-wing, black-robed judges have now officially imposed their perverted view of law and morality on America. As recently as 2010, over two-thirds of the United States had banned homosexual marriage, with Americans overwhelmingly "rejecting same-sex marriage" at the ballot box. Amazingly, the Supreme Court arrogantly, against the will of the people and traditional values since the inception of this country, has now made same-sex marriage the law of the land.

Even though some people are looking at civil law versus God for moral direction, most Americans strongly reject the idea that any marriage other than that of a man to a woman is the right idea. The majority understand that homosexuality defies nature. It's not natural in the animal kingdom, and it's not natural through the eyes of God. A truly wise man will follow God's guidance. An unwise man ignores it. That said, we have some extremely blinded and unwise politicians and judges in this nation.

This is just another step toward their assault on Christianity, their true objective. Look for the rights of Christians to be even more challenged as this insidious same-sex marriage ruling now provides impetus. Look for them to manufacture hate crimes against Bible-believing Christians in the future.

> *There must be repentance, and it needs to start in the church.*

We have the leaders we have because of the spiritual condition of America. God often gives a nation the leaders they desire/deserve. There must be repentance, and it needs to start in the church. Churches/Christians, please pray for America. May God have mercy on this nation.

***

Transgender Movement Wrong

Apparently, a female student who transitioned to identifying as a male was crowned prom king recently at a Massachusetts High School. According to an article by Calvin Freiburger, the transition started in eighth grade. Nicole, now Nicholas, legally changed her name, and after years of consultation with a primary care doctor, endocrinologists, psychologists, therapists, and a support group, she underwent testosterone treatments and gender-transition surgery.

My heart is touched when I read about a story li
it's wrong. Mainstream media may spin this as a
in reality, it's not. God allows mankind the freed(
mankind often chooses wrong. Acts of transition
treatments, therapy, and gender-altering surgery is w.o..ᵤ

Many in society today say it's all right to do your own thing. There are no moral absolutes. After all, one should please oneself. I differ because I believe there are moral absolutes. They are derived from the Bible. The Bible gives definitive guidance on morality and ethical values. Our criminal justice system is derived from the Judeo-Christian values of the Bible.

Many factors affect one's perspective on their being, including social pressures, environment, and demonic influence. Sex change is not in one's best interest. Studies are already proving the negative effects from these transitions.

***

Sexuality of Men Has Been Cultivated

"My name is Bond, James Bond, and I'm a model for all men who want to be cool and masculine," so says James Bond. "Further, women fall for me whenever I look at them and will do for me whatever I desire."

"Freedom of the press has allowed me to publish *Playboy,* and I will influence men and boys throughout their lives with images of lust for the female body, and it will help me get rich." So Hugh Hefner might say.

Commercials consistently and continually stress sexuality throughout our society. Why? Sex sells. After all, men who want to be real men will buy our products when they see these voluptuous women that we use in our commercials. This is about manhood, man.

Recently, we've seen numerous men being accused by many women of sexual improprieties. Why should anyone be surprised by these accusations? As a nation, we've cultivated a society where men are to look toward women as an expression of their masculine identity. Sexual conquests add value to man's self-worth as a man. After all, that's what men have been taught since boyhood.

A society that teaches and cultivates morality contrary to biblical direction will reap the results of those efforts. Thus, society raises men to be men according to their teachings, and now wants to condemn some acting out their masculine desires and fantasies. What hypocrisy.

...an who values biblical direction will value women and treat them ...respect. It appears, as a nation, that we've strayed from biblical direc-...n and values.

***

Pornography's Evil Lure

Today, there's an ever-expanding display of pornography, or sexually-explicit material in print, in theaters, and on television. America's social structure is continuously being bombarded by powerful and lustful stimuli. To say the least, this bombardment has adversely affected thousands of individuals and families when one considers one's eyes and ears are the way to one's heart or inner being.

Let's revisit the Garden of Eden. One will quickly recall that Satan used the eyes of Adam and Eve when he tempted them to eat forbidden fruit. It was through their eyes that Satan first reached their souls. Opening one's eyes to doors of evil has negative consequences. It was through their eyes that their minds became awakened to evil and shame.

Before 1954 sexually explicit pictures were not readily available to mainstream America like they are today. That's the year *Playboy* magazine hit the newsstands. Porn soon gained new levels of acceptance as a result of *Playboy's* marketing strategy. By placing their magazine on newsstands with respected magazines and periodicals, respectability soon rubbed off on *Playboy*. Playboy's strategy worked, but at great expense for this nation. Most assuredly, pornography has ruined inordinate lives and shattered numerous families in its wake.

Pornography continues to expand like an ominous and growing storm. Today, the entire spectrum of pornographic material is available on the Internet, including images of soft-core nudity, hardcore sex acts, and much, much more. Textual pornography with graphic and extremely sensual details is readily accessible.

Who can access pornography on the Internet? Virtually anyone can access material. This means children too. What's to prevent a child from accessing cyberspace when there are no enforceable age checks or verification procedures in place?

Some of the online community and many of the media are opposed to any proposals to regulate the Internet or children's access to pornography. I strongly disagree. Pornographic material should be kept away from children on the Internet. Some may argue that technical fixes are less intrusive than a regulatory or criminal law approach but consider that software programs that regulate children's access to pornography can be bypassed by users with some knowledge of the Internet and some technical sophistication.

One may argue that parents should control their children regarding how their children use the Internet. True, but parents' technical ability often pales in comparison to the children's expertise. A child also has the ability to walk down the street to another computer, like the local library's computer.

Yes, libraries and some public schools now offer tremendous opportunities for porn profiteers to solicit new addicts for their products. Incidentally, this free access to hard-core pornography in public libraries is promoted by the ACLU and American Library Association. I'm sure porn profiteers truly appreciate all federally-funded tax dollars for computer access to the Internet.

The Adult Video News, the trade magazine for the porn industry, reported in 1996 regarding three U.S. presidents, "There have been fewer federal prosecutions of the adult industry under Clinton than under Reagan and Bush. With no reason to change his hands-nearly-off porn policy, vote for him." Let's face it; the Clinton-Gore administration has not aggressively enforced current federal obscenity laws.

One must always remember that without regulatory or criminal law enforcement that pornographers aren't discouraged from peddling their indecent materials to children. What can be done to alleviate this problem? First, current obscenity laws must be more aggressively enforced. Second, there needs to be a more regulatory approach to the Internet on behalf of children.

My comments should not be that difficult to understand. After all, regulatory guidelines exist for alcohol and tobacco use, driving and voting privileges, and entrance into the armed forces. In summation, Internet pornography needs to be aggressively regulated and dealt with on behalf of children.

***

Gay "Civil Unions": Are They Right?

Recently, the Vermont House approved a gay "civil union" bill. This legislation basically recognizes same-sex couples and grants them the same rights and benefits of marriage. Gay-rights activist groups believe this set a moral as well as a legislative example for the rest of the country to follow; however, I strongly disagree.

To grant special protection to gay behavior, "undermines the institutions of marriage and family." To grant special protection is to open the door to anything goes, and then there is no logical stopping point. Perhaps a man should be allowed to marry two women, or perhaps a woman should be allowed to marry two men. Opposition to granting special protection is not based on bigotry, but it's based on informed judgment about homosexual behavior and the political agenda of gay-rights activists.

The idea that homosexuals are born appeals to the American sense of fairness and tolerance, but in reality, this approach has flaws. First, there's no solid scientific evidence that homosexuality has a genetic basis. Second, even if this was true, homosexuality still should not be promoted as correct behavior. Do we urge alcoholics to give into alcohol abuse? Do we urge kleptomaniacs to give into theft? Do we urge pyromaniacs to give into setting destructive fires? Inclination does not make a homosexual. It's behavior that marks one as such.

People like to be treated fairly; thus, the homosexual community attempts to draw on the sympathy of the public by saying it's oppressed by bigotry. In reality, this is not an oppressed minority. Homosexuals have the same rights as everyone else. They have freedom of speech, freedom of religion, and a host of other rights. They get the same police protection as other citizens. One may say that the military doesn't give them proper rights. First, the military is a privilege or duty. It's not a right. Second, the military bars numerous groups from service that detract from the mission and preparedness, e.g., elderly, youth, single parents in some cases, and others.

The "gay rights" movement still contends it's truly oppressed as a minority group. Let's examine this more closely. As a whole, this community is not typically economically deprived. Research by marketing firms shows that homosexuals as a group have higher than average per capita annual incomes, higher than average household incomes, are more likely to hold advanced degrees, and are more likely to hold professional or managerial positions. Openly gay politicians hold numerous high-level government positions. In other words, as a group, they're highly advantaged people.

Minority groups share immutable characteristics such as race, ethnicity, disability, or national origin. Homosexuals surely can't claim immutability since "thousands of people have come out of the homosexuality lifestyle." No, homosexuals claim minority status based on behavior. Sorry, but this justification falls far too short.

Furthermore, God also calls homosexuality an abomination. This isn't bigotry on God's part. In reality, God loves people so much and desires to help them, but he doesn't love sin. Homosexuality has a destructive nature to it, and God desires to steer people clear of it. AIDS, other sexually transmitted diseases, drug and alcohol abuse, and shorter life spans are not uncommon in this group. I share this with compassion and no malice towards anyone.

Based on common sense and Judeo/Christian values, one must conclude that homosexual behavior is immoral, unhealthy, unnatural, and destructive to the moral fiber of this nation. A nation that cannot discern "right from wrong" will eventually become a more chaotic and disruptive society. In summation, our politicians need to recognize the wrongful nature of homosexuality and "not grant special or government-enforced" protection over gay activities.

***

Marriage Glorifies God

The Bible has a central theme in defining man's purpose for life. That purpose is to know and glorify God; thus, marriage should bring glory to God. As marriage vows are properly entered into, vows kept in purity, and biblical guidance followed by spouses, then God is glorified.

Marriage should bring happiness and wholeness to a united relationship, but it goes beyond that in the eyes of God. It should also bring glory to God. You see, marriage in today's society is not how God ordained marriage to be. It was not meant to be some quasi-legal contract where one can easily drop out on a voluntary whim. It was not meant for spouses to be totally self-centered and hostile towards each other.

Today's culture centers on the "Me" generation. Many are concerned solely about their own pleasures, fulfillments, and priorities. As a result, marriage is not greatly respected by many. Cohabitation is easier as it reduces obligation and gives latitude of self-expression and pursuits. Divorce is an out when emotions no longer answer the bell.

In today's hedonistic society, marriage is criticized as outdated and oppressive since it denies people personal freedom, autonomy, and fulfillment. Look how entertainment, advertising, and graphic art exploit sexuality and promote these values today.

God meant marriage to be a source of great happiness. Sin corrupts what God meant marriage to be. A marriage grounded in God's guidance brings strength, enjoyment, and stability to the relationship as well as glory to God.

***

Being Able to Forgive Is a Necessity

The Bible has much to say about unforgiveness. It makes it clear that we must forgive. This is not subject to debate if one is a Christian. One must forgive.

That said, sometimes it's difficult to forgive. One may say that "You don't know my situation." You're right, I don't, but I do know that one must forgive in order to proceed toward inner healing. In essence, unforgiveness keeps one prisoner while the other goes free.

So how does one forgive when the flesh doesn't want to let go. First, acknowledge that unforgiveness is a sin. Second, realize that the Bible directs forgiveness. Third, make a decision to forgive regardless of how wronged you feel. As a start, release forgiveness through your voice. One might start like this, "Father, in the name of Jesus, I forgive (fill in blank) for doing that to me. By faith, I hold no unforgiveness. I hold no grudges, and forgive (fill in blank)." When thoughts of unforgiveness return, refuse to receive them, but say, "Oh, no, no, I've forgiven (fill in blank)," and go your way.

Holding unforgiveness inside can affect health, and ultimately take one to hell if it is not dealt with. Your flesh was hurt, true, and feelings may take years to get over, but one must forgive if one is ever to be set free from its bondage.

Unforgiveness has separated family members, former friends, and business associates throughout time. It need not be so. Unforgiveness is a choice, and I urge you to forgive.

***

A Wonderful Testimony of Forgiveness

When my mother died suddenly of what we think was a heart attack, I was living in Atlanta, Georgia. I flew into town to attend her funeral. Before I went back to Atlanta, I wanted to spend time with friends and attend my old church. I reconnected with a lady who had been like a mother to me. We went to evening service, and afterward, she invited me to spend the night at her home with her family. Around 6:00 a.m. Monday morning, I was awakened by an argument she and her sixteen-year-old son, Johnny, were having. I heard her scream his name, then silence. I got up to investigate what was going on. Being a guest in their home, I asked her son's permission to see about his mother. The house was silent. I went to the basement, going through various rooms looking for my friend. I finally found her covered in blood, lying face down on the floor. From her son I demanded to know what happened. His response was that he didn't know. Standing in the middle of the floor in my pajamas, I didn't know what to do, so I headed upstairs. Before crossing the threshold of the kitchen floor, Johnny began stabbing me.

The first hit I took was to the side of my face. But this is the strangest thing that I had ever experienced before. There was an entity speaking to me (God) telling me (three things) what to do while I was being stabbed. I didn't move; I followed the instructions I was being given. He had the knife in midair, about to strike again, but suddenly, he stopped and walked out of the kitchen. That is when I heard the last of the instructions I was being given, which was to "go," so I did. In my bare feet, I began running down the street, knocking on doors in a strange neighborhood trying to get help for my friend who was bleeding to death in the basement. Twenty years later, I went to the prison to talk to her son to find out why he killed his mother, and without provocation, why had he stabbed me. The little chubby boy I had known twenty years ago was a tall young man now. In talking to Johnny, he wasn't the monster I thought he was going to be. He cried more than I did and asked for forgiveness for his actions against me, and I forgave him. He said my visiting with him has caused him to finally be able to forgive himself and to heal as well.

—— Based on an actual testimony

***

In Hedonism We Trust

Welcome to America, a land of hedonism. Webster's New World Dictionary defines hedonism as:

> *Welcome to America, a land of hedonism.*

"The doctrine that pleasure is the principal good and should be the aim of action." In other words, hedonists seek to live a life of pleasure, a life of self-indulgence. Does this apply to America? You bet it does.

One of the main causes of family breakdown in America is the desire for pleasure. When sports and entertainment stars make millions of dollars per year in comparison to salaries of policemen who put their lives on the line for the populace day after day, one must ponder this nation's priorities. Something seems out of balance. Pragmatically speaking, it just doesn't seem right or make sense.

Sex and pleasure are consistently used in advertising to attract people to products. The lure of pleasure is not new. Satan used this ploy on Eve in the Garden of Eden. The food of the tree was pleasant to her eyes. It appealed to her senses, and advertising uses the same ploy on millions daily. It appeals to a person's senses. If there's pleasure involved, then how can it be wrong?

Use of drugs, alcohol, and pornography is rampant in our nation. Why is this so? It is the pursuit of pleasure. This is the root of a person's obsession in many areas of bondage. Drugs, alcohol, and pornography are merely tools used by this hedonistic and idolatrous god of pleasure.

Many have observed that the decline and fall of the Babylonian, Greek, and Roman empires can be greatly attributed to obsession with pleasure. It was during Belshazzar's drunken orgy that the Medes and Persians broke through the gates of Babylon, and the empire came tumbling down. Who can forget how thousands were sacrificed in the gladiator days of the Romans simply for the perverse pleasure of those watching the arena events? Is the collapse of America next?

Entertainment seems to become more perverse all the time. People want more. They lust for more. Notice how many of these talk shows have become more lewd and raucous on a regular basis. Notice how wrestling has become more wild and bizarre. There's a diminishing return in pleasure. It takes more and more to get less and less pleasure out of something. That's why these programs have developed as they have. Entertainment has become big business, and the wilder, the better. People thirst for the next level.

Is America's obsession with pleasure leading us to a moral, spiritual, and financial bankruptcy? For sexually abused children, it spells trauma. For the cocaine user, it spells addiction. For the wife of an adulterous husband, it spells heartache. For numerous families in pursuit of better televisions, video cassette recorders, digital video disc players, Nintendo games, automobiles, and other products of pleasure, it spells excessive debt. Something appears to be wrong with this picture.

Pleasure costs big dollars and often claims much quality time from the family unit. How many hours does one commonly glue oneself to the television set in America thirsting for entertainment? Have you priced tickets for a professional football game lately? You bet entertainment costs money, and people are willing to pay big bucks for it.

It used to be that Sunday was the Lord's Day for many. It now appears to be a day of pleasure for multitudes all across America. Some of the best sporting events are commonly scheduled on television, and movie theaters are vigorously attended on Sunday. Which way to the golf course? Which way to the amusement park, where one can stand in line an hour and get a two-minute ride.

It appears that hedonism has become a god for many. To put it bluntly, hedonism is just that. I'm reminded of Moses, who had a choice of serving hedonism or the God of Israel. Moses was surrounded by luxury. Being the son of Pharaoh's daughter, he had pleasures set before him for the taking. He could have lived a life of abundant pleasure or suffer with God's people by leading them out of bondage. Moses realized that pleasure was just for a season and would not last. He had his eyes on a greater reward that would come later. Incidentally, his name is mentioned over 800 times in the Bible. I believe God was pleased with his decision of priorities.

I guess we all serve something. Who or what are you serving? It's a question we all should ask ourselves, and then we should ask ourselves why.

***

Vulgarity Too Common in Today's Society

Vulgarity has become more acceptable in the public realm. Filthy language, crude acts, and lewd habits are considered normalized behavior throughout much of our culture. Why the shift to behavior once considered in violation of good taste? Reasons exist for the change. Simply put, where there is cause, there will always be effect.

One catalyst toward increase in vulgarity is the broadcast media. Television and films can be used to educate and edify, but they can also be used to negatively influence and corrupt. Notice the steady stream of irresponsibility, illicit sex, violence, divorce, and rebellion that pours through the television channels daily. Negative behavior is so often glamorized, but what about the real-life results of such behavior? What about the shattered lives of people who emulate their screen heroes?

The entertainment just reflects the culture, some say. Don't swallow that pill. Yes, there is violent crime and perverse behavior, but in comparison, this coverage far exceeds that of typical American life. There are more volunteers helping others in society than there are criminals or prostitutes, but one would never know that from the screen.

According to Robert W. Peters, president of Morality in Media, based in New York City, the increase in vulgarity shows the values of those who produce and act in the entertainment industry. "Mainstream media corporations have largely abandoned their standards," he stated. "They have chosen the low road in significant measure because it reflects their lives. They have a distorted perspective of reality."

L. Brent Bozell III, chairman of the Parents Television Council in Los Angeles, said the television rating system is ineffective because producers of episodes, unlike the movie industry, determine the ratings themselves. Many evening television programs carry a Parental Guidance (PG) rating, even though the programs are full of vulgarity.

In many real-life American families, children are reprimanded for cursing. Adults are often corrected by spouses for inappropriate outbursts. Yet, situation comedies so often portray this behavior as totally acceptable and funny. Children see and emulate the entertainment stars. Just because a program depicts a lifestyle of promiscuity and irresponsibility as acceptable doesn't make it right. Children have impressionable minds, and there are consequences to pay in real life.

Music has played a serious role, as well. Vulgar-laden albums are available and listened to. According to John W. Kennedy, a recent Federal Trade Commission study indicated that 85 percent of children ages 13–16 who attempted to buy music labeled "explicit" made the purchase without being questioned. Most assuredly, there's a plethora of music out there that promotes violence, vulgarity, rebellion, and other negative behavior.

John Nieder, host of the "Art of Family Living" radio program in Dallas, says the rise in vulgarity is symptomatic of the godlessness, abusive behavior, and lack of restraint predicted in 2 Timothy 3. Grant Jones, a licensed psychologist and associate professor at Evangel University, says vulgar language disrespects the respect God intended humans to have in interacting with each other. Vulgarity can hinder or harm relationships. It influences the way one preserves one's character, intelligence, and maturity, according to James O'Connor, author of *Cuss Control: The Complete Book on How to Curb Your Cussing*.

So, what are people to do if they have children? First, lead by example. Start by eliminating casual swearing. Think positively and use alternative words. Cope, don't cuss. Timothy Jay, in his book *Cursing in America*, says

13 percent of the leisure conversation of American adults concerns cursing or obscenities. Second, limit a child's television viewing time in favor of family activities. Parents need to take time to influence their children to act wisely when they aren't in parental company. Further, monitor what they watch and what music they listen to. Rules must be set and explained in order to cultivate proper behavior and speech.

One's eyes and ears are the keys to one's heart. What one plants in one's heart eventually comes out one's mouth. Ephesians 5:4 tells us that "obscenity, foolish talk or coarse joking are out of place" (NIV). Ephesians 4:29 says, "Do not let any unwholesome talk come out of your mouths" (NIV). The Epistle of James says praise and cursing should not come out of the same mouth. Clearly, there's a lesson to be learned here if we'll listen and apply.

***

Hollywood and Its Stars Are Eroding Nation's Moral Fabric

Hollywood movie stars and musicians who actively demonstrate and speak out against American's current military endeavors would not be allowed to do so if they lived under the leadership of Saddam Hussein or Osama bin Laden. Freedom of speech was given to them through the blood of American soldiers who sacrificed their lives on the battlefield. It should never be taken for granted.

Civilian casualties will occur during war, but it is quite obvious America did its best to protect civilians. Why would some of these movie stars want to go to Iraq and serve as "human shields" to protect a dictator like Saddam? Do they really understand the total picture? I think not.

Let's go back to September 11. Let's get these movie stars out to New York City. Now let's see if they're willing to be human shields against the acts that caused falling debris and bodies from the World Trade Center. I venture to say we would only see policemen, firemen, and other underpaid civil servants who gave their all, with nothing in return.

We must understand these are the same people who are for animal rights but against the rights of the unborn. How can they be against war because of loss of life and then be equally in support of abortion? The liberal and often decadent mentality can be seen throughout their movies.

A plethora of Hollywood's movies have subtle themes that are integrated into the overall fabric of them, designed to subvert basic family and Christian values. Movie after movie attests to these shrewd and targeted assaults. I realize Hollywood is out to make a profit, but while doing so, it tactically promotes its liberal agenda, which tears at the morality of society.

It seems Hollywood likes to portray Christians as flakes or weirdos. A psychotic stalker (Robert DeNiro) is tattooed with Bible verses and a cross in *Cape Fear*. Then there's a serial killer (Kevin Spacey) in *Seven*, who kills his victims based on sins. In *Contact*, Palmer (Matthew McConaughey), a new-age minister, makes it clear he has no hang-ups about extramarital affairs. The list goes on, but suffice it to say, Hollywood takes shots at fundamental or dogmatic Christianity. Don't tell Hollywood there are moral absolutes. They don't want to hear that song.

Hollywood is quick to find receptive audiences in the promotion of homosexuality. Use a well-known star as a platform, and message conveyance is greatly enhanced. In *Philadelphia* and *The Birdcage*, Tom Hanks and Robin Williams, respectively, were employed in their full star power to attract plenty of viewers. Another Hollywood technique is to introduce homosexuality through a supporting role character such as George (Rupert Everett) in *My Best Friend's Wedding*, starring Julia Roberts. Character portrayals such as these are designed with purpose and, regardless how one views it, that purpose undermines Christian values.

Marriage is regularly placed in the rifle sight of Hollywood. *The Horse Whisperer, The Prince of Tides, The English Patient,* and *The Bridges of Madison County* all deal with characters who find true love (so to speak). However, their perfect attractions are married to someone else. Is the point that romantic love is more important than a sacred covenant taken before God? Should people take away from these movies the belief that romantic bliss is more important than marriage?

How does Hollywood view the family? In *Instinct*, Dr. Ethan Powell (Anthony Hopkins) is an anthropologist who is extradited from Rwanda back to the United States after apparently going insane and committing a multiple homicide. Dr. Powell reveals how he came to live among gorillas, which eventually accepted him as one of their own. He committed the homicides to protect his loved ones. Three bachelors show they can parent a child as good as parents in *Three Men and a Baby*. What about parents, children, brothers, and sisters? Is the nuclear family now to be construed as anything where there is a presence of affection of love?

Parental authority, pro-life stance on abortions, and their moral issues have also been subverted by Hollywood. I've just drawn some attention to sly and subtle gestures the movie industry uses in order to communicate its liberal ideals.

When I think of these shrewd approaches to the movie audience by Hollywood, I think about a military tactic known as a diversion. A diversion is set up by a combat force to draw attention away from its main assault area. Much in the same manner, Hollywood disguises these assaults within the larger story. Keep the audience focused on the bigger picture and tear away at pro-family values. Judging by moral values in today's society, it certainly appears to have had to an effect.

***

It's Time to Reject Immoral Entertainment

Organizers of the Cannes Film Festival earlier this year recognized the film *Zoo*. The film centers on a supposedly true-life incident in which a forty-five-year-old man was involved in an act of bestiality with a male horse. It appears that the filmmaking community is now attempting to normalize the abhorrent lifestyle of bestiality.

One of the cast members of *Zoo* went so far as to say that the animals were "willing participants" in the sex acts. It seems this is the same type of irrationality that pedophiles use when trying to justify child-adult sex. Judeo-Christian values, based on the Bible, clearly indicate that bestiality is wrong.

The entertainment industry has gone to great lengths to normalize the homosexuality lifestyle. Now it's attempting to normalize bestiality. Is there any moral compass left in the entertainment industry?

The Internet also provides a means for pornography producers to inundate the marketplace with decadent material; thus, pornographic addictions have significantly increased among Americans and the world. As such, perhaps the entertainment industry now believes it can capitalize on bestiality.

It's clear that the entertainment industry and Internet have a great influence on morality. Why? It's because what goes through one's eyes and ears goes into one's heart. Out of the heart come the issues of life. Morality is important, individually, and corporately as a nation. Guard your heart. Reject immoral entertainment.

Righteousness exalts a nation, and yes, there's a vice versa to that as well. God's Word remains true.

***

Be Aware of Dangers of Sex Trafficking

Sex trafficking is more common in the United States than people really have imagined. A report of a missing teenager in Tulare County, California, in late 2016 culminated into the uncovering of one of the largest sex trafficking rings in the Western United States, according to a recent announcement by the Los Angeles County Sheriff's Department. Thirteen young women and girls, including the missing teen, were freed from captivity as a result of an extensive investigation.

Investigators in the Los Angeles Sheriff's Department discovered a sizable human sex trafficking network that extended from Nevada to California. During the course of the investigation, detectives discovered that apartments were used as brothels by the ring in many public areas.

"Human trafficking, which includes sex and labor trafficking, is one of the fasting growing crimes in the world. Its reach is not limited to foreign countries," California Attorney General Xavier Becerra said. "In California, human trafficking is reported here in our state more than in any other."

The *Los Angeles Daily News* reported that since the Los Angeles Regional Human Trafficking Task Force was established in 2015, there have been 697 arrests, and of those, about 30 percent were male buyers. In addition, there have been 185 victims rescued, a majority of them youths who were sex trafficked.

This case probably just scratches the surface of how extensive sex trafficking is in America. Parents need to be attentive to what their children are doing online and elsewhere. Depraved predators are out there and will prey on children.

***

Battle for Moral Conscience

Most Americans are familiar with the Ten Commandments. That said, while many may know about them, they cannot quote them. It's also obvious that many people do not adhere to them.

Advertising, television shows, movies, and mainstream media, over time, have helped hardened the conscience of this nation. Advertising encourages coveting, while well-known television actors ignore the ban on adultery, fornication, and murder. How many in a television series or movie today honor their parents? God's guidance in today's society is repeatedly shown in mocking ways.

The eyes and ears are key to one's heart. Whatever one sees and listens to goes into the heart. Thus, it's not surprising that the moral conscience of America has been hardened, given the plethora of material that has been released into the airways and society.

For advertising, television shows, movies, and mainstream media, it seems virtually anything goes versus the moral guidance of the Ten Commandments. Libraries have used transvestites to read books to young children encouraging acceptance of all lifestyles. Gay marriage and transgender men having babies are pushed as totally acceptable today. They push the theme that no matter what the lifestyle, it's now acceptable because they create the norms. This thinking is perverse and repudiates their belief in God.

Our Founding Fathers would not agree with the moral direction of America. George Washington, James Madison, John Jay, and others saw the exceptional importance of our Judeo-Christian values in government and society. America must morally reverse course, or it will not stand. America is in great need of prayer.

***

Evil Is Celebrated as Good

Evil is being celebrated as good and good as evil in America today. It used to be that everyone in society basically knew what was good and what was evil, even if they didn't play by the moral values of the nation. That has significantly changed.

> *Evil is being celebrated as good and good as evil in America today.*

If you choose a lifestyle that is morally wrong, you are celebrated by the media, entertainment world, and progressive left. If you choose to speak out against the sexual sin that is greatly increasing in America, then you are considered to be a hater, phobic, bigot, racist, or prejudiced.

Notice in the transgender world, how Caitlyn Jenner (formerly known as Bruce Jenner) is commonly interviewed and celebrated with numerous awards. Notice how Barack Obama put the rainbow lights (in celebration) on the White House after passing of the same-sex marriage law. Gay lifestyles are now more commonly accepted throughout society. Many people have been indoctrinated to accept immoral lifestyles as just commonplace living. Be assured that Hollywood movies and the media have done their part to push these themes as acceptable throughout the populace.

To expand this further, governments all over the world are now passing "hate speech" laws that are making it a crime to speak out against sexual sin. This conveys that there has been a global elitist policy put in place to break down morals throughout western nations. It's part of their agenda as they push toward a New World Order. Even so, it doesn't change how God sees things.

***

Morality: Russia Versus America

I was not pleased with Russia's anti-Christian terrorist law. I vehemently oppose this policy, but on the other hand, I support Vladimir Putin on some other moral issues.

Here are some things that Putin supports:

- Promotes the sanctity of life in the mother's womb.
- Does not fund "Planned Parenthood" abortion mills.
- Does not support sodomy.
- Does not support nor use Russian funds to support many of the American sexual perversions, like LGBT men in women's restrooms and locker rooms. Putin has common sense and knows the difference between a man and a woman.
- Keeps Russian national borders as secure as possible, not accepting "Syrian Refugees" (Muslim migrants/terrorists) that America freely pursues/welcomes without proper vetting.

In America, bakeries, photographers, bed and breakfasts, and other private Christian businesses cannot honor their faith by refusing to do business with homosexuals; they have been criminally punished, and many put out of business.

A newly born-again Christian woman clerk in Kentucky, because of her faith, refused to issue marriage licenses to same-sex couples and was thrown in jail.

So, as Christians, let's evaluate what we see in America. We tolerate separation of church and state even though it's not in the Constitution; we've allowed over fifty million abortions, and we've acquiesced to sodomy becoming the law of the land through same-sex marriage.

So when we point a finger at Russia, please remember there are three pointing back at us.

***

Transgender and Related Issues

Transgender and related issues seem surreal. These are issues that our founding fathers could never have envisioned since so much of this is ludicrous and exceptionally challenging to common sense. Christians in America are faced with horrible laws today. There's an anti-God assault in America. You see, America no longer encourages religious liberty, but in reality, only reluctantly tolerates it. Religious freedoms have been greatly reduced in this nation.

Many Christians today seem to be making their own version of God. Thus, to them, does it now mean that God has changed His mind, and many things are now acceptable, even though these things have been labeled as sin throughout the Bible? In essence, some Christians, being influenced by the media and society, are calling sin as righteous behavior. That said, Jehovah does not negotiate with nor compromise with sin.

Christians who fall into this category need to look at Scripture again, and this time, more closely. Christians have a duty and responsibility to share God's truth with others in society. As such, they need to stand strong on God's truth and share with others. They need to use prudence and wisdom and stand strong with their convictions of truth derived from God's Word. They must not compromise Scripture.

Christians are the ones with the light, and that light needs to go forth and dispel darkness. Our nation is under assault from the demonic kingdom. It's quite obvious. Christians must stand strong in God and pray fervently for this nation.

***

Living in a No-Fault Society

It started a long time ago in the Garden of Eden. Most know the story of Adam and Eve. God approached Adam in the Garden of Eden about the forbidden fruit being eaten. He did not approach Eve. Adam then blamed it all on the woman God gave him. "It's not my responsibility, God. The woman you gave me is to blame, not me." Is it really different today? The

United States has become a no-fault society. Something or someone else is to blame.

Many people are set free in criminal cases because of their pasts. Lawyers repeatedly go into court and say it's not their client's fault. Perhaps their client had a bad childhood, and as a result, committed the crime because of built-up frustration against society, or something else that has a good ring to it. Yes, social ills are to blame, but not the one holding the gun. His client was just a victim of circumstances.

Numerous states even have unilateral no-fault divorce laws. In other words, one spouse can obtain a penalty-free divorce, even if the other spouse wants to work at preserving the marriage and has done nothing to give the deserting spouse grounds for divorce. No one, in reality, is really to blame. It just hasn't worked out. Nothing else needs to be said.

What about all these deaths that occur on the highways? Automobile companies are to blame for many of them because they didn't protect people well enough. True, there are some legitimate cases, but never mind in many of them that people were speeding or in violation of the law. Bring suit against the automobile companies anyway. It's really their fault, and as such, they should pay a great settlement.

Look at the tobacco lawsuit victories in recent months. It's the tobacco companies' fault people were suffering lung diseases. Since it's their fault, then the tobacco companies should pay substantial settlements. Never mind that cigarette labels clearly warn that smoking may be hazardous to one's health. Never mind that the media repeatedly has addressed smoking hazards in numerous newspaper articles and radio and television programs. It's not the smokers' fault; it's the tobacco companies that provide the product. Put the blame on them.

Now the government is looking at gun companies. To my understanding, the gun companies really haven't broken any laws. Even so, it's the gun companies' fault that people are getting shot in our society today. After all, they allow guns to get into the hands of criminals and other elements. Bring lawsuits against the gun companies. Yes, the gun companies are to blame for numerous deaths in low-income and other areas. It's really not the fault of these people who misuse firearms. They're victims of the gun companies. The gun companies should pay substantial settlements to them.

I haven't seen any lawsuits against the major running shoe companies yet for runners who sprain their ankles. Perhaps I will in the near future. Sometimes runners suffer some nasty sprains, and after all, it's those shoe companies that sell them their running shoes. Perhaps, if the shoes had just a bit more support, these sprains wouldn't be quite as severe. Running shoe companies better take heed. You may be next.

Then, let's not forget about these companies that make these appetizing desserts. One must remember that many of these desserts have a high number of calories. Calories contribute to weight gain. People with tendencies for weight gain may be taken advantage of by these companies. Let's face it; these companies shouldn't make such appetizing desserts with high calories. Dessert companies better take heed. You also may be next.

Where does responsibility for one's actions and choices begin in our current-day society? It appears lines are becoming fuzzier all the time. I don't think this trend is good for individuals or our nation. This "no-fault" mentality is getting out of hand. Responsibility and accountability for one's actions and choices need to be accepted and acknowledged. This applies to all levels of government, as well as to citizens.

Accepting responsibility for one's actions and choices makes a character statement. Equally, the reciprocal is true. Remember, when one points a finger at someone, then there are three of them pointing back at oneself. It's time for people to accept responsibility for their actions and choices. Let's all learn a lesson from Adam.

***

The "Normans" of Our World

I recently saw a video at church about a man named Norman. Norman was a man people did not want to have much to do with. You see, Norman was about seventy and did not take care of himself too well. He didn't bathe regularly, and his house was not well maintained. As a matter of fact, his house was dirty, and empty food cans were plentiful throughout his kitchen. His clothes were dirty and old. To put it bluntly, Norman was a lonely man who people shunned.

It happened that a Christian man lived near Norman in the neighborhood. God started to move on this man's heart to reach out to Norman. This man started to be convinced of God's love. He pondered how one can do all sorts of things for God, but without love, it means nothing. Even though he didn't want to reach out to Norman, he did and gradually started to build a friendship with him.

As God moved on this man's heart, he reached out to Norman in different ways. He invited Norman to a professional baseball game.

He helped clean and fix things in Norman's house. He invited Norman on the family's vacation. There were things that this man did not, in his flesh, want to do. Even so, as he did, it progressed to where Norman's life was greatly improved. As a result of this man reaching out to Norman, Norman also received Jesus Christ into his heart as Lord and Savior.

Locally, I've monitored the story of Wesley Troxell in the newspaper. Wesley was a twelve-year-old boy who died not long ago as a result of a gang initiation. I did not know Wesley, but perhaps I can make some plausible observations about this situation. Wesley was probably a boy who needed to belong as do most gang members. Judging by his young age in comparison to some of the others involved, Wesley may have been regarded as a black sheep. In other words, Wesley didn't get much respect and perhaps was picked on. It's like the kids picked last on the team after all the others have been chosen.

People are people, no matter how one cuts it. People as adults shun certain adults, and kids as kids shun certain kids. Adults are quick to criticize others without walking a mile in their shoes. Kids can be vicious to one they consider odd or a little bit different. People shoot deadly arrows at others and often have little regard for how others receive them. So what if feelings were hurt! So what if lives are destroyed!

I'm thankful Anderson has charities like Operation Love, Christian Center, Dove Harbor, and others that reach out to hurting and needy people. I'm sure they've helped multitudes in the course of time and have changed many lives for the better. However, I think it wise to occasionally evaluate ourselves in how we are affecting and reaching out to others in our personal lives.

Do we shun others and treat them as outcasts? Do we criticize and put others down without knowing much about their backgrounds and situations? Are we concerned just about our sphere of the world and care nothing about others? These are questions we should periodically ask ourselves, especially if we claim to be Christians.

People can make a difference in the lives of others if they choose to do so. There will always be a Norman or a Wesley out there. How do we react to them? We can make a difference if we choose to reach out. An initiated kind deed here or there often goes further than one perceives. Indifference won't contribute, but determined action certainly will.

People can reach out to others through organizations like Operation Love, which depends on "charitable donations and volunteer support."

Being a part of organizations like this extends a helping hand throughout the community.

Matthew 25:40 says, "……Assuredly, I say to you, inasmuch as you did it to one of the least of these My brethren, you did to Me."

***

Children Need Fathers

Fatherhood affects our society in so many ways. Although fatherhood is officially acknowledged on Father's Day, it's a subject that bears serious scrutiny in the ongoing family and social issues of this country. With that in mind, I now address fatherhood in greater detail.

According to a 1987 Bureau of Justice Statistics Special Report, seven in ten juveniles in long-term correctional facilities did not live with their father while growing up. One just needs to visit long-term correctional facilities to determine this to be so. One will find that females from father-less homes are more likely to have children as teenagers out of wedlock than those who grew up with fathers.

The disappearance of fathers and the drifting away from religious teaching have removed restraints on behavior. Place children in an environment awash with violence, sexually exploitive movies, rebellious music, and one has the making of future problematic children. The development of productive and responsible children doesn't just happen. A father who spends time with his children helps build their self-esteem and character. A father can and should help teach his children "right from wrong" values through godly discipline. A fatherless child will not have this benefit.

You see a difference in the school system atmosphere today compared to a few decades past. In the 1960s, running in the hallway was the problem. Today, children and teachers are getting shot. Why the change in the school atmosphere? A number of reasons exist, but I'll focus on lack of moral guidance in the home as one.

Today, this is more important than ever when one considers all the negative influences vying for the child's attention. Unfortunately, apathy and lack of time with the children have settled into the family, and things are just accepted as normal. It need not be this way. The problem with the youth of America starts before they ever get to school. The heart and soul of this nation is founded in the home.

It's unfortunate that fatherless homes have increased with many children born out of wedlock. In many cases, due to divorce or other reasons, a single woman will have to raise children by herself while maintaining a full-time job. This can be an exceptionally challenging task, and many men who shirk their responsibility to their children are wrong and need to learn a lesson about this subject from Adam.

One may recall that God approached Adam in the Garden of Eden about the forbidden fruit being eaten. He did not approach Eve. Adam then blamed it all on the woman God gave him. "It's not my responsibility, God." A young man will get a girl pregnant today and say it's not his responsibility. It's her fault, not his.

Something or someone else is to blame. One will never mature in life until one accepts responsibility for one's actions and quits blaming others for one's mistakes. Fatherhood accepts responsibility.

It's unfortunate that many in society downplay the role of the father in the family. Notice how situational comedies portray the father as a buffoon or superfluous to the family. The eyes and ears are channels into one's heart or inner being. What one hears and sees has a direct impact on one's perceptions and beliefs in life. Children, especially in a fatherless home, who grow up watching these kind of programs, certainly will not have good role models to learn from. Hollywood, directly or indirectly, has done an injustice to the American family through these obnoxious character portrayals.

Fatherhood is important to God in the role of the family. If not, then perhaps he would only have made Eve, instead of Adam and Eve. A father is to bring provision and protection to the home. He is to bring masculinity with love. He is to take responsibility and promote moral values within his home. Most assuredly, true fatherhood brings a blessing to the family.

***

Our Nation's People Are Living in Lies

Our nation is grounded in lies. Lying pervades our government and media. People are being deceived, and in so many ways, don't feel the worse for it. In other words, they want to believe the lies. They don't want to face truth. Many people want to live in a make-believe world and pretend things are as presented by the government and press. That's because they want to live what they're being told, given, and allowed to participate in.

There's something about truth, however, because truth is absolute. Eventually, many will be awakened to truth, and it'll startle them immensely when this occurs. It'll be like awakening someone out of a stupor, only the truth they'll face will cause them great dismay and rob them of their pseudo peace.

> ***People have been desensitized to morality and sin in this nation.***

People have been desensitized to morality and sin in this nation. Many in society believe that freedom of expression sets people free, and it's the exact opposite. Homosexuality brings people into bondage; it doesn't set them free. Adultery, drugs, or alcohol brings people into bondage; it doesn't set them free. Sin seems fun for a while, but it eventually takes one further than one wants to go. One always pays the piper for the music, and in many cases, there will be stiff payment.

To follow biblical guidance and morality is what brings real peace and sets people free. As one turns from God, one turns to bondage. As one turns to God, one gets set free. This goes for individuals and nations.

***

A Godly Nation Starts in Home

America celebrates special days honoring mothers (May) and fathers (June). Parents mean so much for children to be brought up in a healthy and supportive environment. Needs are met, and values are taught.

That said, parenthood goes beyond just providing a roof over heads and food on the table. One glaring error seen in many American families today is the lack of child discipleship. Christian instruction starts in the home. The results from the lack of it is commonly revealed in crime throughout our nation.

Parents need to rear their children in a godly environment. They must point them to Jesus Christ and guide them in the ways of God. The love of God exemplified in a home depicts a beautiful picture of grace and redemption. Sharing the good news of Christ's resurrection and the love that He has for us starts in our homes.

How can parents have an impact in this manner? Parents can model discipleship in their homes. Do parents trust in God? Do parents take things to God in prayer? Where do parents place their priorities? Is it taking children to a soccer game on Sunday morning, or instead, taking them to Sunday School and church?

Parents need to live by biblical instruction. They need to address heart issues with their children. Formative instruction is required to fix the sin problem. Prayer and hugs should be requisite in establishing a godly and loving environment. Teach children while doing daily activities, and help them to see things from God's perspective.

Chapter 2

Christianity

Note: This chapter has 34 separate newspaper editorials and are not presented in a specific order of when written.

America Needs Spiritual Revival

People have different opinions and perspectives on the main problem in America. Some say it's drugs. Others point to gun control. Thoughts become quite extensive as one ponders this question. The media regularly covers and reports on numerous problems, but still, the question remains, what's the main problem in America?

It's true drugs are a problem in our society. Drugs ruin lives. America has spent millions of dollars on fighting the infiltration of illegal drugs into this nation and advertising against drug use. Even so, as long as demand is there, then supply will be there, too.

America may even take its case overseas. Let's put on our "Uncle Sam" hat and go to Bolivia. Let's talk to a Bolivian peasant family growing coca leaves. Let's tell José to grow corn and not coca leaves. After all, it's not good for the United States. José, who may not even know where the United States is, has to feed his family, and the man down the road will pay him more to grow coca leaves than corn. He's just trying to make a living in his country and provide for the needs of his family.

Many in the United States see gun control as its main problem. Guns kill, or do they? A gun is an inanimate object. Perhaps the same could be said of the automobile. A car kills, or does it? A car is an inanimate object as well. Oh, but criminals use guns to carry out crime, and gangs use guns in gang violence. True, and the hunter uses a gun to put some food on his family's table. Others use guns to target shoot. So is the problem really with the gun?

Then there's the increase in gang membership. True, there must be reasons membership in gangs has increased. There must be reasons why gangs use violence in their gang activities and operations. Now, if we could just uncover those reasons and truly address them, then maybe gang violence wouldn't be as much as of a problem as it is today.

What about the breakdown of the nuclear family? Perhaps that's the main problem in our society that causes all these other problems to exist as much as they do. After all, in recent decades, there have been significant increases in divorce and children growing up with only one or no parents. Children are commonly born out of wedlock today. If they had better supervision and parental care, maybe gang membership and violence wouldn't be as prominent as it is.

Alcohol is perhaps the main problem for those who have grown up with an alcoholic parent. Money that should be used for the family is spent on alcohol; thus, many of the family needs aren't being properly met. Then there's the continual abuse and strife that besets a family in this situation.

One might say that immoral lifestyles are the root of many of these problems. People only go around once in life, so why not live life to the fullest? That means having a good time in any way one can. After all, one has rights. One's lifestyle is a matter of choice, and there should be laws to protect one's lifestyle. I guess this kind of thinking ties into the "me" generation. If it feels good, and I like it, then nothing must be wrong with it.

The main problem in America is not any of the ones I've previously mentioned. The main problem is a spiritual one and not a physical one. Change the spirit, change the man. Don't change the spirit, don't change the man. America attempts to correct problems through Band-Aid fixes. To get rid of the weeds, one must get to the roots.

American needs a spiritual revival that would sweep this land with the gospel of Jesus Christ. That would be getting to the root of the problem. This would begin to remedy many of the aliments in society.

***

Real Meaning of Christmas

Without Christ, there's no Christmas. Without salvation, there's no celebration. Those who celebrate Christmas without these realities will celebrate in vanity. They may enjoy the season and have a good time, but it'll have been in vanity.

My first assignment overseas as a young Navy lieutenant was in the Middle East. During this time, I lived in Egypt, Israel, and Jordan, visited Cypress and Syria, and worked in Lebanon for certain periods of time. I was a young Christian, and during my free time, I traveled extensively on my own to see what I could see regarding biblical areas.

I came to realize something remarkable about the Bible. In reference to prophetic Scripture, I saw how it was backed up again and again by archaeological and historical evidence. Considering that there is no holy book in the world that deals effectively with prophecy except the Bible, I found the fulfillments supernaturally impressive.

The prophetic fulfillments further confirmed that this was not a "pie in the sky" book. I came to realize that man records history, but God writes it.

I often ask people what's more important—sincerity or truth? Without question, truth is more important. You can be sincere as a suicide bomber, but that doesn't mean that you're operating in truth.

"Behold, I bring you good tidings of great joy which will be to all people. For there is born to you this day in the city of David a Savior, who is Christ the Lord" (Luke 2:10–11, NKJV). Make Jesus a reality in your life this Christmas.

***

When Life's Final Bell Rings

I sometimes think of a prizefight when I visit a funeral home. As I approach a casket, I think within me that for that particular person, the bell has rung in the twelfth round. Now, it's time for the decision.

What's the most important decision in that person's life right now? I guarantee it's not about having a new car or shopping for groceries the following day. Their primary concern is their status in the afterlife.

So what's that dead person's status? Is that the real person we see all fixed up to look nice in the casket, or is it just a lifeless shell that person lived in? Is the spirit that lived in that body the real being that is now living in heaven or hell? If it is, then it would have behooved that person to have found out the truth before life's last breath.

Perhaps questions of this nature were not a priority. Perhaps this person was too busy to be concerned about afterlife questions. Perhaps this person avoided discussions about politics and religion. You know, many people don't like to talk about these two subjects. Perhaps this person was reaching for the gusto and living for the world, thinking you only go around once in life.

I'm not a politically correct person. I believe truth is absolute and will always prove its course. To hide behind political correctness is too often to hide behind lies. Ultimately, hiding from truth will only hurt oneself in the long run. One must confront truth to ultimately be set free.

I have strong Christian beliefs, and fortunately for me, earlier in my life, I came to realize that the Bible was the inspired Word of God. It's not a "pie in the sky" book. Most assuredly, it's backed up by history and archeological evidence. As a result of living in Israel, Jordan, and Egypt, the Bible also became geographically alive to me.

One key item that sets the Bible apart from other holy books is that of prophecy. Other holy books don't deal with it, but the Bible does so in a grand manner. Over and over again, the Bible is backed up by history and archeological evidence. Many do not realize the significance of this because they haven't closely studied it. It's an amazing book.

The Bible talks about heaven and hell as being real places. I will now discuss with you some real-life testimonies about heaven and hell. These testimonies only confirm what's already been said in the Bible.

I heard Mary Kathryn Baxter speak in San Diego at a church one evening. She said, as part of her testimony, that Jesus actually took her into hell, and that she was to tell the people that hell was real. She conveyed how the fear and torment she saw was horrible beyond words.

I remember one key item about that evening that will stay with me throughout my life. I was near the front of the church when she gave the altar call for those who had not yet received Jesus Christ as their Lord and Savior. She had tears of flowing down her face, pleading with people not to leave the building if they didn't know Jesus as their personal Savior. This woman was sincere with a capital "S." As her voice quivered, one could easily tell that her heart yearned for people to avoid hell.

In another testimony, I recall the words of the Rev. Kenneth E. Hagin when he was about sixteen years old. He said he left his body and descended into hell. It's an exceptionally impressive testimony, and the terror of hell was deeply impressed into his heart at that time. The testimony of Bill Wiese, who said he was in hell for about twenty-three minutes, is even more gripping. If an agnostic or atheist after listening to this testimony would not change, then I'm not sure what would reach their heart. This is one serious testimony.

On the other side of the coin is the testimony of Evangelist Jesse Duplantis visiting heaven in 1988 for about five hours and fifteen minutes. If you want to listen to something that will bless your socks off, this is it. Those in Christ Jesus have a bright future. Nothing, absolutely nothing this world has to offer is worth missing heaven for.

Two interesting books by Maurice Rawlings, M.D., are *Beyond Death's Door* and *To Hell and Back*. Here's a medical doctor who discusses real life experiences he has encountered in the medical field over time. Is there life after death? Dr. Rawlings became thoroughly convinced that there is. He found out that there was a heaven to gain and a hell to shun.

To anyone who reads this, I say to you that there is life after death. There is a heaven to gain and a hell to shun. If you have not received Jesus Christ into your heart as Lord and Savior, then I encourage you to do so. Jesus is real and loves you with a wonderful love. Don't wait until the bell of your twelfth round rings. Get right with God while you yet have breath. It's the wisest decision you'll ever make. You'll be glad you did.

***

Funeral Home Visit

As I made a funeral home visit this past week, I pondered some thoughts as I extended condolences to parents who had tragically just lost their daughter. First, even if someone is nice, was that person saved? Second, which I pondered later, who consoled the Father when Jesus was brutally beaten and then put to death on the cross?

Being just nice doesn't necessarily mean one gets to heaven. The Bible makes it very clear that the way to the Father is through His Son, Jesus Christ. One must receive Jesus as Lord and Savior, believing that He died on the cross for their sins and rose from the dead for their justification. If one does not have a relationship with Jesus before one dies, then it's too late when one gets to the funeral home. There's a heaven to gain and a hell to shun.

We humans do not fully understand what was going on in the spiritual realm when Jesus died. I'm confident that there was great pain in the Father's heart as Jesus was horribly beaten and then crucified. Love between each other was phenomenal for lack of better expression. This cannot be denied. Separation between the Father and Jesus took place during this traumatic period of time when Jesus took the sin of mankind. Heartache must have been tremendous.

I believe condolences to the Father can be best expressed in this manner. First, receive Jesus as Lord and Savior. Second, give our heavenly Father much praise and worship.

***

Life Has Three Most Important Decisions

I've often thought that there are three most important decisions in life. It's important to get these three right because your quality of life will greatly emanate from them. Yes, there are many more important decisions along the way, but these three, in my mind, are ones that provide the foundation and key direction in one's life.

The first decision is the acceptance of Jesus Christ as one's Lord and Savior. Unequivocally, this is the most important decision in one's life. It will greatly affect one's quality of life presently, and in the life hereafter.

The second most important decision in one's life is who one marries. Lives are destroyed through marital strife and divorce. For a Christian, it's so important not to become unequally yoked. Having the same goals, objectives, and values in life is requisite to success. It's better being unmarried than being married to the wrong person.

The third most important decision is what one does for a vocation, i.e., what one does to earn a living. I've told adolescents to look within themselves and consider what they really like doing. Based on personal desires, then I often recommend considering that as a pursuit in life. Oftentimes, as a natural consequence, one will have the innate skills to pursue what they really enjoy. One who really enjoys working on cars may have been called to be a mechanic. One who really enjoys building things may have been called to be a carpenter. Check the desire and pursue.

***

Choose This Day

Choose this day whom you will serve. May the words of Joshua challenge America?

People believe that they have the right to do evil the same way illegal immigrants believe that they have rights to be here in violation of law.

> *People believe that they have the right to do evil the same way illegal immigrants believe that they have rights to be here in violation of law.*

Talk show hosts get on the radio and tell you what needs to be done in our government. This scene goes on without substantial progress election after election. Globalists pit group against group and watch the fray from the sidelines, probably amused by and enjoying their orchestrated arrangements.

It's clear that the church has had little or minimal impact on the direction of this nation. Based on various reasons, could it be said that the church has been, on a whole, quite anemic, lethargic, or inept?

One is told from the Bible that God is a jealous God and hates evil. This statement is worth pondering as one considers the morality and direction of this nation, as a government, and as a people. Further, in light of this last statement, is it possible for man to solve the problems of America? I answer this with a resounding, "No." It's quite obvious that this nation is heading for a tremendous train wreck.

The only answer, and I cannot be more emphatic, is for America to repent immediately before the Living God, as a government and as a people, and serve God Almighty with their all of their hearts. The divine providence of God is requisite to the future of this nation.

***

Skeptics Oppose Crucifixion Story

Christmas celebrates the birth of Jesus as Savior coming into the world. However, almost as intriguing as the virgin birth is his crucifixion. Skeptics have argued throughout time, opposing the biblical story of the crucifixion. Did Jesus merely faint from exhaustion on the cross?

What was a Roman flogging like? A soldier would use a whip braided with leather thongs with metal balls and sharp bones woven into them. The whip would cut the flesh and bruise it at the same time. The back would become so shredded that part of the spine was sometimes exposed along with the ribs. The victim would commonly receive thirty-nine lashes. The entire back, buttocks, and back of legs would be torn to shreds. Muscles, sinews, and bowels were open to exposure. Many people would die from this kind of brutal beating before making it to the crucifixion.

Crucifixion is a slow, agonizing death by asphyxiation. The stresses on the muscles and diaphragm put the chest into the inhaled position. For the victim to exhale, he would have to push up on his feet so the tension on the muscles would be eased. Doing this would cause the nail in the feet to tear through against the tarsal bones. Continuation of this procedure was requisite in order to breathe. Exhaustion would eventually come, and then death.

The birth of Jesus is cause for celebration, and rightly so, but the reason that Jesus came was so that He could die for mankind.

***

Story of the Wise Men Not a Myth

The Lamar Outdoor billboard near New York showed silhouettes of the traditional images of three wise men approaching the Nativity scene during this past season. Its message, "You KNOW it's a Myth. This Season, Celebrate REASON!"

People have a right to decide on their beliefs. They have a free will to choose, and I totally agree with this. I would not have it any other way. As I say this, I'm also aware that truth is more important than sincerity. Build your house on lies, and in time, your house will fall. Truth is absolute and always proves its course. In other words, always build your life on the solid foundation of truth.

People will tell lies and lead many people astray. Make sure, especially in light of eternity, that you choose wisely what you accept and believe.

The evidence that Jesus came to earth, died on a cross, and was resurrected is overwhelming if you earnestly study the biblical story and history that supports it. I submit to you, to believe a message on a billboard, such as the one previously mentioned, is to choose unwisely.

Wise men approaching the Nativity scene from the east happened. It's not a myth, but truth. You may join that group of wise men by choosing to believe the rest of the story, as Paul Harvey would say, and to receive Jesus as your Lord and Savior. This will be the wisest decision in your life if you haven't already done so.

***

Consider This: Jesus Is an Extremist

This is a news report from Jerusalem. We've just noticed the man called Jesus turning over tables of money changers in the temple. He's chasing those out of the area who were buying and selling in the temple. We're told He did this as a result of zeal for God. According to one bystander, He did this because He believed these merchants were profaning the temple.

Another witness has shared some other interesting things about this man's behavior. We understand that on numerous occasions, He has boldly spoken out against the Pharisees. Needless to say, this is not politically correct. He has boldly called the Pharisees hypocrites and has repeatedly cast them in unfavorable light. Who does this man think He is?

The Pharisees are not the only group that Jesus has upset. He has also upset the Sadducees and the lawyers. Where does this man stop? He has challenged these people about their attitudes and beliefs systems and has really rocked their boats in front of many people. He's definitely not afraid of what they think of Him.

Here's another individual who has observed Jesus throughout the Galilee region. He states how Jesus has boldly proclaimed the kingdom of God and confronted the evil in the land. It's clear that Jesus is not one who remains silent about the depravity of many accepted practices throughout the region. He calls sin for what it is. There're no cat and mouse games in His attitude or behavior. He's definitely not trying to please everyone.

While Jesus has confronted the evil and ungodly practices of the land, He has also shown a sincere compassion for helping others. It has been said he has healed and encouraged many. He has fervently taught multitudes godly values and has directed them toward proper morality and the things of God. Let it be said that He has a heart for people, and at the same time, the courage and conviction to speak out against the evil of the land and mankind.

Something else we've noticed about Jesus while covering this news story is His commitment to God. It has been said that Jesus regularly communes with the heavenly Father. It's not unusual for Him to spend hours in prayer. Based on His behavior, it's easy to see that he's a very disciplined and focused man. There's nothing lax about His commitment and dedication to the heavenly Father or things of God. His commitment and dedication are exemplary, and He knows where His priorities are.

After observing Jesus and interviewing others who have closely observed Him, we've come to the conclusion that Jesus is an extremist. He's extreme against the evils of mankind and the ungodly practices of those in authority. He's extreme in His compassion for mankind. He's extreme in His zeal and commitment to the heavenly Father and the things of God. Most assuredly, Jesus is in extremist. This concludes our news report from Jerusalem.

Now back to news in America for a short analysis.

That was good coverage by our news team in Jerusalem, but let's turn over a few more stones for a moment. Based on what we've just heard, how would Jesus react to things currently going on in America?

Would Jesus support abortion? Do you think He might have some comments to say about partial-birth abortion procedures that occur in this highly civilized country? Although many in churches may remain silent in their pews and not pray about this subject, I don't think He would. Jesus was an extremist.

Would Jesus support separation of church and state in this so-called Christian nation? What would Jesus think about the school prayer situation? Think about it, but don't think too long. Jesus was an extremist.

Would Jesus support pornography and homosexual marriages? Go to the Bible, and I think you'll find your answer. Remember, Jesus had a zeal for the things of God, and yes, Jesus was an extremist.

Would Jesus become a mundane Christian in America, or would He remain steadfast, dedicated, committed, and on fire for the things of God? Would He serve others and show compassion to those in need? Would He be concerned about the salvation of others so that they wouldn't have to go to hell? You know the answer. Jesus was an extremist!

***

Stewards of Our Belongings

Did anyone see a U-Haul® trailer behind Howard Hughes' hearse when he passed away? No, I don't think so. Nor did they see one in the wakes of Princess Diana, Frank Sinatra, or John Kennedy Jr. Sorry, U-Haul® trailers loaded with possessions could not be seen anywhere near these wakes.

I've come to the conclusion no one owns anything in this life. People, after working for years, might say they own their own homes but, in reality, not so. The same goes for cars or anything else. Basically, people are merely stewards of the things to which they have access. They use things in this life but can't take things with them when they depart. Someone else then becomes the new steward, and the cycle goes on.

Life and possessions are so dynamic. Consider America as an example. Native Americans were here long before the Europeans came. Colonists came and claimed new land, but the Native Americans used it before the colonists. Conflict and war have a way of changing things. To the conqueror go the spoils, and then to the next conqueror go the spoils, and so on. Use of land and possessions is only temporary.

With all that in mind, I think it is interesting how people approach material possessions throughout their lives. Some people just save and save. True, it's good to save and plan wisely, but some people become obsessed with savings out of fear of not having enough. Many people in this category are often classified as "tight," and in some cases, "greedy." Some may develop this kind of attitude out of growing up in an impoverished home. Regardless, no matter how many thousands are accrued in one's savings account, it's all left behind when one passes on for someone else to enjoy.

Some people are loose with their funds and possessions. Often money seems to slip through their hands quite easily for persons of this nature. People in this category often have advantage taken of themselves. Where does the money go? A bit more discipline and some savings would go a long way in helping one do better in this situation.

Many people focus their lives on things and the pleasures they may bring. If they could just get a better home or a better car, they would be happy. If they could just get a bigger boat or more expensive jewelry, they would be happy. Many, with this nature, continually strive for bigger and better things.

On the reciprocal, others are happy when their needs are met. Many of these folks desire to have nice things but are content with what they have. Bigger toys are not necessarily their desire.

Attitudes and focus on possessions are as different as are people. One could easily ponder the diversities of this subject for quite a while and why people approach possessions as they do. Even so, while people can't take things with them, they can surely leave an imprint of their lives behind them after they depart this life.

There are many people who live a comfortable lifestyle and bless others along the way. While meeting the needs of their families, many people will still give of their resources to help others who may not be as fortunate. Many will share much of their time, so others may have a better life. Lives have been changed throughout time because of people reaching out to help others. Their priorities are not strictly living for the world and what they can gain from it solely for themselves. History books will not record many of their names, but they will live on in the hearts of those they helped.

I'm reminded of a story about a stingy, rich man who peered out his window and saw people in need all around him. He then looked into an old mirror that was really only glass with a silver coating. He suddenly realized that when the silver was added, he saw only himself.

One of my favorite Christmas stories is that of Ebenezer Scrooge. Scrooge's transformation was exceptionally noteworthy and serves as an example from which we can all learn. No, you won't see a U-Haul trailer behind a hearse. Mr. Scrooge grew to realize that he couldn't take it all with him and chose to help others along the way.

***

All Stays Here When You Depart

Sam had done well in life. He had invested well and made some great business decisions along the way. Sam had become financially wealthy. As a result, Sam began to live for himself and all the fun he could pursue. He built things that brought him even more profit. In the world's eyes, Sam had it made. Wine, women, and song were common themes in his life. He could afford virtually anything one could imagine and pursue any pleasure one could perceive. He lived for himself and all the pleasures his money would bring.

Sam had just become fifty-two when he had a fatal heart attack. Just like that, Sam was dead. His bank accounts were substantial. His investments were doing exceptionally well. He had accumulated great wealth. After his casket was taken from the funeral home, it was loaded into the hearse. A string of cars followed it to the cemetery.

Interestingly, there was one item conspicuously absent. There was no rental trailer behind his hearse to take his great wealth with him. All Sam's great wealth was left behind. He had lived for himself, and now he was dead.

How does fifty-two years compare to eternity? It's like a grain of sand from all the beaches in the world. It's nothing. To live for this world and not the next is foolery.

To live for this world and not develop a relationship with Jesus Christ is foolery. Nothing this world has to offer is worth that trade.

***

Anti-God Assault Growing in America

Transgender and related issues seem surreal. These are issues that our Founding Fathers could never have envisioned since so much of this is ludicrous and exceptionally challenging to common sense. Christians in America are faced with horrible laws today. There's an anti-God assault in America. You see, America no longer encourages religious liberty, but in reality, only reluctantly tolerates it. Religious freedoms have been greatly reduced in this nation.

Many Christians today seem to be making their own version of God. Thus, to them, does it now mean that God has changed His mind, and many things are now acceptable, even though these things have been labeled as sin throughout the Bible? In essence, some Christians, being influenced by the media and society, are calling sin as righteous behavior. That said, Jehovah does not negotiate with nor compromise with sin.

Christians who fall into this category need to look at Scripture again, and this time, more closely. Christians have a duty and responsibility to share God's truth with others in society. As such, they need to stand strong on God's truth and share with others. They need to use prudence and wisdom and stand strong with their convictions of truth derived from God's Word. They must not compromise Scripture.

> *Our nation is under assault from the demonic kingdom. Christians must stand strong in God and pray fervently for this nation.*

Christians are the ones with the light, and that light needs to go forth and dispel darkness. Our nation is under assault from the demonic kingdom. It's quite obvious. Christians must stand strong in God and pray fervently for this nation.

***

Tsunami Leads to Other Questions

Recently, I was pondering how horrible the tsunami tragedy was in Southeast Asia. Of course, I was thinking in different terms than our mainline secular press. I was thinking about how many thousands are now in hell because of this disaster.

This led me to think about patriotism and religion and a similar manner. Patriotism and religion are not always necessarily good. Patriotism can be used by leadership to stir emotions and lead many toward a desired course of action, often using deception and misinformation to accomplish its goals. Religion, in similar manner, can be used to accomplish objectives by pushing the right deceptive and emotional buttons. How many thousands are now in hell because of the misuse of these powerful forces?

America, in recent decades, has been involved in aggressive and repeated military action. Immediately, there's Vietnam, Libya, Grenada, Bosnia, Afghanistan, and Iraq that come to mind. Was our participation in these conflicts truly of a righteous nature? Did we have the approval of God before we administered deadly force in these areas?

I know how the news media prepared the hearts of the civilian populace before we went forth into these conflicts, but then I know that I was not behind the closed-door meetings. Were there unscrupulous motives purposely hidden before the commitment of force?

Based on multiple accounts and valid sources of information, there are indications of a plethora of governmental cover-ups in our nation, that include in recent decades, the John and Robert Kennedy assassinations, Martin Luther King assassination, mysterious deaths of Vince Foster and Ron Brown, TWA Flight 800, and Oklahoma bombing incidents.

In light of these, I ponder the validity of the 9/11 report. Were there things purposely hidden from the American populace? Did we get the total truth, or was the media again deceptively used to mislead the American people? Do we have the full story on Afghanistan and Iraq?

Let's say for the purpose of unity that we have the correct report. Let's say we went into Afghanistan and Iraq for all the reasons the government said we went in with. Will this course of action resolve our security problems? My answer is a resounding—No!

America has only one answer and one answer only for its future. The answer lies within and not outside its borders. America must have a spiritual recrudescence, or it will perish. The answer for America is a spiritual one. Get right with God as a nation, and God will do things outside the borders that a nation can only hope to do through billions of dollars and sacrifice of lives.

After Iraq, where to next? Iran? Syria? At the same time you're pondering this, continue to pursue legalized murder through abortion, laws that favor homosexuality and pornography, keeping prayer out of schools, separating God out of public life and other unrighteous pursuits, and it doesn't matter.

I will tell you America's future if it continues its apostasy, decadent, and hedonistic ways as a nation.

Look for more and intense natural disasters to occur on its shores. The media will say it's just Mother Nature, but the media won't realize that God has lifted His hand of protection. When a nation rebels against God, nature rebels against that nation.

Second, after a series of intense national disasters, look for foreign troops on this soil. They will come in as a surprise attack with a coalition of forces fighting together against us.

At this time, America will truly wail and fall to its knees. Many will then cry out to God, but then it will be too late as smoke from burned-out city buildings will cover the skies of a once-great nation. Blood will flow on its streets, and famine will be extensive. America will be overtaken and divided into sectors. Foreign flags will fly over its soil.

There are three real tragedies in all this.

The first tragedy is that it did not have to take place. There's a simple answer, a simple solution, an easy answer to all of America's current woes. The answer is a spiritual recrudescence unto Jesus Christ. It must be of heart service and not lip service.

The second tragedy is that the pulpits of America did not effectively convey this message to the American populace. It's a message that needs to be preached from many more pulpits than it currently is so that Christians will intercede and pray.

The third tragedy is that many Christians did not intercede and pray for this nation as they should have done.

Forget the words "God bless America." Change the words to "America bless God" and live unto righteousness. America's future depends on it. It's the only answer for this nation.

***

Go to the Roots of Nation's Problems

What made America great? It's the God of Abraham, Isaac, and Jacob.

We cannot fix America because we're not the ones who made it great.

What made America great? It's the God of Abraham, Isaac, and Jacob. Today, all sorts of humanistic and secular solutions are being discussed, and sometimes acted on, in order to supposedly get America going in the right direction again. Unfortunately, these proposed solutions continue to ignore the root of the problem. In addition to the government, the majority of Americans have fallen asleep and can't see the root of this nation's problems.

The government ignores the solution, while the spirit of apathy has seized the hearts and minds of most Americans. Unless there is a sincere spiritual recrudescence unto the gospel of Jesus Christ, this nation will continue on its road toward becoming a slave nation.

In recent decades the church has shown a great deal of impotence. Has it made a great difference in changing this nation's direction? You be the judge. Many secularists and humanists, inspired by the demonic realm, have had victory after victory. There has been the taking of school prayer out of school; abortion laws developed, executed, and maintained; homosexual rights vigorously promoted; extensive pornography condoned; and other unrighteous areas that violate basic biblical and moral guidelines.

Families have broken down in our society. Churches are compromising the gospel of Jesus Christ. There is sin in the church. Our nation is floundering out of control.

The root of the problem is spiritual. I urge churches and fellow Christians to fervently pray for America.

***

Universities Changed Their Foundations

What do Harvard, Yale, Princeton, and Oxford universities have in common? They all were established as religious institutions but now advocate evolutionary thinking. Why the change? For that matter, what happened to cause so many other Christian universities to abandon their roots as well?

It's clear that changing of world views had significant influence. Universities across the board fell first in the area of science. Naturalism opposes God's Word in Genesis, the foundational book of the Bible. Psalm 11:3 states, "When the foundations are destroyed, what can the righteous do?" (HCSB).

Cracks began to form in the foundation, leading to the collapse of the Christian worldview in schools. The cracks started to appear in the late 1700s and early 1800s. Belief in old-earth concepts seriously wounded widespread acceptance of the flood and biblical chronology. Old-earth thoughts permeated universities by the mid-1800s and set the stage for Darwinian evolutionary ideas. As universities accepted these views, gravitation to naturalism soon followed.

Compromise in the belief of an ancient earth and evolution contributed greatly to the spiritual downfall of Christian universities. These institutions had given up the Bible as their starting point, and had accepted natural science instead.

Genesis was written as literal history and should be taken as such. Beware of any doctrine that is not biblically sound. Second Timothy 4:3–4 states, "For the time will come when they will not endure sound doctrine ... they will heap up for themselves teachers; and they will turn their ears away from the truth."

***

Follow Wisdom of Solomon

It appears that the wisdom of Solomon would be requisite in dealing with the many domestic and foreign policy issues that America faces today if our nation is to be successful.

Solomon, in all of his glory and riches, came to some interesting conclusions about life. He struggled to find significance in daily living but came to the conclusion that he was doing so in vanity and grasping for the wind.

Solomon learned over the course of his life that he could not live as if there were no God. He came to realize that our ultimate purpose is wrapped up in our relationship with the God who made us. This applied to all areas of life.

It's on this point that I will focus. I'm confident, first and foremost, that Solomon would advise his people to get right with God, and then he would take steps to ensure godly leadership for his nation. You build a solid foundation before you build the next level of the house. If you do not, then that house will eventually falter.

America once had a solid foundation, but today it does not. It has built its house on secular and humanistic sand. As a government, it has defied the living God. As a nation, it has gone astray from its source of grace and protection. Its house will not stand if it continues on its present course.

Message from Solomon to America—get right with God, individually and corporately as a nation.

***

Worry: Give It to God

What is worry? Most would agree that worry conveys a feeling of uneasiness, apprehension, or dread. These feelings bring on negative thoughts of tension that grip one's mind. It preoccupies one with painful consequences of what might happen in the future. Typically, worry centers around threats, choices, past experiences, or lack.

Why does worry occur? We worry because we're vulnerable physically, emotionally, and spiritually. Human beings are susceptible to all kinds of conditions that can threaten one of these areas in our lives. Even so, worry is sin, and in essence, demonstrates a distrust of God.

The Bible says to cast all our burdens on the Lord. There is no situation that He cannot deal with. People need to remember that God is everywhere, that He knows all, and that He is all-powerful. He wants us to trust Him because He only wants the best for us and loves us so much.

Worry is actually unbelief in disguise. Instead of worry, God would have us to come to Him in prayer and cast those burdens into His hands. As we release them to Him, we should replace worry with thanksgiving because we trust Him to work things out. Feeling overwhelmed, then give that anxiety to the One who has the power to burst through any situation.

Trust in the Lord, and give Him all your cares. He can handle each and every one of them and bring peace into your life. Do it now.

***

Lesson from Nineveh Is Guideline for All

The Bible provides the best guideline for living that I know of for individuals and governments. That said, I'm confident in saying, unequivocally, that America, as a government and nation, needs to learn a lesson from Jonah and Nineveh. What happened when Jonah warned the king of Nineveh? The king led Nineveh into repentance before God, crying out for mercy. As a result of this leader's actions, Nineveh was spared many more years.

What needs to happen in America is the exact same thing. President Obama needs to call this nation to repentance. He needs to call on the mercy of God for this nation in a national news conference. The symbology in all this is that he is the leader of this government, which represents the nation. President Obama needs to ask forgiveness, on behalf of America, for all its abortions, its sins, and great irreverence toward an awesome and holy God, deserving of all reverence.

Some people may consider these words trite, but they're not. This kind of action is more requisite than many can possibly conceive. The train is on the track. It's moving, and America has been found wanting in its arrogance and pride. Be assured, America's not above judgment from an Almighty God.

There must be repentance because as a nation, it has sinned, forsaken, and greatly disrespected the gospel of Jesus Christ and what it stands for. If no repentance, then there will be great mourning and cries of despair throughout this land.

***

Christians Need to Work Together

I've pondered why the church has not had a greater effect on the direction of America today. Based on history, it's clear that the church had a much greater effect on politics in the earlier history of America. Why isn't the church having a greater effect today?

First, Jesus taught love, forgiveness, sacrifice, unity, and humility. One thing that immediately jumps out is that the church has overlooked these professed virtues to some extent while giving much attention to non-essential denominational differences. The church needs to fight the enemies of the gospel and not fellow Christians. Unity generates power while disunity weakens.

Second, through all the comforts and distractions of America, it appears that spiritual apathy has set in among many believers. Modern society provides many conveniences and secular entertainment; thus, less dependence on God for one's needs.

Third, the voice of the church has become almost silent in its public proclamation against sin, while many are going to hell and society crumbles. Many Christians have become indifferent while the secular world mocks the truth, robs freedoms, and claims more converts for itself.

There needs to be repentance, commitment, prayer, and adjustment of priorities in the American church today. Christians need to work together and remember that they are to be a light throughout all society. The body as a whole should not leave all the work to just a few but should all get involved and use their talents and resources to exalt Jesus Christ in America.

***

Truth Outweighs Sincerity

What's more important—sincerity or truth? I submit to you that truth is more important. Sincerity is certainly commendable, but truth is absolute. People can be sincerely wrong. It can cost people their lives. It can lead to poor decisions. It can lead to poor investments. A doctor, for example, may be sincere in his diagnosis, but if he misses in his assessment, then a patient may die. In essence, this is not philosophical discussion but just practical living.

If truth is more important than sincerity in this life, then what about the afterlife? Again, I submit to you that truth is more important. One may be sincere as can be in regards to all sorts of beliefs. One may sincerely believe that there's no afterlife. One may sincerely believe one way while another sincerely believes another way in accordance with their particular religions. Regardless, I get back to my premise that truth is more important than sincerity in the afterlife as well.

Let me get to the point. The Bible clearly states that there is salvation under no other name than Jesus Christ. If you choose to ignore God's plan of redemption, then I assure you that it will adversely affect your eternal destiny. The veracity of the Bible and its prophecies are consistently backed up by history and archeological evidence, and be assured; truth always proves its course.

***

America: Repent

Some years back, Muslim Sulejman Talovic fatally shot several people in a Salt Lake City shopping mall. FBI agent Patrick Kiernan said the bureau had no reason to believe that he was motivated by religious extremism or terrorism even though he was armed with a .38 caliber pistol, a shotgun, and a backpack full of ammunition. I wonder if the people shot considered this an act of terrorism.

Hundreds of thousands of illegal aliens have entered America, and many are here with the explicit purpose of terrorism. There are indications that many are pre-positioned and awaiting orders to launch a nationwide campaign. I cannot be more emphatic in saying that Allah is not Jehovah. The spirits behind Christianity and Islam are as different as night and day; thus, so is the spiritual influence.

What did we see after 9/11? Some churches had a few moments of silence and some lit candles. America missed the cue.

You see, there is a true God, and He is the only source of protection and solution for the current ills of America.

Unless there is a true spiritual recrudescence in this nation unto Jesus Christ, then there are bleak days ahead with hundreds of thousands dying horrible deaths in America. You see, there is a true God, and He is the only source of protection and solution for the current ills of America. Human plans will not be able to protect this nation from its current irreverent path. America must repent if it is to have a future.

***

Resurrection, True or False?

Many people have come up with different theories in trying to refute the resurrection of Jesus Christ. However, one will find that the evidence, upon close examination, overwhelmingly supports the resurrection. Furthermore, pure logic refutes opposing theories.

Some say that the disciples stole the body from the tomb. This means that the disciples, who had just fled for their lives, would have had to penetrate a Roman guard in a clandestine manner, push away a huge rock without being detected, grab the body, and run. Not likely.

Some say that the authorities took the body. If this was true, then why didn't the authorities show the body and disprove the claims of the disciples just a few weeks later? What turned the downcast disciples into fiery proponents of the resurrection if they had not seen Jesus again? Again, not likely that the authorities took the body.

Some say that Jesus only fainted, or went into a deep swoon. What caused the soldiers to misinterpret the evidence and certify that Jesus was dead? One even speared His side to ensure death. How could Jesus, who had been severely beaten and near death, push away a huge rock by himself from inside the tomb and walk away in perfectly good health? Again, not likely that Jesus only fainted.

Consider how the disciples, including Paul, turned the world upside down in the spreading of the gospel after having an experience with the resurrected Christ.

The correct answer to my question is: True.

***

Nothing Nobler in Life

Christians can operate by fear, or they can operate by faith and love. That said, one of the worst disablers to well-meaning individuals is the fear of man. Many people, when sharing their faith, start to think this way: What will they think of me if I invite them to church? Are they going to think I'm strange if I give them a gospel tract? I don't know if I should say something about Jesus because I feel nervous.

Typically, that is the flesh talking to you when you become fearful of sharing Jesus. If the flesh is talking to you, then you need to make a decision in those moments to die to self. Jesus Christ gave you life, and Romans 12:1 instructs us that it is our "reasonable service" to live for Him. Those are thoughts of fear, but remember, the primary motivation is love.

If you love others, you will tell them about Jesus. If you love people, you should share with them what Christ has done for you. If you care about those around you, that crippling fear should be replaced with a love for them regardless of their reactions. God has given you a spirit of love, and the greatest thing you can share with others is the gospel of Jesus Christ. We still have freedom to share that message in America. We need to take advantage of that freedom to do so.

There is nothing nobler in life than to share the gospel with someone.

***

Demonization of America Continues

Where is the church? Hollywood has been developing and promulgating anti-Christian movies for many years now. Although this assault has targeted adults and youth, in reality, Jesus Christ is the main target, along with the damnation of souls. That said, Christians have been taught, by their leadership, to be passive, non-violent, and to offer no resistance, as if to do so would be sin.

There has been a flood of spiritual evil at work in America. From Harry Potter witchcraft stories, the scene has now moved further into werewolves, vampires, walking dead, ghosts, evil spirits, demons, and so forth. Popular icons are being developed for the youth through these efforts. Again, where is the church? It has remained incredibly silent.

Christians are banned from public displays of faith in any form. Christians are now incrementally being criminalized for being Christians. It's interesting that Muslims can become aggressive in public square forums, and there's nothing said by the media.

Based on the anti-Christ spirit operating behind our government, Hollywood, and media, there's a strong satanic attack against Christian attitudes, behavior, and actions. Many Christians see this as an advance of liberalism, secularization, and socialism. They really need to look deeper. The spiritual foundation of these assaults has nothing to do with movements. It has everything to do with Satan and his plan to destroy the Church and Christianity in America.

Here's the tragedy: Most of the nation are in agreement with Satan, and many of these are in the Church.

***

Eternity: Heaven or Hell?

Some perceive me as being arrogant or self-righteous when I write about Jesus Christ as being the way of salvation. Some even consider me insensitive toward others when I discuss eternity. Let me say that I'm not politically correct because eternity is brutally frank. Thus, in reality, I have great concern for others.

Two plus two equals four. There are many different answers to that equation, as there are many different religions from Christianity. Regardless, four is the correct answer. It's also that way in the Bible. Jesus Christ is the way of salvation, and there is a heaven to gain and a hell to shun. It's as clear as can be in the Bible.

The Bible is such an impressive book. History and archeological evidence back up Bible prophecies over and over again. There's no holy book that uses prophecy like the Bible. Further, there's an abundance of evidence that supports the crucifixion and resurrection of Jesus Christ. It's a true story.

There is life after death, and I'm confident in saying that if people do not find Jesus Christ as their Lord and Savior in this lifetime, then they won't find him in the next. If I could scare people out of hell, I would flat do it. Some will scoff at my comments as being foolish, but I say unequivocally, they're not.

Life on this earth is short. Eternity is forever. You will spend eternity either in heaven or hell. The choice is yours. Choose wisely.

***

Love, Security, and Significance—A Christmas Gift

Love, security, and significance are important words for a human being. A human being will even compromise, manipulate, lie, steal, and deceive as that one earnestly pursues these values in one's life, trying to fulfill these requisite aspects of life without not totally understanding why. As one examines human behavior, it's quite easy to figure out why humans do this if one considers God in their lives. Without God, it's not so easy to figure out.

Man or woman in the beginning never had a need to pursue love, security, and significance in their lives. Love, security, and significance were all provided by God and completely fulfilled in those early relationships between God and mankind. When Adam fell, it brought separation from God. With that separation came the need for love, security, and significance. People were now on their own to fulfill these areas in their lives. Why do love, security, and significance have to be fulfilled in one's life, one may ask? It's because of our DNA. God put those desires in the human DNA. People were wired that way from the beginning.

As Christmas Day comes near, let us remind ourselves that God did not leave us in that condition. Through Jesus Christ, God brought us back into relationship with Him. As we accept Jesus Christ as Lord and Savior, we can once again have those aspects of love, security, and significance reinstated into our lives the way it should be. Thank God for Christmas.

***

Life After Death

Many people in society plan ahead for their retirement years. Many plan for the future education of their children. Many plan for summer vacations. Yet, with all that planning, many fail to investigate or earnestly research about life after death. Even so, life after death should be the most important question in one's mind. If one is uninformed about this subject, then one should do some thorough research on this subject before one arrives at the funeral home.

Based on my exposure to a plethora of sources, I've come to the conclusion that the Bible is the valid source for answers to life after death. One thing that sets the Bible apart from other holy books in the world is prophecy. Archaeological and historical evidence backs up the Bible over and over again. I doubt many who criticize the Bible have done much research on fulfilled Bible prophecy, or they could not have a negative attitude about the Bible.

Many criticize the Bible by saying it contradicts itself. Dr. John Warwick Montgomery, a well-known Bible scholar, has said, "I myself have never encountered an alleged contradiction in the Bible which could not be cleared up by use of the original language of the Scriptures and/or by the use of accepted principles of literary and historical interpretation." Dr. Montgomery is an extremely qualified scholar. He holds two doctorates and seven undergraduate degrees, has written forty books, and is a founding member of The World Association of Law Professors.

The Bible tells us that Jesus died on the cross for our sins. You see, all have sinned and fall short of the glory of God. Adam sinned in the Garden of Eden, and the sin nature then became part of the human race. God is a holy God and cannot condone sin. That's why He sent His only begotten Son, Jesus Christ, in the form of a man to die on the cross for the sins of mankind. God provided atonement for each and every individual who will accept the blood sacrifice of Jesus Christ on the cross. God forgives our sins as we accept and confess Jesus Christ as our Lord and Savior. This is not a pie in the sky story but one of great truth.

Now, let's go back to life after death. The Bible is clear on this. Please listen to these words very carefully. One will spend eternity in either heaven or hell. Heaven will be the abode for those who have received Jesus Christ as their Lord and Savior. Hell will be the abode of those who have not. Heaven will be a wonderful place of love, joy, and peace beyond anyone's imagination throughout eternity. Equally, hell will be a horrible place of indescribable pain and torment with no hope, peace, or mercy throughout eternity.

Someone will say, what about a person in a South American jungle who may not have heard about Jesus. I would say, don't worry about that person. God is a righteous God. He will deal righteously with all. The question should be what will you do about Jesus Christ in your life?

***

Thoughts as We Celebrate Christmas

America is a land of great privilege. We have the freedom to worship freely. We have religious liberty to preach the gospel and be a voice for and to the oppressed. We live in a nation exceptionally blessed by God.

On holidays, such as the Fourth of July, Memorial Day, and Veterans Day, one often thinks of loyalty and patriotism. Many gave their lives for these ideals, but in essence, they gave their lives for freedom. Across this great land, that's the one word that silently resonates within every heart—freedom. That said, as a Christian, I have a responsibility to be a good steward of the freedom that I enjoy within America.

How do I use my freedom in reference to time? One can use their time in so many different ways when given the freedom that Americans daily enjoy. Everyone has twenty-four hours in the day. Thus, our freedom allows us to choose what we do, where we go, and what we say in so many different ways.

As a Christian, not taking my freedom for granted, I need to use my time efficiently and effectively to further God's kingdom. I have the freedom to spread the gospel and share God's love.

As we celebrate Christmas, let us remember why Jesus came. Let us use our time wisely to spread the gospel and share God's love. When life is gone and freedom no more, will there be remorse or joy for what you did with the freedom God gave you while you lived in such a privileged land?

***

Tolerance Takes Souls to Hell

May I put a touch of cyanide in some water? It looks like water, tastes like water, but there's poison in it that one doesn't see. The Christian body, in numerous cases, has developed this "nice" attitude about all things. Tolerance, or political correctness in the political arena, doesn't get the job done when considering the fear of God.

Our nation, to a great degree, is in the situation it is today because of tolerance in the Christian church. In the last several decades, where has the fear of God really been throughout the whole body of believers? Go with the flow. That's not how God approaches things. Is it more important to gain the approval of man or of God? After all, live and let live.

Someone recently showed me an article about nice Muslims and nice Muslim beliefs. Islam, no matter how it's portrayed, is wrong. I've studied the life of its prophet. I've compared its teachings to the Bible. I know that this religion is unequivocally inspired by Satan with one design—lead as many as straight to hell as one can.

Trying to peddle a soft side to Islam is so inspired by Satan. Peddle all the niceness you want, but it has an insidious spirit behind it. That's why when I speak on Islam, I read numerous verses from the Koran. Satan would love peddle this south side and lull more Christians to sleep in tolerance. Excuse me, Christians, while I take a nap.

God told the Israelites to deal with the idols. Thou shalt have no strange gods before thee. Go forth and preach the gospel. Much of the church today needs to consider the fear of God in their lives. We all need to—me included. There's an awesome reverential respect that needs to be shown toward the Almighty.

My, my, today, many Christians won't even verbally confront things clearly not of God. Live and let live. There are many in pews of churches today that have one foot in hell and the other ready to go in, and they don't know it. Is there not a cause to serve the Living and True God? Is there not a cause to confront evil in the land? Is there not a cause to preach the true gospel?

Is it better to have the approval of man or the approval of God? We are not to be fearful of men's faces.

But, Michael, you're being mean to tell someone that Islam is a false religion. You're not walking in love, Michael, get off your soap box. Was Elijah, as he killed the prophets of Baal on Mount Carmel, walking in love? Was Jesus walking in love as he called others hypocrites and a brood of vipers? Was Jesus walking in love as he turned over the tables of the money changers?

I'm not talking about burning mosques or abortion clinics. Don't take things out of context. I'm talking about the fear of God and taking a stand for things that matter. Today, many in this country are calling evil as good and good as evil. This ought not to be so. Where is the voice of the church and its people?

True, we are to walk in love as believers, but love also confronts. This attitude of "tolerance" is allowing and taking many souls straight to hell. Thank God that the disciples, after the departure of Jesus, did not have this same attitude that is so prevalent throughout the church of modern-day America.

***

Christians Wrongly Labeled

Christians who stand up for biblical values in this nation are considered "extremists" by liberals and their supporting news media. What a bunch of bunk! In reality, it's those folks who

> *Truth is absolute.*

are the extremists. Truth is absolute. When one recognizes that to be so, then one as a starting point for furtherance of this conversation.

What is truth? Don't go looking into some philosophy or psychology book for the answer to that question. Forget about those rabbit trails that take one down the wrong path. Truth can be found in the Word of God, the Holy Bible. If one doesn't believe the Bible is the inspired Word of God, then one can take it up with God after one leaves this life. If one doesn't believe in God, then one can discuss it with Him after one's death. For those who discount the death, burial, and resurrection of Jesus Christ as fallacy, I say, prove that didn't take place. In my opinion, the evidence to support this event is overwhelming for those who have a heart to receive.

I recall the story of Frank Morison, who wrote the book *Who Moved the Stone?* He was an English journalist who set out to prove that Christ's resurrection was nothing but myth. Even so, his detailed and incisive investigation led him to discover the validity of the biblical record in a convincing and personal way. Stubbornly, his perception changed, almost imperceptibly, as the facts led him to the truth.

Over time, America has accommodated other religions and liberal ideas into its melting pot. As a result, these things have tainted biblical ideals in this nation and its government and have led to compromise where compromise should not be made. This reminds one of Israel when God warned them against mixing with heathen nations. God knew their false gods would have an effect on Israel, and the direction it would take as a nation unto God. A small bit here and a small bit there and, before one knows it, there's a completely different picture than from the beginning.

God wants Christians to stand up for biblical values today forevermore. If Christians don't stand up for the things of God, then who will?

Christians who stand up for godly standards and show their light are classified as "normal" and not "extreme" in the eyes of God. Refer to the Bible if one believes abortion, homosexuality, and related-type issues are pleasing to God. Edmund Burke once said, - "The only thing necessary for the triumph of evil is for good men to do nothing." Yet, if one stands against immoral and ungodly issues, then one is considered extreme by the press.

Some might say that some Christians don't see things that way. After all, some ministers, for example, even endorse homosexual marriages. That's their prerogative, but, like all, they will stand before God and give an account. The Bible I read is very clear about living and standing up for the things of God. Revelation 3:16 states, "So, because you are lukewarm—and neither hot nor cold—I am about to spit you out of my mouth" (NIV). God was talking to the church of Laodicea, not unbelievers. It still applies today. Let me say God's Word is uncompromising for those who want to continually compromise His direction and ideals.

I still don't buy into this separation of church and state issue. Let me also interchange the word "Church" for "Christianity." Right from the beginning of this nation, they knew how important it was to have godly direction and ideals incorporated into this new government. Make no mistake about it. This is not an extremist position. If so, then the Founding Fathers were extremists by today's standards.

John Adams once said, "Our Constitution is made for a religious people. It is wholly inadequate for governance of any other." Christians should not be considered extremists if they push their ideals. In 1860, slave owners attacked Abraham Lincoln and the abolitionists for wanting to push their religious views. Thank God, Abraham Lincoln and the abolitionists did. Judeo-Christian influence is important to America—much more important than liberals and the news media fully understand.

If I'm not being politically correct in the eyes of the liberal entourage, then so be it. This "politically correct" stuff has gotten out of hand. Again, truth is absolute and will always stand its ground under all attacks. One should never be afraid to confront truth because, in truth, one is set free. To hide behind falsehood is to set up for failure sooner or later. One should never build one's house on lies, or eventually, it will fall. This applies to all, governments included, even if it's the government of the United States of America.

***

Court Rulings an Assault on Christianity

The same-sex marriage law was just a continuation or the assault on Christianity in America. The ultimate desire is to take Christianity down and all moral values associated with it.

These attacks seek to weaken Christianity and limit what ministers can say and do publicly. It's about undermining the religious liberties of Christians. Efforts will continue attacking Christian schools, Christian nonprofit organizations, such as Family Talk, and Christian businesses, hospitals, charities, and seminaries.

In society, Aaron and Melissa Klein, who refused to bake a wedding cake for a same-sex ceremony, were targeted. Melissa was fined $135,000 for this "offense," but has now been slapped with a gag order so she can't even tell her side of the story. Where's her freedom of speech?

There's a Catholic organization known as the "Little Sisters of the Poor." They, like Family Talk, have been involved in a suit with the federal government to avoid providing abortifacients (such as the morning-after pill) to their employees. These contraceptives can cause the deaths of tiny embryos, which, in those instances, is abortion. That violates the consciences of the nuns, and they sought protection according to their First Amendment rights. On July 14, 2015, the Tenth Circuit Court of Appeals ruled against the nuns.

It's time for Christians to awaken and allow our collective voices to be heard. We must "pray fervently" for our nation and for national revival. We must defend our beliefs in a spirit of Christian love, but with deep conviction and committed effort.

***

Churches Hurt by Judge's Ruling

Have you heard about the administrative law judge? This is a special judge who tries a person on behalf of the government. No jury required. This court is part of the executive branch and not the judiciary. This brings me to an interesting case.

Two lesbians asked to be married at a church-owned camp meeting. The church refused. The case was then hauled into court. In essence, should a private Christian organization be forced to violate its own religious beliefs? Religious groups should have the right to use their private property in a way that's consistent with their beliefs.

Even so, administrative law judge Solomon Metzger incredulously ruled that the Christian organization had violated the civil rights of the lesbian couple. Metzger ruled against the Christian organization. Not only that, but the organization also lost part of its tax-exempt status.

Churches are feeling heat from government. Will this heat increase? You bet. Message from government is you'll do things our way, or you'll lose your tax-exempt status. Stay in your corner, church, and don't make any opposing political sound. If you do, government will put you in your place. Never mind if you're forced to do things against your religious beliefs.

Things have gotten progressively worse for the church ever since the "absurd separation of church and state doctrine" was established. This was by design. Eventually, the globalists intend to develop a one-world religion as part of their global program. Christianity has, and will continue to be, strongly dealt with.

***

Christians Need to Vote and Pray

I strongly urge Christians to vote in the Indiana primary on May 3, leading to the presidential election. At the same time, I strongly urge Christians to pray for all the primaries leading to the presidential election. Please, earnestly consider the following prayer points:

- We vote for a person of decency and honor (integrity matters).
- We vote for someone that cannot be bought or sold.
- We don't jump from the frying pan of failed government to the fire of another chameleon who changes colors at will (the political spirit).
- We remember that not everyone in Washington, D.C., has been part of the problem—be wise and discerning (God has been sending some good men and women to D.C.).
- We vote for humility (which God exalts), morality, and righteousness (which exalts a nation).
- We choose substance and specific ideas over shallow rhetoric, fame, show business events, and exciting promises (does anyone remember 2008?).
- We vote for a strict constitutionalist (it was born through prayer and based on Scripture).
- We remember that we are also voting for the next two or three Supreme Court justices, who will undoubtedly shape our nation and lives for decades.

- We vote for an uncompromising, consistent, radically pro-life person.
- By God's grace, we end up with a born-again, praying, Bible-reading, moral, humble, honest, and wise person in the White House.

Put race and any other issues aside. Use the Bible as the key reference for your prayers. We greatly need leadership firmly grounded in Judeo-Christian principles and values.

***

Time for Black Robe Regiment to Arise

The Black Robe Regiment was the name that the British placed on the courageous and patriotic American clergy during the Founding Era of our nation. They were the pulpit preachers in the colonies who not only spoke God's Word but also spoke against those who put themselves before or above God. They were a vital part of, indeed, the voice and soul of the movement to secure liberty from British tyranny.

These men saw themselves as the "watchmen on the wall" for God and country, and they took their calling seriously. It's time for current day pastors to not only preach God's Word but also "what's going on in their country." Put away political correctness, or you won't have religious freedom.

There's an ongoing coup to break the sovereignty of this nation, destroy Christianity, and lead us into the globalist and godless New World Order. It's time for pastors to understand that this is not about race; this is about moral direction, basic values, freedoms, and the future of America under God.

Put away the political rhetoric. These violent demonstrations are an extension of Democrat policies, their attitudes, their tactics, and disdain for morality and righteous direction in America. It's time for pastors to tell their congregations the truth of what's going on in America, and who to vote for. Racism, orchestrated violent demonstrations and looting, and the incessant propaganda, designed to generate division and hatred, are being used as tools by the globalists toward their end objective.

The pied piper of mainstream media, with their propaganda, has deceived and influenced many Christians to ignorantly vote against the best interests of this nation. The elections this November are critical against the road to Marxism.

May the spirit of the Black Robe Regiment arise within the American clergy. No more apathy or casual lip service, please. Tell your people the truth, and urge them to pray.

Chapter 3

Islam

Note: This chapter has 13 separate newspaper editorials and are not presented in a specific order of when written.

Practical Differences Between Christianity and Islam

Christianity teaches heartfelt obedience and living faith to God. In essence, people can't force someone into becoming a Christian. However, you can force someone to become a Muslim. All five pillars of Islam are behavioral. Each one can be fulfilled without heartfelt conviction. Christianity promotes discipleship—teaching others to follow. Islam promotes conquest (internal and external).

Christianity has seen decline in some areas of the world. That said, it does not go to physical war to reclaim those areas for Christ. Instead, Christians pray and evangelize because Christ's kingdom advances not in territory, but in and through the people who claim him as their King. It's not the same with Islam. If Islamic nations become less Muslim, that's a direct affront to Islam, and that must be strongly confronted, sometimes with much aggression.

Rejection or mockery of Muhammad or Islam is a personal attack on Islam. Every person who leaves Islam to become a Christian shames Islam because he conveys that it's unworthy of belief. Christ teaches us that to be shamed by the world for the gospel's sake is honorable.

Violence has been a distinguishing mark of the human race throughout time. In other words, Islam does not necessarily make people violent. Sin does. As a man-made religion, Islam is just one more tool people use to harden hearts and embrace sin. Even so, not all Muslims are given over to the violence, just as atheist/secular people don't fully embrace every sinful behavior that their non-religious worldview could justify.

***

Don't Confuse Allah and Jehovah

Many in America believe that Muslims and Christians serve the same God under different names, but that's not so. Most assuredly, Allah of the Koran is not Jehovah of the Bible. I strongly disagree with those who believe they're the same deities.

I've lived in Egypt, Jordan, and Israel and have conducted liaisons with the Palestinian Liberation Organization and Israeli Defense forces. I've formed some pretty strong opinions on the differences between Muslims, Jews, and Christians. I will now share a few thoughts on Islam, as objectively as I can. Nothing is intended to be offensive to anyone.

Muhammad, the prophet of Islam, was born in A.D. 570 in Mecca. Muhammad's father died before he was born, and his mother died when he was still young. According to the *Cyclopedia of Biblical, Theological, and Ecclesiastical Literature* by John McClintock and James Strong, Muhammad's mother often claimed she was visited by spirits and that she had visions and religious experiences, too. Some scholars today believe she was actually involved in occult practices and that this basic orientation was inherited by her son.

According to tradition, Muhammad would often fall down on the ground, his body would begin to jerk, his eyes would roll backward, and he would perspire profusely when he was about to receive a divine revelation from Allah. *The Shorter Encyclopaedia of Islam*, published by Cornell

University, points out that the Hadith, another collection of Islamic sacred writings, describes "the half-abnormal ecstatic condition with which he was overcome." Based on this type of bodily action during his trances, some scholars believe that he was having epileptic seizures.[2]

According to tradition, Muhammad would often fall down on the ground, his body would begin to jerk, his eyes would roll backward, and he would perspire profusely when he was about to receive a divine revelation from Allah.

It's interesting to note, that on one occasion, according to scholar Alfred Guillaume, Muhammad claimed that a heavenly being had split open his stomach, stirred his insides around, and then sewed him back up.

The Koran in Sura 4:3 forbids the taking of more than four wives. Muslim scholar Ali Dashti indicates Muhammad had at least sixteen wives and additional slaves and concubines. Aesha, one of his wives, was only eight or nine years old when he consummated the marriage. This is interesting since the Koran was supposed to have come "to" man through Muhammad.

Westerners heard the term "Holy Jihad" from Saddam Hussein during the Gulf War. Westerners, in most cases, do not understand how that term came into being as part of the Islamic religion. Basically, Muhammad tried to get people to accept his prophethood and follow his teachings through persuasion, but that didn't work out too well. People weren't as receptive as he desired. He then turned to force violence to subdue the people into following his teachings. To participate in jihad was to conduct religious fighting on behalf of Allah's cause. The Hadith even reveals that Muhammad wanted his religion to be spread primarily by the sword.

Muhammad demanded that Muslims force Jews, Christians, and pagans to embrace Islam or to submit to violent consequences if they didn't. Americans regularly see this principle of jihad at work throughout the world today in Islamic countries. Look at the countries of Nigeria and Sudan. Hundreds of thousands of Christians and pagans have been brutally slaughtered or enslaved in the name of jihad because they would not convert to Islam.

---

[2]Sam Shamoun, "Revisiting the Issue of Muhamad and Epilepsy Pt. 1," Answering Islam, https://1ref. us/1fn (accessed November 4, 2020).

Westerners will never understand why Muslims think and do the way they do until they acknowledge that Islam is a distinctly Arabian cultural religion. Seventh-century Arabia shows up whenever fundamentalism Islam is in power. You see, Muhammad took all the secular and sacred customs of the culture around him and incorporated them into Islam. All aspects of life are dictated by Islam. It's a way of life. Look at Iran under the Islamic clergy as a case in point.

Notice how Islamic countries do not have democracies. Muhammad took the political laws of seventh-century Arabian tribes and made them into the laws of Allah. The one in charge of the tribe or group had absolute authority over those under him. There was no concept of personal rights in seventh-century Arabia. This is why today you see Arab nations ruled by dictators or despots.

Many will notice a crescent moon symbol on some Middle Eastern flags and mosques. In reality, the crescent moon was a pagan symbol of moon god worship in Arabian culture and elsewhere throughout the Middle East. The moon god was known as "Allah" by many in pre-Islamic Arabia. According to Middle East scholar E.M. Wherry, pre-Islamic Allah worship and the worship of Baal were both astral religions in that they involved the worship of the sun, the moon, and the stars. The historical background concerning the origin of the Arabian "Allah" reveals Allah cannot be the same God of the biblical patriarchs, Jews, and Christians.

So much can be said on this subject. I've only provided a few comments to provide some insight on Allah and the Koran. I do know that there are significant differences between Islam, Christian, and Jewish religions. I also know that there are significant doctrinal differences between the Koran and the Bible. Review and study of each book reveal this to be emphatically so. Look into it for yourself.

***

Nation of Islam's Deception

The black community has been deceived by the Black Muslim Movement. My heart goes out to them because I know many of them are being deceived and misled.

Although it may not be politically correct, I believe it is important to address these issues. Truth is important, and one will never be free until one accepts the truth.

I think it necessary to deal with the background and history of the Nation of Islam, or the Black Muslim Movement, in order to gain insight into the deception of this movement. However, up front, let it be known that those of the Black Muslims Movement are not viewed by Orthodox Muslims as true Muslims or as part of Islam.

Let's start with Elijah Muhammad, who profoundly influenced this movement. Born Elijah Poole, son of a Baptist preacher, in October 1897, around 1930, he moved from his native state of Georgia to Detroit. It was there Poole came under the influence of an interesting teacher by the name of Wallace Fard.

Not a great deal is known about Fard except that he was a peddler of "African" clothing, who claimed that he was a brother from the East, born in Mecca, but no proof was ever shown. He promised relief from oppression and poverty and urged followers to renounce their birth names and adopt Muslim names, such as Muhammad. This helped create an African identity and black pride among his followers.

Using cult-based Christian teachings, Fard tore down his black followers' faith in the gospel of Jesus Christ. Denying the trinity of God and the deity of Jesus Christ provided an excellent foundation to deceive his believers.

Fard was a "white man" who introduced clever theories mixed with overtones of Islam as a way to sway his followers away from true Christianity, which he mocked as "the white man's religion." Basically, Fard took them from cult-based Christian teachings to a form of Islam, from the Holy Bible to the Koran, and from Jesus Christ to Muhammad, using the driving force of "racism" to fuel the process.

Fard then mysteriously disappeared in 1934. Many think he was murdered to get him out of the way. Regardless of why or how he disappeared, his disappearance gave Elijah Muhammad the perfect opportunity to take over the Black Muslim Movement.

The movement grew tremendously over the years as a result of Elijah Muhammad's guidance and organizational skills. It continues to grow and prosper today under the leadership of Louis Farrakhan. Elijah Muhammad died in 1975.

One big embarrassment to the Black Muslim Movement was the sudden disapproval of Malcolm X, who was eventually murdered. Malcolm X, born Malcolm Little, served the movement faithfully for twelve years until he woke up to Elijah's main moral problems, such as his thirteen illegitimate children, his greed and jealousy, and the constant strife that filled Elijah Muhammad's life. It was during his pilgrimage to Mecca that, for the first time, Malcolm X clearly saw the heretical and racist nature of the Black Muslim Movement in America.

Subsequently, he publicly renounced the teachings of Wallace Fard and Elijah Muhammad and begin to warn the black community about the heretical and racist nature of the Nation of Islam. As a result, Malcolm X was assassinated on February 22, 1965.

There are some bizarre teachings in the Black Muslim Movement. For example, Black Muslims claim Elijah Muhammad was prophesied to come, according to the book of Malachi 4:5–6 of the Holy Bible. Close examination and scriptural reference will prove they have the wrong Elijah. Elijah of the Holy Bible was a righteous man.

Closely examine Elijah Muhammad's life, and one will quickly ascertain a life filled with deception, fraud, racism, greed, immorality, and spiritual error. Nevertheless, it is true that racism and slavery are forever a shame and disgrace to American history. Yet, to combat white racism with black racism is to release the spirit of degradation and death from one generation to another. This does not promote dignity, but only stirs hatred and more strife. Furthermore, the rejection of the gospel denies people of any color the opportunity to find true dignity. For it's through the gospel of Jesus Christ that true dignity is truly found.

***

Jehovah Is Not Allah

I read the article on the Muslim religion printed in *The Herald Bulletin* on November 13. Ramadan and the lunar calendar were referred to in the photo. The Sabeans, pagans, in the pre-cultural time of Muhammad prayed five times a day and celebrated a month of fasting based on the lunar calendar. This appears to be where Muhammad got that practice. He used the same prayer times and the month of fasting like the Sabeans.

If Muslims serve the same God as Christians, then I ask—was Jesus Christ crucified or not? The Koran says he was not. Does that mean God was drunk when he wrote the Koran? Jehovah is consistent. There are too many differences between the Koran and the Bible to say it's the same god. Most assuredly, Islam is following a different god than the one of Christianity when one compares the substantial differences between the Koran and the Bible.

The Bible says that Noah's ark landed on the mountains of Ararat, and not Mount Judi as the Koran says. The Bible says Abraham went to sacrifice Isaac and not Ishmael as the Koran says.

The Bible says that the flood occurred during the time of Noah and not during Moses' time as the Koran says. These are just a few of a plethora of differences between the Koran and the Bible.

I respectfully refer Muslims who are seeking truth to the following websites:[3]

FaithFreedom.org: https://1ref.us/1fo

Answering Islam—A Christian-Muslim Dialogue: https://1ref.us/1fp

***

Sharia Law Should Be Banned

Sharia is the religious law of Islam. It deals with crime, politics, and economics, as well as personal matters such as sexuality, hygiene, diet, prayer, and fasting. Where it enjoys official status, Sharia is applied by Islamic judges. In western countries, where Muslim immigration is more recent, Muslim minorities have introduced Sharia family law, for use in their own disputes, with varying degrees of success.

Guidelines for American law are based on Judeo-Christian principles and values. With the increase of the Muslim population in America, there has been an increased push for Sharia law. I personally oppose the passage of Sharia law legislation as it commonly opposes the Judeo-Christian principles and values that the American judicial system was based on since inception. People who oppose making Sharia law legal in America are, in reality, not moved by hatred and fear; they are simply aware of the tyrannical nature of Sharia law and its practices.

Simply put, liberty and ethical justice are products of biblical and Christian influence in America. Influence of Christianity can be seen in the Magna Carta, Declaration of Independence, Constitution, and yes, in the laws of America. Sharia law often produces inequitable, barbaric, and cruel results, especially for young girls and women. For example, brutally beating a wife by her husband for a slight transgression would be considered "for her good" by Islamic law. I believe that Sharia law should be

---

[3]Both accessed November 11, 2020.

banned from our judicial system and land. Any inroads into our judicial system should be denied.

***

Opposed to Advertisement

Recently, the *Washington Post* printed a two-page color ad celebrating the Prince Alwaleed Bin Talal Center for Muslim-Christian Understanding, a $20 million "think tank" at Georgetown University. The ad shows one of Georgetown's beautiful Gothic buildings, topped by a stone cross. In the night sky above Georgetown is a crescent moon and star, symbols of Islam.

This is offensive to me. The cross identifies with the death, burial, and resurrection of Jesus Christ. The crescent moon identifies with Allah. There was a pre-cultural god known as Allah, the Moon god, during the time of Muhammad.

The Bible was not translated into Arabic until around the ninth century A.D. time frame. At that time, the translators felt pressure to place Allah into the name for God in translation. Remember, Muhammad had died in A.D. 632. Thus, Islam had already been in place for a long time in that region of the world.

If there is no connectivity between Allah and the Moon god, then why is the crescent moon a symbol of this religion? You'll see it on flags, on top of mosques, and literature.

You'll notice that the Bible does not confuse Jehovah with Dagon, Molech, or Baal. If the Koran was a continuation of the Bible, then why did Jehovah's name get changed in translation?

Muslims will say that the Bible was corrupted. The Dead Sea scrolls prove otherwise. God preserved His word. Jehovah is not Allah. Following Allah will lead multitudes straight to hell.

***

Muslim Raised from the Dead

I understand my editorials on Islam are considered hateful by a particular Muslim. I apologize if my opinions are taken that way, but that is not my intent.

I want to share an interesting story taken from the book, *Like a Mighty Wind*, by Mel Tari, a citizen of Indonesia, who was caught up in a mighty move and revival of God among Christians in that nation during the 1960s.

Mel and some fellow Christians went to a Muslim town to witness about Jesus Christ. Once there, they found out a Muslim chieftain had died of a heart attack in the jungle three days before. Jesus spoke to Mel, asking him and the others to pray for the man to be raised from the dead in the name of Jesus. They obeyed.

As a result, the Muslim was raised from the dead. The chieftain told the astounded Muslims that when the Christians prayed for him, Jesus Christ came into hell and took him back to earth. The chieftain, while in hell, said that he could see when Christians died, they ascended to heaven, whereas when Muslims died, he saw them fall into hell's flames. As a result, the whole community converted to Christianity.

The story is not submitted with animosity whatsoever. I urge all to receive the truth and revelation of Jesus Christ into their hearts before they pass on from this earth. It's the most important decision anyone will ever make in one's lifetime.

***

Islamic Persecution Continues Against Christians

Al-Qaeda attacked a church in Baghdad on October 31, 2010, killing at least fifty-eight people. Since then, other attacks have been carried out against Christians in Iraq. One gunman was reported to have said, "We will go to paradise if we kill you, and you will go to hell." Let's get to the point: Many Muslims believe it's Allah's will to carry out attacks against Christians. Their reference is the Koran.

My heart goes out to the Iraqi Christian community. In 2003, there were an estimated 800,000 Christians in Iraq. Many Christians have since fled that country. Iraq is not an isolated story by any means.

In another recent story, a Christian mother named Asia Bibi in Pakistan was given a death sentence for blasphemy. The police claimed that she called the Koran a "fake" and made negative comments about Muhammad. The Voice of the Martyrs reports that she had a religious debate with Muslim women which ended when she was physically attacked for proclaiming Jesus Christ to be "the true prophet of God." A cleric then reported her to authorities.

In Iran and the Palestinian territories the story is not much different. Christians continue to face brutal persecution from its Islamic persecutors.

Ayatollah Khamenei publicly called the "network" of house churches in Iran a threat to Islam.

Why are so many Muslims fearful of conversions to Christianity? Again, their reference is the Koran which strongly teaches against conversion from Islam, with severe consequences against those who do.

***

No Public Christian Churches in Afghanistan

According to the U.S. State Department, there is not a single, public Christian church left in Afghanistan. This reflects the state of religious freedom in Afghanistan ten years after the United States first invaded it and overthrew its Islamist Taliban regime. In the intervening decade, U.S. taxpayers have spent $440 billion to support Afghanistan's new government, and more than 1,700 U.S. military personnel have died serving in Afghanistan.

The last public Christian church in Afghanistan was razed in March 2010, according to the State Department's latest International Religious Freedom Report. The report, covering the period of July 1, 2010, through Dec. 31, 2010, also states that "there were no Christian schools in the country ... There is no longer a public Christian church; the courts have not upheld the church's claim to its ninety-nine-year lease, and the landowner destroyed the building in March [2010]," reads the State Department report on religious freedom. "[Private] chapels and churches for the international community of various faiths are located on several military bases, PRTs [Provincial Reconstruction Teams], and at the Italian embassy. Some citizens who converted to Christianity as refugees have returned."

Religious freedom, beyond Islam in Afghanistan, is dealt with harshly. This is the nature of Islam as inspired by the Koran and Hadith. In reference to military operations in Afghanistan, U.S. personnel are also prevented from proselytizing in any way. Point, this is a dark country in need of light.

This is a sad commentary on Afghanistan and the nature of Islam.

***

Christians Being Slaughtered

Christians have been slaughtered throughout the Middle East with hardly a notice from the Executive Branch since President Obama came to office. Nigerian human rights activist Emmanuel Ogebe recently reported that more Christians have been killed by Islamist Boko Haram than NATO troops have been killed in Afghanistan.

It wasn't long ago that President Obama was supporting war efforts in Libya to protect Muslim rebels, some with radical al-Qaeda links. Reason stated was for "humanitarian" protection. Furthermore, Mr. Mubarak, please step down and allow the Muslim Brotherhood to come forth.

> *Christians have been slaughtered throughout the Middle East with hardly a notice from the Executive Branch since President Obama came to office.*

Thousands of Christians have fled Iraq. Operation Iraqi Freedom has not protected them. In fact, their situation has been made much worse since America took out Saddam Hussein and allowed, in fact, required a new Iraqi constitution containing a "repugnancy clause." State Department advisers, I understand, insisted upon this clause. It says that notwithstanding anything else in the new constitution, nothing shall be done by the Iraqi government that is "repugnant" to Islam. Well, saying "Jesus is Lord" is repugnant to Islam. That can cost you your life.

Recently, Egyptian television showed the horror of a young convert from Islam to Christianity being beheaded. The Egyptian news anchor, exclaimed: "Is this what we want here?" And he asked the obvious question: "How will these people govern?"

It seems stories like this are largely ignored by the American media because the media, controlled by the globalists, is, in my opinion, anti-Christian. Yes, America, there is an agenda.

***

Christian Genocide Continues in Middle East

Forty-five Egyptian Christians were murdered by ISIS while attending church services on Palm Sunday and many others were wounded. It seems whenever Christians are killed by Islamic terrorists, it only receives scant news coverage. In reality, Christian genocide has been ongoing in the Middle East for many years now, yet most Americans remain sadly uninformed.

ISIS wants Christianity eradicated. This should be a big story in America, but it's not. The Islamic terror attack on the Brussels airport last year, killing more than thirty people, was heavily covered by mainstream media. The Islamic terror attack in France, when a driver plowed his truck into hundreds of people in Nice, killing more than eighty, was also heavily covered by mainstream media. The bloody footage, including dead children lying in the streets, was continuously highlighted.

Why is the mainstream media almost silent when Christians are being slaughtered throughout the Middle East? This is a compelling humanitarian story that should be extensively covered, but it's not. Thousands of Christians have been displaced, exiled, attacked, maimed, tortured, starved, and murdered. This is a crisis of epic proportions, yet the news coverage of this ongoing tragedy is almost negligible. Christian genocide receives less coverage than a Sean Spicer misquote at a news briefing, or a passenger being forced off an airline due to overbooking.

Even so, I strongly encourage Christians to pray for fellow brethren in the Middle East. If you don't pray for them, then who will? Pray for strength, encouragement, protection, and for their needs to be met.

***

Where's Outrage for Murdered Christians?

Mainstream media in America was rampant with extensive news coverage about the terrorist attack on two mosques in New Zealand that occurred on March 15, 2019. Apparently, fifty people died, with others being treated for gunshot wounds. Police took a white male, labeled as a white supremacist, from Australia into custody. Although this attack was wrong, this coverage falls right in line with the reinforcement of "Islamophobia."

Don't say anything wrong against Islam, or you'll be labeled "Islamophobic." Political correctness has been put into play for a long time now on this subject by the global elitists, or Deep State.

Interestingly, on the same date of March 15, 2019, Samuel Smith in *The Christian Post* reports that at least 120 people have been killed by alleged Fulani militant attacks since February in Nigeria, with the latest attacks resulting in the deaths of more than fifty and the destruction of more than 140 homes. Where is the outrage for the Christians being murdered by the Fulani Muslims?

I think it's time to coin a new term, "Christian phobia." Maybe mainstream media could help with this. That said, they won't because Christianity isn't important to them.

The Deep State, in effect, is anti-Christian. They'll use propaganda, ignore concerns, promote adversarial laws, pursue court cases, and steadfastly oppose Judeo-Christian values in their attacks against Christianity and promotion of their agenda.

***

Homegrown Islamic Terrorism Threatens U.S.

Jamaat ul-Fuqra, known in the United States as Muslims of America, has purchased or leased hundreds of acres of property throughout this nation. Sheikh Mubarak Gilani boasts of conducting the most advanced training courses in Islamic warfare.

Based on research, a documentary called "Homegrown Jihad: Terrorist Training Camps Around the U.S.," provides impressive evidence of how Muslims of America operates with impunity inside America. The recruitment video shows American converts to Islam being instructed in the operation of AK-47 rifles, rocket launchers, machine guns, and C4 explosives. It provides instruction on how to kidnap Americans, kill them, and conduct sabotage and subversive operations.

A 2006 Department of Justice report states that this organization has more than thirty-five suspected communes and more than 3,000 members spread across the U.S., all in support of one goal: the purification of Islam through violence.

Wall Street Journal reporter Daniel Pearl was attempting to interview Gilani in 2002 when he was kidnapped and later beheaded. One year later, Lyman Faris, member of Jamaat ul-Fuqra and al-Qaeda, pleaded guilty in federal court to a plot to blow up the Brooklyn Bridge.

Gilani was at one time in Pakistani custody for the abduction of Pearl. Intelligence sources further suggest a link between Jamaat ul-Fuqra and Richard Reid, the "shoe bomber" who attempted to explode an ordnance onboard a Paris-to-Miami flight on December 22, 2001.

Any of this information should not surprise anyone. Islamic leadership has already told you their goals: American government. Need I say more?

Secular researchers have also dated Lyuba, a baby woolly mammoth, at 40,000 years old. Creationist researchers argue that this mammoth actually died around 2,000 B.C., during the Ice Age that followed Noah's flood. Lyuba's remarkable lack of decay supports a death much more in line with the biblical timescale.

Scientific evidence supports the biblical story of Noah's flood.[5,6]

***

Humans Created in the Image of God

No creature is designed like a human. Our ability to communicate, understand, feel emotions, and to logically think seems to demonstrate that we were created for a particular purpose. Evolutionists, however, believe that human beings just evolved with no special design or purpose. Which is true?

Humans are creative, emotional, and spiritual beings, very distinctive from the animal kingdom. Humans have the unique ability to communicate thoughts and emotions through meaningful verbiage. Consider how human speech and writing contain complex sounds, developed thoughts, and an abundance of words. Notice that humans have a noticeably long throat, flexible tongue, defined, shaped lips, and distinct vocal cords. There's flexibility in the mouth, tongue, and lips to create a wide spectrum of sounds. A multitude of muscles work together during communication, while the brain and neurons process information and actions at a tremendous rate of speed. Verbal skills like these don't just evolve from monkeys.

Consider how humans are capable of a wide range of emotions, ranging from jubilation to desperation. Then consider how the different ways of expressing emotions sets humans apart from animals. The limbic system is a group of interconnected structures located deep within the brain; it's the part of the brain that's responsible for behavioral and emotional responses for humans.

Humans derive pleasure in many unique ways. Things are appreciated through the five human senses—sight, hearing, touch, smell, and taste. Humans may stop to marvel at a great man-made structure like the pyramids in Giza, or a beautiful scene from nature like the Niagara Falls, while animals won't process in like manner.

---

[5]Dr. Marcus Ross, "Two: Those Not-So-Dry Bones," Answers in Genesis, *Answers* magazine, January 10, 2010, https://1ref.us/1bo (accessed November 4, 2020).

[6]"Mammoth Tour," Answers in Genesis, *Answers* magazine, April 1, 2010, https://1ref.us/1bp (accessed November 4, 2020).

Humans also exhibit perceptive thought and conscious behavior. Animals are different in that they're more programmed to instinctive behavior. The migration of birds proves this point as they fly thousands of miles in their annual travels, often traveling the same route year after year with hardly any deviation. Their instinctive clock kicks in, and they're off.

Further, consider the number of extensive and verified cases of one's spirit leaving one's body in hospital emergency room situations. Numerous people can tell you what they saw when their spirits left their bodies during those periods of time. Yes, man has a spirit, also known as one's conscience.

Why were humans created? We were created to know and glorify God in a personal relationship.

***

Breath of Life Defies Definition

There's something exceptionally intriguing about life and the willingness to live. Whether it be in human beings or the animal kingdom, species strive to survive. Creatures regularly seek food and water in their efforts to subsist. Notice how endangering situations are carefully avoided when life is threatened. Dangerous situations are clearly shunned in efforts for protection of life.

God is so awesome. He created life, and I'm quite sure that He put this instinct into species; however, there's another aspect to life and God in regard to the breath of life. Let's take the subject of a human being born. I personally believe that God breathes life into that body at conception. At death, I believe that breath of life is drawn back into God, leaving just a corpse and departure of the person's spirit. In essence, God is the breath of life. Without His breath of life into a body, there could be no life, for He is the complete source of life.

This, in essence, separates species from inanimate objects, so to speak. Without the breath of life into a species, that species would be just a collection of matter with no feelings of existence whatsoever. It would be inanimate, and basically, just occupy a space like a rock. The breath of life from God cannot be covered by science textbooks. It cannot be covered by evolution. It defies humanistic definition because it extends from deity in the fullest sense of the word.

***

subject. However, I believe that there are definitive answers for strong consideration.

With that in mind, there's something that stays with me as I approach life. When something significant happens to one in life, one should always refer to the Bible for guidance. I know that it has been my foundation for living. What does the Bible say about different situations? Equally, what does the Bible say about certain phenomena throughout time?

Based on the Bible, over 4,000 years ago, God judged the wickedness on the earth. Many believe that Noah's flood occurred somewhere between 3,000 and 2,000 B.C. One must consider that this Great Deluge destroyed everything on land because of the pervasiveness and depth of the water coverage over the earth. This makes sense.

Genesis 7:11 says, "In the six hundredth year of Noah's life, in the second month, the seventeenth day of the month, the same day were all the fountains of the great deep broken up, and the windows of heaven were opened."

This indicates that fountains from below the surface broke up, and the windows of heaven were opened. This means enormous volumes of water came forth from beneath the surface of the earth and from the above atmosphere. The rainfall must have been immense, to say the least.

Huge earthquakes could have caused great rifts in the earth's crust, exploding the release of waters from beneath and setting off volcanic activity. When the earth opened up, coupled with seismic plate shifts, volcanos probably erupted and put hot lava and volcanic ash and dust into the atmosphere. Interbedded within the sedimentary rocks is evidence of incredible volcanic activity that has no parallel today. Vast, unusually thick layers of volcanic flows and ash interlayer sedimentary rocks and fit the worldwide flood paradigm very well. It appears that at the end of the flood, the world was covered by huge volumes of volcanic ash and gas that had spewed into the atmosphere. This volcanic ash and dust would naturally block the warmth of the sun from reaching the surface of the denuded earth.

Now consider the remaining water bodies (oceans, seas, lakes, rivers, ponds) that had been warmed from all the volcanic activity. These water bodies then send warm water vapor into the atmosphere. With cold air already over the land mixing with warm water vapor, then one has the potential for great snowfall.

With the atmosphere filled with volcanic ash and dust shielding warmth from the sun reaching the earth, then the snow remains and builds, and eventually, sheets of ice develop in great portions of the earth.

One may recall when Mount St. Helens erupted on May 18, 1980, that volcanic ash and dust were blown thousands of feet into the air and eventually spread extensively to multiple states. Sunlight was greatly shielded as one revisits this scene. This was just from one mountain erupting. Imagine multiple, and even stronger and more intense eruptions, happening throughout the earth during the Great Flood. Then consider the extensive amount of time it would take for the fallout to settle.

David Keys makes a case that a massive volcanic eruption in Indonesia caused the darkness, cooling, crop failures, and social upheaval that was recorded in A.D. 535.

My point is that there is a viable biblical explanation for the Great Ice Age. Much more can be discussed on the Great Ice Age; however, if you research this subject in greater detail, you'll find additional detailed information supportive of this narrative–that the Great Ice Age followed Noah's flood.[8]

[8]Michael J. Oard, "Chapter 7: The Genesis Flood Caused the Ice Age," Answers in Genesis, *Answers* magazine, October 1, 2004, https://1ref.us/1bq (accessed November 4, 2020).

come from the heart of man. God looks on the heart. Putting some token words on printed money, or offering a token prayer, doesn't necessarily make a godly nation. God looks deeper. He looks into the heart.

So what happens to a nation that banishes God from its government? Expect to see dramatic increases in violent crime, divorces, drug use, teen pregnancies, abortions, and immoral lifestyles. Expect to see what has happened in America during the past four decades.

One cannot live in one's past, or one forfeits one's future. Therefore, we as Americans need to look to the future. People who have a concern for the future of our nation are exhorted to pursue the following:

- Pray for America. Don't underestimate the power of prayer. The spiritual realm, in reality, is the most prominent realm and has more impact on the physical realm than many realize.
- Vote and assist in putting godly leaders in government. This may mean working on behalf of godly candidates.
- Raise your children in the ways of God. This means spending time with them and giving them godly direction.
- Stand up for godly values. Don't underestimate your part in the restoration of America. Each citizen can play a part. It's a team effort. America's future depends upon it.

In summation, I'll close with a statement from George Washington, the first president and commander-in-chief of the United States, "It is impossible to rightly govern the world without God and the Bible." Politicians and Supreme Court, please take note.

***

Scandalous

Let's go back to the late 1700s. Can anyone, in their right minds, actually envision the Founding Fathers having the Ten Commandments monument removed in one of the thirteen colonies? Emphatically, no. Do you actually think our first Supreme Court Justice John Jay would view the recent action taken in Alabama as correct? Emphatically, no.

Do people realize that Founding Father judges had prayer in the courtrooms with jurors? Do people realize that the U.S. capitol was used as a church building by the Founding Fathers? Do people realize that the Founding Fathers gave speeches, read from the Bible, and prayed at public school graduations?

Once again, we see these unelected federal judges making wrong decisions based on a flawed and incorrect policy. The Founding Fathers never meant the Constitution to be interpreted the way many are attempting to interpret today. The words "separation of church and state" are not even in the First Amendment.

There's an effort going on to ban God and any Judeo-Christian reference from public America. Of course, it's wrong. Simply put, the greatness of this nation can be directly traced back to our Judeo-Christian heritage. That's why, the same day Congress passed the First Amendment (September 25, 1789), they approved a resolution requesting George Washington to proclaim "A day of public thanksgiving and prayer ..."

Incidentally, I recently read where a USA Today/CNN/Gallup poll said that 77 percent of Americans opposed the removal of the Ten Commandments monument in Alabama.

***

Atheist Opened Door to Unwise Policies

Madalyn Murray O'Hair once stated that God was sadistic, brutal, and a representation of hatred.

William Murray said of his mother, "I was born into a home of near-constant rage and violence. As a result of my mother's constant angry outbursts, she could not hold down a job. She, my brother, and I lived with her parents and my unmarried uncle. My grandfather had never filed an income tax return, and most of what he did do during his life was illegal or ill-advised. My grandmother read Tarot cards and sent out demons by burning human hair. My uncle kept hordes of pornography in his room, and my mother filled the house with statues of mating animals, which she worshipped. My mother was an evil person ... Not for removing prayer from America's schools ... No ... She was just evil. ..."

The dismembered bodies of Madalyn Murray O'Hair, Jon Murray, and Robin Murray were found in January of 2001 at Camp Wood, Texas. One of the killers, David Waters, led the authorities to the site.

Even so, is Madalyn Murray O'Hair really to blame for removing prayer out of schools? I think not. The left-wing Court of the day wanted prayer out of schools, and they were just waiting for a case to change America. Ultimately, the blame goes to the Court and an apathetic nation for allowing it to be done.

really justified? It seems to me that the framers of the Constitution knew exactly what they were saying when they penned the Second Amendment. I'm also reminded of a quote by President Harry Truman, "I have little patience with people who take the Bill of Rights for granted. The Bill of Rights, contained in the first ten amendments to the Constitution, is every American's guarantee of freedom." The NRA may, in fact, may be doing the average citizen more of a favor than he realizes. Currently speaking, waiting periods and mandatory background checks for handgun purchases may appear reasonable to many, but where does the government stop?

Is the NRA wrong for trying to get government to increase prosecutions against criminals using firearms? Why hasn't there been greater enforcement of current law violations? It appears that federal prosecution of gun law violations has dropped significantly since 1992. Should new gun laws be put into effect when the current ones aren't being stringently enforced? NRA's support for Project Exile, a noble cause, "adopts a zero-tolerance for federal gun crimes, with federal, state, and local law enforcement working hand-in-hand to prosecute each and every federal violation."

People need to put blame where blame is due. Don't blame the NRA for senseless killings. Eric Harris and Dylan Klebold killed fellow students at Columbine High School. They were responsible for their actions. Are gun locks going to deter criminals from commitment of crimes? Let's get real.

Focusing on school and other senseless killings creates an emotional fervor against the use of guns, but this kind of reporting tells us only a small portion of the story and often a misleading one to boot. For example, in 1997, criminologist Gary Kleck estimated that over 2.5 million people a year defend themselves from an assailant or burglar by exercising their constitutional right to bear arms. According to data compiled by Lawrence Southwick Jr., "Victims using guns were consistently less likely to lose cash or other property than other victims., Why isn't there more reporting of people protecting themselves in this manner?"

One should also consider the countries of Switzerland and Israel before getting overly emotional about this gun control issue. Switzerland has a heavily armed population as well as a thriving gun culture. Shooting contests are a popular tradition for children twelve to sixteen, and yet, Switzerland has one of the world's lowest crime rates. What about Israel? Most adults are either on active duty or in the reserves. They possess weapons, and yet, Israel has a low murder rate among its citizens. It seems to me guns aren't a significant problem in these heavily armed countries.

Does one really think that gun control is going to stop the criminal? One will never effectively keep guns out of the hands of criminals. No matter what, smuggling and black market operations will ensure their needs are met. It doesn't take many weapons to commit crime. Stringent gun control measures could, in many cases, make it easier for criminals to carry out crimes against an unarmed or less defendable populace.

Zacharia Johnson once said during the ratification period of the Constitution, "The people are not to be disarmed of their weapons. They are left in full possession of them." President Jefferson also stated, "No man shall be debarred the use of arms. The strongest reason for the people to retain the right to keep and bear arms is, as a last resort, to protect themselves against tyranny in government." Much thought and foresight went to these statements.

Politicians need to focus on this most important issue of infringing on Second Amendment rights. Don't "grandstand" the gun control issue, but closely examine what can be done at the "causes and roots" of our society's problems. That's where a wise politician will do this nation a greater service.

***

Thanksgiving Lesson from Thanksgiving

The Mayflower, carrying 102 pilgrims and thirty crew members, landed at Provincetown Harbor off the coast of Massachusetts in November of 1620. Many of the colonists barely survived the harsh winters of 1620 and 1621. Many died.

Governor William Bradford subsequently implemented a collectivist policy in 1622 where he allotted each family a plot of land and mandated that all profits must be given to a common storehouse for all to equally draw from. This policy almost destroyed the Plymouth settlement. Why? It's because collectivism only works in theory, not practicality.

The less diligent members of the colony came late to their work in the fields and were easy in their labors. Knowing that they were to receive an equal share of whatever the group produced, they saw little reason to be more industrious in their efforts. The harder working among the colonists became resentful that their efforts would be redistributed to the more malingering or slothful members.

and local rights. The states had not fought Parliament only to submit to another centralized government in the area of religion. Every state was prejudicial toward its own Christian framework: those who did not agree could move to another state or into the territories.

The First Amendment did NOT separate church and state. It says with respect to religion: "Congress shall make no law respecting an establishment of religion or prohibiting the free exercise thereof." This meant that the federal government was barred from interfering with Christian laws and establishments of the thirteen states. This was a matter of states' rights exclusively.

Sorry, Supreme Court, there's "no separation of church and state" in the Constitution. Further, let me say, although America had some shortcomings, Christianity still prevailed in both the hearts of Americans and the laws of their government.

***

Mayflower Compact Gives Us Roots

Go to your roots, America, lest you forget who and what once made you great.

"In the name of God, Amen. We, whose names are underwritten, the Loyal Subjects of our dread Sovereign Lord King James, by the Grace of God, of Great Britain, France, and Ireland, King, Defender of the Faith, etc. Having undertaken for the Glory of God, and Advancement of the Christian Faith, and the Honour of our King and Country, a Voyage to plant the first Colony in the northern Parts of Virginia; Do by these Presents, solemnly and mutually, in the Presence of God and one another, covenant and combine ourselves together into a civil Body Politick, for our better Ordering and Preservation, and Furtherance of the Ends aforesaid: And by Virtue hereof do enact, constitute, and frame, such just and equal Laws, Ordinances, Acts, Constitutions, and Officers, from time to time, as shall be thought most meet and convenient for the general Good of the Colony; unto which we promise all due Submission and Obedience. In witness whereof we have hereunto subscribed our names at Cape Cod the eleventh of November, in the Reign of our Sovereign Lord King James, of England, France, and Ireland, the eighteenth, and of Scotland the fifty-fourth, Anno Domini; 1620."

Please notice that these new settlers in America undertook this venture for the Glory of God, and advancement of the Christian faith. That's Christian faith; the faith that was significant in the founding, and settlement of the United States.

***

The Supreme Court on Trial in God's Court for Its Decisions

Scene: The Supreme Court is on trial before Almighty God in heaven for treason. The trial is about to begin. All are welcome to listen in.

God: "Supreme Court, do you know why you're here?"

Supreme Court: "Yes, God, but we do not agree with the charges."

God: "Are you familiar with how America came into being?"

Supreme Court: "Of course, we are, God."

God: "Are you familiar with the Mayflower Compact, your Declaration of Independence, and your Constitution?"

Supreme Court: "Of course, we are, God. We interpret and rule on the Constitution."

God: "Let me say, up front, you've twisted the Constitution to say things it doesn't say, and as a result, you've led America down a decadent and immoral path. Who do you think inspired the Founding Fathers in the formation of America and the writing of the Constitution?"

Supreme Court: "I guess You did, God."

God: "Correct. Now let's talk to some witnesses."

Founding Fathers: "No way, God, we never would have allowed millions of babies to be murdered through abortion and take God out of our society through that crazy separation of church and state doctrine they put on the American people."

God: "Supreme Court, what do you have to say about this?"

Supreme Court: "God, we had to represent the people. After all, there are atheists, agnostics, Muslims, Buddhists, and many others, who live in America, who have rights too. Many in America don't believe life starts in the womb, or see you as God. We don't want to offend them."

God: "Let me make this clear. I was involved in the formation of America and blessed this nation from the beginning. It's currently a perversion of what I had in mind. You've helped in that perversion. You've allowed false doctrines to influence your decisions and rulings.

young student, voted for Barry Goldwater when he ran against Lyndon Johnson. Of course, the class overwhelmingly supported Lyndon Johnson, as did the populace. I was in the minority as Lyndon Johnson easily won.

I think we can learn some keen political lessons from students. As such, I want to submit to you a third-grade mock presidential election. However, in this case, I'll submit to you a scenario where one student runs against another student for the high office.

The two candidates were selected from the third-grade class. One we'll call Sam, and one we'll call Jimmy. Sam spoke before the class on how he was going to improve the class and make things better. It was an articulate and methodical presentation, considering his age. He took some time and brought out a lot of good points. It was an impressive presentation. The next candidate, Jimmy, then got up to make his presentation. The class prepared to listen intently. Jimmy then said, "If you elect me, then I'll give you free ice cream." Jimmy then sat down. The votes were cast, and Jimmy won overwhelmingly.

In reference to the free ice cream, I want to add that there are no free lunches. Someone has to ultimately pay. If Jimmy brought in free ice cream to the class, then someone paid for it.

***

CPUSA Endorsement Telling

The Communist Party (CPUSA) has been broadcasting its support for the Democratic Party and candidates Hillary Clinton and Bernie Sanders. However, for some reason, our media have failed to take notice. The liberal media writes about Donald Trump and support from white nationalists. So what gives?

The CPUSA endorsed Barack Obama in 2008 and 2012 and now supports both Mrs. Clinton and Mr. Sanders. Donald Trump has been questioned about support for his campaign from figures such as former Ku Klux Klan leader David Duke, but the open and admitted involvement of communists in the Democratic Party gets completely ignored by the press. Does this tell you something, America?

The CPUSA is based on Marxist doctrine, which calls for the elimination of private property and the overthrow of capitalism. Cultural Marxism seeks to eradicate traditional adherence to Judeo-Christian values and silence those individuals who are in favor of traditional families, as well as those who recognize differences between males and females. Can you see the influence of these Marxist values in our politics? These values are not prudent for society.

As suggested by its endorsements of President Obama in 2008 and 2012, the CPUSA has been very pleased with Mr. Obama. He's their kind of person, and so are Mrs. Clinton and Mr. Sanders. The communists believe that Mr. Obama, who was influenced at an early age by CPUSA figure Frank Marshall Davis, has transformed America into a socialist state through Obamacare and other initiatives, and has changed U.S. foreign policy by establishing relations with anti-American regimes in Cuba and Iran.

***

Trump Made Right Decision on Paris Agreement

President Trump put American interests above the desires of the global elitists by pulling out of the Paris climate accord. That said, President Obama tried to undermine Trump with some foolish, leftist rhetoric.

Obama cited his past negotiations on the Paris agreement as "principled American leadership." His negotiations would have bound America to a jobs-killing, economy-constraining, wealth-redistributing deal—all without the consent of Congress. This isn't principled leadership. It's doing what the global elitists want in efforts to help them accomplish their anti-American and globalist objectives. American patriots don't make deals like this.

The Paris Agreement was exceptionally costly and would accomplish virtually nothing in regard to climate change. If carried out, the deal would destroy hundreds of thousands of jobs, harm American manufacturing, and destroy trillions in gross domestic product. In another gross move, the Obama administration gave $1 billion in taxpayer dollars to the Green Climate Fund in support of negotiations leading up to the Paris conference without authorization from Congress.

Mainstream media attack Trump with the fact that the only countries not participating in the Paris agreement are Syria and Nicaragua. On a reciprocal thought, Trump could have gone along with Iran and North Korea, who signed onto the deal. Of course, they wouldn't play that in a negative way because it wouldn't serve their interests. Mainstream media

the American people are really in rebellion, when in reality, it's happening because of their staged events. Mainstream media will cover what's best for their agenda and remain silent on exceptionally important issues and matters for America.

The Democrats and RINOs, who are part of this group, faithfully serve as obstructionists against prudent policies designed for the improvement and best interests of America. They pretend to serve the American people, but in reality, they seek their demise. They use deceptive rhetoric against common-sense solutions in order to stir the emotions of citizens in a negative manner.

The Bolsheviks, ultimately, want control of the American people. They want America to become a third world nation. They want to place America under the globalist umbrella and take away her sovereignty. They're not patriots, and their flag has the hammer and sickle.

***

Contraceptives for Health Coverage?

As the federal government, let's have grocery stores give away food this week to people who have a need. Then for home builders, let's have them build an add-on room for those who have a need. Now for furniture stores, we'll have them donate free sofas for those who have a need. Anyone need a car, well, we'll take care of that one, too. We'll just direct the auto dealers to comply. It's as simple as that.

Our national leadership has lost the bubble. The federal government has no right to have an employer or insurer cover anything. There are no free lunches, America. In reference to this contraceptives debacle, be assured, all insured folks will absorb the cost. Action taken by the federal government in regard to this contraceptives issue is totally unconstitutional. Why do certain groups get favor from the government?

In reference to health, cancer and heart disease certainly qualify as health issues, but what do contraceptives have to do with women's health? There is no law preventing the purchase of contraceptives. Why is the government involved in this? Let's get to the point—the federal government has no constitutional authority to order any kind of insurance or insurance coverage, and especially at no cost.

There is an agenda, America. The global elitists are diligently working to speed America more quickly toward the New World Order.

Their representatives in leadership are incrementally destroying the Constitution. Evidence is in abundance for those who will perceive.

***

Democrat Party Supports Infanticide

The Democrat Party ensured that the Born-Alive Abortion Survivors Protection Act failed passage in the Senate. Only three Democrats voted for the bill: Sen. Bob Casey Jr. (D-PA), Sen. Joe Manchin (D-WV), and Sen. Doug Jones (D-AL).

What did this bill do? The legislation read, "This bill amends the federal criminal code to require any health care practitioner who is present when a child is born alive following an abortion or attempted abortion to: (1) exercise the same degree of care as reasonably provided to any other child born alive at the same gestational age, and (2) ensure that such child is immediately admitted to a hospital."

In essence, the Born-Alive Abortion Survivors Protection Act would mandate doctors to attempt to save born-alive children instead of allowing them to die. This bill recognized that a newborn baby is a baby, no matter what the circumstances were of the birth. For those who voted against this bill, a baby scheduled for extermination before birth is still fair game even after birth. This is infanticide, and it's— "MORALLY WRONG."

> *Knowing the Democrat Party platform and how it leans, it still amazes me how a Christian can vote Democrat.*

This bill would have ensured that babies who were purposely induced, or survived abortions, would've been provided appropriate medical care and treatment. How can anyone, ethically and morally, deny them this support?

The Democrat Party should also be known as the "Infanticide Party," "Party of Shame," and "Party of Death" after this vote.

Knowing the Democrat Party platform and how it leans, it still amazes me how a Christian can vote Democrat. The global elitists have a nefarious agenda.

***

civil. It's about the globalist agenda and retention of power. It's sinister and opposes true constitutional values.

Trump won the election—let it be.

***

LGBT Being Used as a Pawn for Policies

It used to be that when I went to school that men used men's bathrooms and locker rooms, and women used women's bathrooms and locker rooms. The global elitists are using the lesbian, gay, bisexual, and transgendered (LBGT) agenda to advance their policies. The LGBT community is being used as a pawn in a bigger scheme of insidious efforts. These policies are designed to break down the moral fiber of America and to continue the assault on Christianity and Judeo-Christian values.

The LGBT community is only a small percentage of the masses. It's like the tail wagging the dog. The masses don't want these policies. Laws are being passed against the will of the people. This flies in the face of America as a republic. In a republic the people elect officials to represent them and what their desires are. This is not being done in America. The masses don't want these policies; yet, they're being forced upon them.

Many people live their lives in deception, thinking it's truth. This pertains to some in the LGBT community. Some say that they were born that way. They, over time, as it continues to be reinforced by progressive thought, believe this lie, but they're living in deception. God would be unjust to make people that way, and then in the Bible, speak against it. God doesn't do things that way. LGBT lifestyles are a choice based on influences outside of God. Demonic influences, model behavior, family problems, and other factors influence LGBT lifestyles.

***

Obama Presidency Mired with Scandals

President Obama recently stated, "I'm extremely proud of the fact that over eight years we have not had the kinds of scandals that have plagued other administrations." This is blatantly false. Some scandals are as follows:

• Operation Fast and Furious: Armed drug cartels while trying to undermine the Second Amendment.

- Benghazi: Requests for security repeatedly denied while Americans died; citizens were lied to.
- IRS targeting of conservative organizations: Tea Party organizations were targeted.
- DOJ seizure of Associated Press records: Phone and e-mail records of Fox News reporter James Rosen were seized.
- NSA conducted mass surveillance against American citizens without a warrant: This was in violation of the Fourth Amendment.
- Obama administration seemingly paid ransom to Iran for hostages and lied to American people about it: Obama didn't reveal the details of deal with Congress and Iran; this had ransom all over it when $1.7 billion was given to Iran, supposedly settling a failed arms deal.
- Hillary Clinton e-mail scandal and compromise of highly classified material: Her server was unapproved and unsecured with blatant disregard of security.
- EPA poisoned a Colorado river: Three million gallons of toxic mine waste was dumped into the river.
- GSA scandal: Lavish spending occurred involving decadence in Las Vegas.
- Secret Service scandal: Prostitutes and unguarded classified material were involved.
- NSA caught spying on Congress: A law was broken by eavesdropping on private conversations between American lawmakers and Israel.

Some politicians are above the law.

***

Obama Caught Spying on Congress

Senator Burr, Republican chairman of the Senate Select Committee on Intelligence, told Breitbart News that his panel will investigate whether President Obama's National Security Agency broke the law by eavesdropping on private conversations between American lawmakers and Israel.

I remember when Richard Nixon spied on Democrats with the Watergate tapes. What did Congress do? They pursued impeachment. Here we have Obama caught spying on members of Congress. What will Congress do? Will Congress impeach him?

Here's how the scenario will probably unfold. The congressional committee will go through the motions. They'll express much concern, but what will they do—nothing. They'll come up with some reason to excuse Obama's actions.

Congress caters to Obama's wishes. There are some in Congress, although not many, who will stand up for the American people. There are some who have solid morals and principles and will attempt to do what's right for America, although, shamefully, not enough.

Congress is supposed to give checks and balances within our government. It has failed miserably during the Obama years. The key reason is that the global elitists have their hands in both political parties. The global elitists intend to take America into the New World Order and transform our government and nation into third world status. These people are entrenched, have deep pockets, and control the media.

God is our only answer out of America's current status. Pray for repentance, mercy, and assistance. Without God, America faces a bleak future.

***

Secretive Administration with an Agenda

In a recent interview with Al-Jazeera America, Jill Abramson of *The New York Times* described the Obama administration as "the most secretive White House that I have ever been involved in covering" and said it's inconceivable to think President Obama himself isn't directly responsible for the cloak-and-dagger policies that have made it difficult for even publications like *The New York Times* to get a straight answer.

There has been scandal after scandal. I've heard that there have been seven criminal leak investigations during this administration. Couple that with the hidden agenda this administration has, and it's not surprising this is an exceptionally secretive administration. That said, leadership starts at the top, and for one not to think that President Obama is personally involved with much of this seems to be totally naive.

Part of this administration's agenda has been the National Defense Authorization Act. The indefinite detention provisions need to be challenged. This law, in effect, establishes the legal framework for the establishment of a police state and the subjugation of the American citizenry through the threat of indefinite military arrest and detention, without the right to counsel, the right to confront one's accusers, or the right to trial.

The National Defense Authorization Act is not moral nor constitutional in my opinion. It's an assault on the freedoms of American citizens, and this law should be rescinded. It leaves American citizens vulnerable to arrest and detention, without the protection of the Bill of Rights.

Someone in Congress, please stand up for the American people!

***

U.S. Foreign Policy Is in Shambles

The Muslim Brotherhood is an international political, financial, and terrorist movement whose goal is to establish a global Islamic State (Caliphate). Their front group has infiltrated the U.S. government at high levels. According to retired four-star U.S. Navy Admiral James Lyons, under President Obama's guidance, every U.S. security agency has been penetrated by this radical anti-freedom organization. Obama ran on change in 2008, and the transformation of America continues to be in full swing since.

It's obvious to anyone monitoring what's going on in America that the Muslim Brotherhood exerts tremendous influence over the American government's foreign and domestic policies under President Obama. Much of the violence in the Middle East and across North Africa can be directly attributed to the Muslim Brotherhood's effective control over American foreign policy in the region.

I served as a civilian observer for the Multinational Force and Observer Group in the Sinai during 2007. I observed how President Mubarak had to exert a strong grip over the Muslim Brotherhood in order to maintain stability in Egypt. Then in 2011, I noticed how the U.S. Executive Branch and media were portraying the Muslim Brotherhood as moderate and were trying to force Mubarak to step down. I remembered thinking to myself what a lie to the American people. This group was radical. This is the same group that was affiliated with the assassination of President Anwar Sadat in the fall of 1981.

Then I monitored our support of al-Qaeda-linked rebels in the supposedly "humanitarian effort" of overthrowing President Gadhafi in Libya. Gadhafi had been pretty silent since the Reagan years. I wondered why there was such a strong effort to take him out since he was maintaining stability in the region. Through our direct efforts in Egypt and Libya, we helped to seriously destabilize this region.

Recently, Obama met with American Muslim leaders at the White House, but the administration was unwilling to reveal who attended the meeting, which was closed to the press. After stonewalling for days about the names of participants at the meeting, it was revealed that members of known jihadist groups were in attendance.

I believe it was the following day that Obama delivered his extremely offensive and controversial comments at the National Prayer Breakfast when he told those in attendance to get off their high horse, recalling Christians and the crusades. The Crusades happened hundreds of years ago. If this was an effort to somehow justify or soften current actions in the world, it fell on deaf ears.

Our foreign policy is in shambles. Former allies have been abandoned and are embittered. Under the present leadership in the White House and State Department, Israel is considered the aggressor, and Hamas and Hezbollah the oppressed. Based on demonstrated actions, Obama appears to be consciously anti-American, anti-Semitic, anti-Christian, and broadly anti-Western. Yet, the American public does not understand how this administration consistently finds itself standing against key foundations of America–religious freedom, capitalism, and justice under law.

To the detriment of our safety and well-being, the domestic Muslim Brotherhood front groups in America help dictate counterterrorism policies. In view of this, one may ask why Obama has such an affinity for the Muslim Brotherhood. Even the average citizen should begin to wonder what his beliefs truly are and who he really works for. He came to us with a mysterious and shrouded background and does not stand for the great values of this nation. George Soros and the global elitists have their man in the White House.

I strongly urge Christian pastors to conduct prayer in their congregations for our nation on a designated and ongoing basis. I strongly urge Christians to intercede for America on an ongoing basis. The root of America's troubles is a spiritual one. That's why we have the government leadership we have today. We must cry out to God in earnestness for repentance and divine intervention in our nation. If no repentance or divine intervention, disaster awaits.

***

American People Still Don't Know the Full Truth

I think the presidential election in 2012 may have been exceptionally corrupt. Numerous reports came out shortly after the election regarding corruption and voter fraud. Of course, much did not come out of those reports other than just rhetoric of words.

Judging on what has been seen during this current administration, was this election stolen at the polls? There has been scandal after scandal. Just like voter fraud during that election, people still don't know the full truth of Benghazi, Fast and Furious operation, targeting by IRS of President Obama's enemies, attacking of Libya without congres-

> *I think the presidential election in 2012 may have been exceptionally corrupt.*

sional approval, National Security Agency surveillance operations, and other matters of concern.

How do they get away with not telling the American people the truth or ignoring their requests for the truth? How can they hide things like they do? They can because they're protected. As long as this administration, like other previous administrations, carry out globalist elitist objectives, they'll be fine. Globalist elitist influence is prominent throughout our government, and most assuredly, our media. These people are ultra-rich and have an agenda that they're perpetrating on the American people through incremental change of laws and policy in our nation.

The only way out of this situation is a spiritual repentance unto the Lord Jesus Christ in this nation. Without this, America is headed for a tremendous train crash. Repentance is absolutely requisite. Without repentance and divine intervention, this nation will not change the direction it's currently headed.

***

Bill of Rights Being Nullified by New Law

Americans should realize that the National Defense Authorization Act (NDAA), coupled with the Patriot Act, for all intents and purposes, completely nullifies a good portion of the Bill of Rights, turns America into a war zone, and places U.S. citizens under military rule.

This law grants the U.S. military the legal right to conduct secret kidnappings of American citizens, followed by indefinite detention, interrogation, torture, and even murder. This is all conducted completely outside the protection of law, with no jury, no trial, no legal representation, and no requirement that the government produce evidence against the accused. It is a system of outright tyranny against the American people, and it effectively nullifies the Bill of Rights.

President Obama signed the NDAA on New Year's Eve. I doubt many Americans noticed its implications because they do not yet comprehend the big picture. This law, coupled with the Patriot Act, is paving the way for America's direction toward tyranny. The 9/11 event was purposely developed and executed, in part, America, to take away your rights. They appear to be getting away with it.

Signed into law by President G.W. Bush, the Patriot Act and Military Commissions Act effectively took away the Fourth Amendment to the U.S. Constitution. Now, the NDAA, signed into law by President Barack Obama, has effectively taken away the Fifth, Sixth, Seventh, and Eighth amendments to the U.S. Constitution.

The only presidential candidate who has expressed concern against this consistent and deliberate erosion of our rights is Representative Ron Paul.

***

Obama Still Working from the Shadows

Many leftists are still calling for President Trump's tax returns. This, of course, is just another ploy, like the Russian-collusion story, to try to get something on Mr. Trump that can be magnified and distorted.

Mr. Trump should consider showing his tax returns—but only after Barack Obama makes public his college records, passport application, immigration status when he was a student, funding sources for his college bills, college records, and Selective Service registration. Of course, would the mainstream press agree with that? Not likely, since they still protect President Obama at all costs.

Exhibit A: The media doesn't dare discuss the "Organizing for Action" (OFA) group. OFA is behind the strategic and tactical implementation of the resistance to the Trump administration that we are seeing across America, and politically active courts are providing the leverage for these insidious efforts. Mr. Obama's message to OFA members: "Organizing is the building block of everything great we have accomplished. Organizers around the country are fighting for change in their communities, and OFA is one of the groups on the front lines. Commit to this work in 2017 and beyond."

OFA is dedicated to leftist change. Its issues are gun control, social-ist healthcare, abortion, sexual equality, climate change, and immigra-tion reform. According to Paul Sperry, who has written for the *New York*

Post, Mr. Obama is intimately involved with OFA operations. OFA is anti-America, like those who support it.

***

Democrats Ignored Bill Clinton's Accuser

Christine Ford appeared sincere during the Senate Judiciary Committee hearing on the Supreme Court nomination of Brett Kavanaugh. Many were sympathetic with her story from something that happened thirty-six years ago. Questioning was done with much care and tenderness toward her during proceedings. Even so, Ford had no evidence, while Kavanaugh had evidence to support his case.

It might be interesting to scrutinize Christine Ford's medical history and political activities/background. They really went after Kavanaugh regarding activities from his high school and early college years in order to possibly discredit him, but shied away from any aggressive questioning toward Ford. Was Ford telling the truth? I can't say for sure.

I know from personal experience while working in Liberia during 2008 that people could look as sincere as could be and be lying through their teeth. I personally saw this in repetitive occurrences that reinforced my thinking on this subject. Just because someone says something, and looks sincere, doesn't make it so. Some people can lie and sell it well as truth.

Juanita Broaddrick was apparently in the hearing area. The Democrats made all over Ford but totally continue to ignore Broaddrick's rape accusation against Bill Clinton. Broaddrick had the who, what, when, where, and how information; yet, the Democrats laughed her off. Her evidence was exceptionally more compelling and substantive than Ford's. Democrats turned their backs on Broaddrick in 1999 and continue to do so.

In essence, Ford is being used to advance their political agenda, while Broaddrick detracts.

***

Some Lawmakers Delete God in Oaths

House Democrats continue their assault against God in the public arena. Some recent efforts focused on the removal of "so help me God" from the House of Representatives' oath witnesses took when testifying before several of the congressional committees, all of which are under Democrat control.

According to LifeSiteNews, the changes to the oaths have been slowly implemented ever since the House Democrats announced the new policy this past January. One America News pointed out in March that Rep. Steve Cohen, D-Texas, chairman of the House Judiciary Committee's Subcommittee on the Constitution, Civil Rights, and Civil Liberties, specifically omitted "so help me God" when swearing in witnesses at the hearing. When Rep. Mike Johnson, R-LA., challenged him, Johnson was publicly rebuked.

Take God totally out of secular society and place Him within a church building, only to be referred to at a Sunday morning service. Is this now the Democrat theme for God in our society? I'm sorry, but I want God involved in all aspects of our society. I want God involved in our government, education system, families, and on the battlefield when our soldiers are in harm's way. America unequivocally has prospered because of the grace of God.

Step by step, assault after assault is being conducted against our Judeo-Christian heritage and Christianity. The Democrat Party has become more socialist and further supports abortion, homosexuals, gay marriage, open borders, and transgender programs. A Christian must take notice.

***

Second Amendment Shouldn't Be Changed

Halls of Fame exist for players who consistently excel in their particular sport. Credit is given to acknowledgment of superior professional performance, and athletes are honored. That said, I want to introduce four members of the "Gun Control Hall of Fame" deserving of recognition.

First, there's Joseph Stalin. He took guns away from his citizens in 1929 and then murdered twenty million of them once they were defenseless.

Second, Pol Pot is a member. Guns were taken away in 1956, and subsequently, two million were murdered once defenseless.

Third, Adolf Hitler was easily inducted. He took away guns from his citizens in 1938 and then murdered thirteen million once defenseless.

Fourth, Mao Tse Tung is also a member. He took away guns in 1935 and then murdered twenty million defenseless citizens.

Gun control continues to be debated in America. The ultimate objective of the progressive movement is to disarm its citizens. They want to deceptively do this one step at a time while hiding their true objective.

Even so, criminals will always have guns, and tyrannical leaders can easily control and dominate a defenseless body.

There have been numerous cases where citizens have used deadly force to defend against aggression, but so often, the media won't cover these stories like they should. Honest, law-abiding citizens aren't causing the problems, criminals are.

The Second Amendment was written by the Founders to protect its law-abiding citizens from the tyranny of government. It was placed in the Bill of Rights with great wisdom.

***

Gun Control Not the Answer

Gun control is not the answer. Look at Obama's Chicago with its strict gun control laws, and yet, its murder rate is off the charts. No, the global elitists, Democrats, and leftists already know that gun control is not the issue. They simply use gun control to attack second amendment rights in support of their godless agenda. Criminals will always have guns.

Here's the issue—it's spiritual. Change the spirit, change the man. Don't change the spirit, don't change the man. School prayer was taken out of schools in 1962. The McGuffey Readers were used for more than 100 years as textbooks in public schools until they were stopped in 1963. McGuffey Readers were widely used in American schools from the mid-nineteenth century to the mid-twentieth century and are still used today in some private schools and in homeschooling. The McGuffey Reader taught biblical values and morality.

The modern humanist culture and mainstream media would prefer that we all forget America's Christian heritage and embrace new pluralism. They would prefer that we forget that the nation was once stronger and safer when Christian morality was taught in government schools. The prohibition of such teaching is one key reason that we have the conditions in society that we have today.

The sad truth is that much of our nation, with its secular and humanistic system, has rejected righteousness in favor of sin. Remove God from your schools and society, and what can you expect? Here's what you can expect—increased crime, immorality, and opposition to the laws of the land.

***

Compare 1935 Germany and 2014 America

Startling comparisons exist between 1935 Germany and 2014 America. Here's a list of some comparisons:

- The demise of capitalism was fine, and the rise of socialism accepted.
- Prayer was taken out of schools in 1935.
- Daycare raised the children of Germany during the 1930s and 1940s.
- Socialized medicine ruined the German health care system. The elderly and handicapped were marginalized.
- Abortion became the new norm and was even expected.
- Private education was gone by 1938.
- Government spending skyrocketed, and taxation increased to 80 percent.
- Gun registration was followed by gun confiscation by the Nazis.
- Free speech incrementally faded as newspapers and other media proclaimed the pro-government spin on things.
- The green agenda was adopted because it was soaked in paganism. Hitler loved paganism.
- Government spying greatly increased.
- Germans were totally taken by the great oratory skills of Hitler. How could he lie to them?
- The church in Germany did not want to cause problems with the government. Pulpits would never address serious issues or politics.
- Churches in Germany were known for compromise. Many pastors in Germany wanted to be popular and find favor with the government. They did not want to offend anyone.

History has shown us that tyranny can come from too much pervasive government, as well as unscrupulous leadership. Today, many people in America look for government to take care of them. In essence, government has become their god.

Request—will churches/Christians please pray fervently for America?

***

Black America and the Democrat Party

In honor of Black History Month, I thought that I would discuss black America and how the Democrat Party has manipulated it through liberalism.

Liberalism ultimately is about controlling the masses. Lies are continually used to deceive and manipulate American citizens. Democrats celebrate themselves as the party of diversity and acceptance, but their actions and history prove otherwise.

First Lie: All Republicans are racists. Wrong. In reality, the Democrat Party exudes racism. Racist quotes have been directly attributed to numerous Democrat presidents and other prominent leaders if one cares to research. Not only is this seen through quotes but also in purposeful divisive action taken to cause discord among the people.

Many believe that birth control activist Margaret Sanger was racist based on her actions and verbiage over the years. Yet, Hillary Clinton expressed her admiration of Margaret Sanger.

Second Lie: Democrats are champions of civil liberties. History shows that the Ku Klux Klan supported the Democrat Party for many years in their creation of mayhem. It's common knowledge that many black and white Republicans were lynched by the KKK in their hateful aggression. Interestingly, the Jim Crow laws in the South were created by Democrats looking to overturn Republican civil rights laws. It's also clear that white nationalism comments by the Democrat Party today are nothing more than election strategies.

Democrat Senator Robert Byrd, a mentor of Hillary Clinton, served a one-year term as leader of his local KKK chapter in West Virginia in the 1940s. No nationally elected Democrat opposed him being president pro tempore of the Senate.

No one today can argue that America is a more racist or white nationalist society than it was in the early 1900s. We've come an exceptionally long way since the segregated bathrooms, but the Democrat Party and mainstream media play the race card every election period to stir up racism and class warfare among the black populace. To prove their

> *The Republican Party was founded in 1854 as an abolitionist movement. The great black abolitionist leader Frederick Douglas was firmly Republican.*

hypocrisy, if the Democrat Party were actually concerned about white nationalism, they would be holding hearings on Antifa, a far-left violent white hate group.

In contrast, the Republican Party is the real party of civil rights. The Republican Party was founded in 1854 as an abolitionist movement. The great black abolitionist leader Frederick Douglas was firmly Republican. Republican President Abraham Lincoln was the one who authored the Emancipation Proclamation, which freed the slaves. Per David Barton, 94 percent of the Republicans endorsed the fourteenth Amendment to the U.S. Constitution, granting blacks citizenship in America, when it came before Congress, while not one Democrat voted for it.

Third Lie: The Democrat agenda is best for black Americans. Black communities haven't really prospered under the Democrat policies. Democrat support of programs that oppose Judeo-Christian values has led to decadence and immorality within both black and white communities. In reality, many Black Americans have remained poor while the majority continue to vote overwhelmingly Democrat.

Liberalism has destroyed black America. Black Americans need to cast off the chains of the Democrat Party and support conservative Republicans who have Judeo-Christian values.

***

Establishment Protects Its Own

This whole charade with Special Counsel Robert Mueller's investigation just proves how entrenched the globalist elitist influence is in Washington.

It's amazing how this whole thing can go on as it does. It should never have been started since it was bogus from the beginning. The Mueller investigation baffles logic and decency and is just a tactic of the global elitists to impede and undermine the Trump agenda.

The Republicans won the election but have allowed the global elitists, leftists, and Democrats, to walk all over them in this investigation. U.S. Attorney General Jeff Sessions recuses himself over bogus charges; why didn't he stand his ground when there was nothing there? Where is the pursuit of truth?

It's obvious Russian collusion and corruption occurred in the Hillary Clinton and uranium deal. This has been out there for a long time, but no substantive action has been taken. It tells you the globalist elitists and the establishment has its hands in both political parties. Trump has a lot to fight against.

The Trump Dossier was bought by Clinton and the Democrats. It doesn't get the attention it should be getting since the global elitists control mainstream media.

What does this tell you? It tells you that the global elitists and establishment are entrenched and that many are above the law, such as President Obama, the Clintons, former Attorney Generals Eric Holder and Loretta Lynch, and former Clinton campaign chairman John Podesta, and others. The establishment protects its own.

***

America Is an Oligarchy

America has become a country led by a small dominant class comprised of powerful members who exert total control over the general population—an oligarchy, said a new study jointly conducted by Princeton and Northwestern universities. In the study, "Testing Theories of American Politics: Elites, Interest Groups, and Average Citizens," researchers compared and contrasted 1,800 different U.S. policies that were put in place by politicians between 1981 and 2002 and found that most benefited the average and wealthy American or the special interest group.

One concluding finding in the study: The U.S. government now represents the rich and powerful, not the average citizen.

I've come to the conclusion that the global elitists have their hands in both parties. It's a charade for the American people—elections and pre-election campaigning is like a play to a great extent. A play entertains people while elections and pre-election rhetoric, with assistance of the media, is put on by the global elitists to give entertainment of free elections. In reality, they put their players in place, sometimes through unscrupulous means, and continue their agenda in Washington election after election.

This is why the Tea Party is politically attacked. This party is not a global elitist team player. I perceive some elected either get on the global elitist bandwagon, or they'll be viciously attacked, or something will be spun to ruin their reputation. As an elected official, if you're not a global elitist team player, then you'll have a "rough road" in Washington.

***

Homelessness on Increase as Economy Downturns

This evening, countless numbers of homeless people will try to make it through another cool night in large tent cities that have been established in the heart of major cities such as Seattle, Washington, D.C., and St. Louis. Homelessness has gotten so drastic in California that the L.A. City Council has formally asked Gov. Jerry Brown to officially declare a state of emergency.

Portland has extended its "homeless emergency" for yet another year, and city officials are really struggling with how to deal with the booming tent cities that have sprung up.

According to the Department of Housing and Urban Development, more than half a million people are homeless in America right now, but that figure is increasing daily. It has also been reported that that the number of homeless children in America has substantially increased in recent years.

If economic downturn continues to accelerate, homelessness is going to spiral out of control. The economy is on thin ice; although, this current administration wants to paint a different picture. Pretty soon, there could be tent cities in virtually every community in America as the middle class is struggling more and more.

Much of this situation can be attributed to our economic policies. Global elitists purposely de-industrialized this nation. Our de-industrialization just didn't happen by chance. It was orchestrated through globalist policies.

Although Barack Obama and Hillary Clinton are global elitists, Donald Trump is not. May God help Trump bring jobs back to the United States.

***

Political "Twilight Zone"

Welcome to the real-life Twilight Zone. During the first scene, you'll notice the Islamic immigration policies of Western nations. The general populace in these countries does not desire these policies, yet the governments force them on their people—despite the fact that they bring an increase in crime and political demonstrations. Notice that the news media promotes these policies and keeps silent on immigrant crimes, such as rape of native women.

In the next scene, politicians use concocted data to push "climate change." They use the idea that if you tell lies often enough, people will believe the lies as fact. Amazingly, many people do.

The third scene takes us to an "attack" mentality. It's a phenomenon used throughout history. If you don't agree with someone, such as President Trump, attack him daily no matter what he does. Never mind that he wants to bring jobs back. Never mind that he wants to restore law and order. Never mind that he wants to appoint judges who will uphold the Constitution. Attack him because he wants to hold criminals accountable. Attack him because you just don't like him.

In the next scene, the strategy of "fake news" is gainfully employed by the news media. No longer news, it really has now become propaganda, and many people still don't get it.

***

Congressional Leadership

Democrat Michigan Representative Rashida Tlaib was sworn into Congress on her personal Koran.

"My swearing in on the Koran is about me showing that the American people are made up of diverse backgrounds, and we all have love of justice and freedom," Tlaib told the Detroit Free Press. "My faith has centered me. The prophet Muhammad was always talking about freedom and justice."

I want people to thoughtfully consider the above statement. It sounds good to many on the surface, as do many political statements. Tlaib states that her faith has centered her as she also talks admirably about Muhammad.

Most Americans are not familiar with the teachings of the Koran or Mohammed. The Koran, specifically Surah 5:51, states to "take not the Jews and the Christians as allies." Surah 9:29 states to "fight those who believe not in Allah." I could list extensive Koran references that should be a cause of concern when leaders of your government are centered in this belief system.

If Muslim leaders are instructed by the Koran to take neither Jews nor Christians as their friends and to fight those who believe not in Allah, then that should be a cause for concern. As more Muslims are elected to Congress, will there be a greater push for Sharia law versus the Constitution?

These thoughts aren't centered in islamophobia; they're centered in pragmatic thought toward our Judeo-Christian heritage and the laws in our nation, which they are based on. As one builds one's life on truth, a nation should do likewise.

***

No Grounds for Impeachment

Numerous Democrat and liberal voices have repeatedly cried out, "Impeach President Trump!" As they do this, mainstream media beat the impeachment drums with the same regularity. My main question—for what reason? They have none.

House Republicans conducted an exhaustive investigation on foreign interference in the 2016 election and found no evidence that Russians colluded with any members of the Trump campaign, and disputed a key finding from the intelligence community that Russia had developed a preference for Trump during the election.

Based on the more than $25 million Mueller investigation, there was no collusion nor obstruction against Trump. Granted, Mueller's ambiguous follow-on remarks gave opportunity for the Democrats and liberals to try and stir the pot for dissension; however, many believe those remarks were political in order to continue their charade against Trump.

There appears to be much information coming out proving that the Mueller investigation was rigged from the beginning. Devious procedures, lies, and criminal tactics were used with motives to go after Trump and take him down any way they could. This, in essence, was a black-operation attempted coup from elements from within the government to purposely take down a duly elected president. They knew there was no Russian collusion from the start, but they vigorously tried to find/falsify/generate/twist information to make something stick to support their insidious objectives.

Here's why they want to impeach Trump. He stands in the way of their globalist agenda. Trump is not a globalist and fights for America's sovereignty. Their actions are criminal.

***

Impeachment Inquiry a Kangaroo Court

There's an internal revolution in America. Not only is it seen in society, but it's also seen in our government. What happened in this impeachment inquiry by the Democrats was appalling. It was insurgent.

The Democrat impeachment inquiry opposed the norms of our government. Republicans were not allowed to call witnesses, constrained in their questioning, and the president did not have fair representation. It was a kangaroo court in search of some crime. The Democrats weren't searching for truth, but for anything they could use in their impeachment scheme.

The Democrats, leftists, and mainstream media are trying to overthrow our government. Their coup efforts against President Trump started right from the beginning of his election. Their actions are about subversion to our Constitution and outright rebellion to America's sovereignty.

Many of the Democrats, RINO Republicans, and mainstream media are controlled by the global elitists. Many of these legislators certainly don't serve the American citizen.

President Trump signed the USMCA bill during 2018 to vastly improve the trade situation between Canada and Mexico. This improved trade arrangement substantially benefits citizens and will bring thousands of jobs to America. Yet, the Democrats won't bring it to vote. They refuse to close loopholes in our immigration policies because they want open borders. They now have a socialist agenda.

Ayn Rand once stated that communism enslaved men by force, while socialism did it by vote. A vote for a Democrat is now a vote for the destruction of America.

***

Citizenship: A Common Sense Question

A citizenship question has appeared in some form or another on censuses throughout our history; however, it was only removed entirely in 2010 during the Obama administration. Its roots reach far back into the founding era. Thus, the citizenship question is not a new concept; it really equates to common sense. So, why would the Democrat Party vigorously oppose a simple, common sense citizenship question on the census?

It's because the Democrat Party has become the party of lawlessness, socialism, and key supporters of the globalist agenda. They seek to erase the sovereignty of America. Their acts and objectives are treasonous under the guise of politics. There's a crisis on our border, and they purposely do nothing about it because they want open borders. They want America flooded with illegal immigrants.

The Democrat Party has been virtually a do-nothing party since 2016 besides obstructing justice, refusing to truly help the American people, and investigating President Trump. These elected representatives were sent to Washington to help improve America; yet, their daily agenda, coupled with mainstream media, have been to get Trump at all costs. Resist Trump on the border and criticize him for anything he tries to do for this nation. They aren't for the American people; they're for the globalists and their agenda.

If their insidious ploys and deceitful schemes of maneuver succeed, you will not recognize America once they put America in their vice-like grip of control. Just ask the Venezuelan citizens for their advice, and they'll tell you to oppose the disingenuous Democrat Party.

***

Clinton Broke Finance Law

Federal Election Commission (FEC) records indicate that the Hillary Clinton presidential campaign illegally laundered $84 million. Yet mainstream media took no notice.

Gary Gensler, the chief financial officer of the Clinton campaign, said the Democratic Party was "fully under the control of the Clinton campaign. The campaign had the DNC on life support, giving it money every month to meet its basic expenses, while the campaign was using the party as a fundraising clearinghouse." In essence, the contributions qualified as donations to the Clinton campaign for purposes of federal campaign finance law, and when properly accounted for, exceeded the legal contribution limits. Thus, based on the 2014 Supreme Court ruling in McCutcheon v. FEC, Mrs. Clinton and the Democrats violated the law.

The Supreme Court stated: "Lest there be any confusion, a joint fundraising committee is simply a mechanism for individual committees to raise funds collectively, not to circumvent base limits or earmarking rules. Under no circumstances may a contribution to a joint fundraising committee result in an allocation that exceeds the contribution limits applicable to its constituent parts; the committee is in fact required to return any excess funds to the contributor."

Mrs. Clinton and the Democrats broke the law in their campaign finance scheme, but the mainstream media are too busy generating bogus news against President Trump to cover the story.

***

Support of Bernie Sanders Problematic

Personally, I was amazed that so many people supported avowed socialist Bernie Sanders for president in the primaries. It speaks loudly that America has grave concerns in regard to the American youth base. Cultural Marxist education and media propaganda have mesmerized too many young Americans who do not recognize the values that once made America great.

Cultural Marxist education and media propaganda have mesmerized too many young Americans who do not recognize the values that once made America great.

President Obama traveled to Cuba in 2016. He was wined and dined by the political elites and enjoyed a festive visit. Many feel that he betrayed many victims of communism in and from Cuba. Today, many freedom seekers are in Cuban prisons because they don't go along with Cuba's communistic control and doctrinal policies. The truth about Cuban politics is hard to find because of media spin and propaganda dominating American press dissemination.

Consider the thoughts of filmmaker and American citizen Agustin Blazquez, who sees a radical shift happening in America, and it reminds him of Communist Cuba, his native land. He says the left has been clever by using "very non-threatening words," like liberal, progressive, and concerned citizens, for advancing government control of American lives. As the "fundamental transformation of America" continued under Obama's governance, Blazquez warned that America is in a precarious situation. Privileges, rights, and property could evaporate fast with America's trend toward erosion of liberties.

Complacency is the first step to captivity. It's time for America to reject leftist propaganda and policies.

***

Give Trump Credit for Oil and Gas Boom

It's incredible that President Obama would take credit for the recent oil and gas boom of America. Recently, Obama spoke at a gala for Rice University's Baker Institute and appeared to take credit for our nation's oil and gas boom.

Data from the Congressional Research Service shows that shares of crude oil and natural gas produced on federal lands dropped from 2009 to 2017, even as production on nonfederal lands greatly increased. According to the Institute for Energy Research, production on federal lands has not been able to fully recover from Obama administration policies that resulted in a moratorium on offshore energy permitting and long delays in approving drilling permits.

One simply needs to review Obama's record on energy. He promoted policies designed to curb fossil-fuel usage and production, including the Clean Power Plan, the federal methane rule, federal restrictions on hydraulic fracturing, the rejection of the Keystone XL pipeline, and the Paris climate accord. His assault against the coal industry was severe.

In reality, the one who should get credit for the oil and gas boom is President Donald Trump. Through his leadership, he has sought to neutralize the Obama administration's energy agenda by pulling out of the Paris agreement, repealing the fracking restrictions, and rolling back the methane rule. Unfortunately, mainstream media refuses to acknowledge Trump's substantial achievements.

Numerous policies from the Obama administration were not in America's best interests. That's because they were globalist policies and purposely designed to be detrimental to America's sovereignty. Trump is for America as a nation and purposely for her prosperity.

***

Let Venezuela Be a Warning

Venezuela is in crisis. Under the socialist regimes of Hugo Chavez and Nicolas Maduro, a nation that in the 1950s was the wealthiest in South America, with vast oil reserves, is now in total poverty. People are without food and medicine after fifteen years of socialist policies. Many have been reduced to scavenging garbage to feed their families. Power outages that last for days at a time have plunged Venezuela into darkness without access to clean water, food, or communications networks. Many people have lost their lives to starvation, disease, and violence.

Recently, America, Canada, Israel, Brazil, and several other nations recognized opposition leader Juan Guaido as the legitimate leader of Venezuela in the wake of Venezuela's disputed elections. Further, Mr. Maduro has closed the border to block access of American humanitarian aid into Venezuela and blamed most of the chaos on American operatives. Last month, Russian forces landed in Venezuela to assist the Maduro socialist regime. What we have now in Venezuela is chaos, poverty, and complete government failure—all brought on by socialist policies.

Americans listening to Bernie Sanders, Beto O'Rourke, Alexandria Ocasio-Cortez, and other congressional Democrats need to reject their political rhetoric. Their policies may sound good to some on paper, but in the end, they'll lead America into an abyss and abject poverty. Capitalism is far superior to socialism. There are no utopian systems, but socialism is unequivocally a dismal failure. It creates a higher elite who manage the peons who work for them.

Reject the Democrats and their socialist policies if you love America.

***

Democrat Party Has Changed

It's time to eliminate the Democrat Party. This is no longer the Democrat Party of the John F. Kennedy era. The Democrat Party has transitioned into the Marxist and Socialist Party of America.

After reviewing the Democrat Party platform from the last presidential election, I found it exceptionally hard to comprehend how a Bible-believing Christian could have voted for a Democrat. The Democrat Party opposes basic principles of morality as set forth in Scripture. It has become the party of activism, obstructionism, and violence. It's easy to see why Communist Party USA consistently supports the Democrats.

While it accuses the Republican Party of racism and bigotry, it's really the party of racism and bigotry. Its past history and current actions of accusations repeatedly corroborate this statement. It's the party that promotes division and disunity while pretending to actually care about the American people.

The Democrat Party doesn't care about the Judeo-Christian values of America, nor the Constitution. They're the party of globalism, and they're anti-American, anti-sovereignty. They use people and causes to promote the godless agenda of the global elitists.

Lenin is reputed to have coined the phrase "useful idiots" to describe those in the West who acted as apologists for the political brutality and economic failure of Soviet communism. It seems that the Democrat Party could equally apply this term to their followers; although they want their followers to feel enlightened.

*****

Democrat, Republican Platforms Vastly Different

There are clear distinctions between the Democrat and Republican platforms. The Democrats passed the most liberal platform in the history of the Democrat Party. Now that the Democrat Convention is over, the Democrats hope to use their party planks to move this nation even more into a liberal direction.

On abortion, Democrats turned their backs on forty years of policy as they call for repeal of the Hyde Amendment—a law signed by President Jimmy Carter that prohibits the use of federal tax dollars for abortion.

Republicans call traditional marriage the "foundation for a free society" and acknowledge traditional families as ideal for raising healthy children who are less likely to get into trouble. However, the Democratic platform calls for expanding rights for LGBT.

The Democrats call for a carbon tax on the environment, while Republicans oppose it.

The Democrats are trying to significantly change the face of America with their progressive movement. Through government, they intend to decimate our Judeo-Christian foundations.

I understand that Rep. Keith Ellison, a Muslim, at the Democratic Convention pushed for more Muslims to run for political office. Does one truly realize the difference between Sharia (Muslim) law and the Constitution? Muslim law and the Constitution are not congruent—vast differences. It's like oil and water. They don't mix. With more Muslims in elected positions, one will see a push for more changes in our society and law.

The visions between the Republican and Democratic platforms have stark differences. Americans have a distinct choice in this election.

*****

Iran Deal Was a Betrayal

President Barack Obama didn't require Iranian leaders to sign the nuclear deal. This is appalling when one considers that the government tried to sell this to America as an official agreement. The Joint Comprehensive Plan of Action was not a treaty or an executive agreement and was not a signed document after all.

Obama, essentially, elevated a sworn enemy of the United States to a "regional power" in what he called a "new equilibrium" that would balance the Shiite regime against Sunni powers and Israel. He thoroughly undermined U.N. Security Council resolutions negotiated by previous administrations that banned any nuclear enrichment at all by Iran, and he then turned a blind eye to Iranian terrorism.

He also made this deal quite profitable for Iran. Billions were ultimately paid to Iran, but the details surrounding these payments remain shrouded in mystery, according to Mark Dubowitz, executive director at the Foundation for Defense of Democracies.

Even so, Iran remained committed to destroying America, as well as Israel. It has the blood of hundreds of American soldiers on its hands. It remained engaged in war crimes in Syria and elsewhere and continued to sponsor deadly terror attacks around the world, including attacks against civilian and diplomatic targets. Yet, Obama was committed to elevating and supporting the Iranian regime even to the point of failing to assist the Iranian opposition when it rose up in 2009.

In reality, Obama betrayed America and Israel when he so obligingly supported the radical theocrats of Iran.

*****

Democrats More Than Sore Losers

There is no evidence that the leaked Hillary Clinton campaign emails are of Russian origin ("WikiLeaks figure says 'disgusted' Democrat leaked Clinton campaign emails"[11]). WikiLeaks said the emails came to them from an inside leak, not from an outside hack, and former top National Security Agency official William Binney has stated that if Russia were the source, the NSA would have conclusive proof.

The left lost the election, voter recount, and the Electoral College vote. Now, it appears time to try the Russian card. Yes, let's now blame our loss on the Russians while we continue to organize demonstrations from behind the scenes. You simply can't trust the current government or

---

[11]https://1ref.us/1fs (accessed November 4, 2020).

mainstream media. I think many people are beginning to get a sense of their unscrupulous actions.

President Obama hypocritically feigns contempt for a so-called Russian connection to these emails. In 2015 Obama spent hundreds of thousands of dollars on sending subversive groups such as One Voice to be "boots on the ground" in Israel to hack Israel's free and fair election process in a lame attempt to oust Prime Minister Benjamin Netanyahu, who was seeking reelection.

One Voice used the money to build a voter database, train activists, and hire a political consulting firm with ties to President Obama's campaign—all of which set the stage for an anti-Netanyahu campaign, according to the Senate Permanent Subcommittee on Investigations.

It's time for the left to quit its shenanigans and give Donald Trump a chance to clean up the mess it has left him.

***

End Mueller Investigation

The whole Robert Mueller investigation was a scam from the start. They knew that there was no Russian collusion from the very beginning. Defying the will of the people, this would be their pre-planned and fabricated scheme to try and oust President Trump from power. Why? It's because he interrupted their globalist agenda. Trump is not a globalist elitist or part of the Deep State. He's red, white, and blue for this nation, while the Deep State is not. The Deep State is subversive to the ideals for what America stands for and against the Constitution.

This whole assault on Trump is criminal with pervasive government corruption. It almost seems amazing and surreal how this investigation keeps going and going like the Energizer bunny. It appears that the Justice Department is out of control. This all-out effort to get Trump is shameful and has become an embarrassment to the rule of law and order. Is Rod Rosenstein in charge of the Justice Department, or is it Jeff Sessions? Jeff Sessions, where are you?

Right from the beginning, Mueller loaded his team with Democrats and proceeded with gangster politics. Ignoring the true Russian collusion between the Clinton campaign and the Russians, they purposely went after Trump while mainstream media rigorously beat the drums for them. They assiduously pretended to look for Russian collusion, while all the while, they were really looking for any dirt on Trump they could find and then bring him down.

Wrong is wrong. The Mueller investigation is criminal and should be immediately ended.

***

Return to Truth, Justice, and the American Way

COLLUSION is defined as secret, or illegal cooperation, or conspiracy, especially in order to cheat or deceive others. That being said, then I ask mainstream media to confirm collusion in the following events:

- Collusion exists when an attorney general meets in secret with the spouse of someone under investigation.
- Collusion exists when the media provide questions to one candidate in advance of a presidential debate.
- Collusion exists when a political party conspires with one candidate to block another candidate in their primary.
- Collusion exists when a sitting president wiretaps the candidate of the opposing party to help their opponent.
- Collusion exists when government officials leak classified information to the media to smear a sitting U.S. President.
- Collusion exists when an FBI director hands out immunity to persons involved in a criminal investigation after they destroyed significant evidence.

SEDITION is defined as incitement of resistance to or insurrection against lawful authority. Again, I ask mainstream media to confirm sedition in the following event:

- Sedition exists when a plot is premeditated, thoughtfully developed, and executed to deceitfully take out a duly elected U.S. President. That they used falsified information, manipulated the truth, and aggressively attacked the U.S. President in unscrupulous manner as verified by the evidence.

Some things would be so obvious if we had honest journalism. Clearly, we need to return back to a 1942 episode of "The Adventures of Superman" radio series when the phrase, "truth, justice, and the American way" was introduced to us.

If we did, then these collusion and sedition cases would be righteously dealt with.

***

Trash Politics

The Democrat Party assault on the Supreme Court nomination of Brett Kavanaugh was nefarious. Let it be seen as it was—trash politics. They've sunk to a new decadent low. Their actions are becoming more lewd and vile all the time, and they don't care what the average citizen thinks.

Kavanaugh has had a stellar record. He has proven to be a man of great character and has rendered outstanding service in the American judicial system for many years now. Yet, because they didn't want him on the Supreme Court, they tried to assassinate his character. Their partner in crime, mainstream media, was right there with them to beat the adversarial drums.

The Democrat Party, in reality, is not for America, or the Constitution. For all the people who have voted for Democrat Party candidates in the past, please wake up. This is not the party of John F. Kennedy. They've changed dramatically over the years. They read from Saul Alinsky's playbook and create chaos and havoc to further their objectives. They use lies, deception, and slander knowingly and willfully. Truth is not requisite for them in pursuit of their political objectives.

> *If you believe in Judeo-Christian principles and care about America, then you conscientiously cannot support the Democrat Party.*

If you are a communist, socialist, globalist, liberal, or leftist, then this is your party. If you're an American patriot, then this is not. Maybe you've voted Democrat all your life, but if you have, now is the time to make a positive change.

If you believe in Judeo-Christian principles and care about America, then you conscientiously cannot support the Democrat Party.

***

Hillary's Wrongs Swept under Rug

With all these attacks against and investigations into President Trump, I wonder about the status of the quid-pro-quo assertions against the Clinton

Foundation. Has anything ever come of it? Or has that news been swept under the carpet? If it's the latter, the uranium deal that Bill Clinton coordinated with Kazakhstan doesn't get any scrutiny, even though it had some significant security implications.

I wonder if any Democrats from Hillary Clinton's team had any liaisons with the Russians prior to the presidential election. I don't hear anything from the news media on this. Maybe no Democrats whatsoever even talked to any Russian diplomats, or if they did, only did so in the normal course of business. I guess all Democrats can be trusted, but the same cannot be said for Trump and his team. Trump wasn't even a politician. He was an outsider who had never been in politics. According to the Democrats, the fact that he has not been entrenched in Washington goings-on for many years seems to mean that he can't be trusted.

Ask yourself, did the Democrats lie to America on Obamacare or Benghazi? Did they lie to America on Hillary Clinton's server or about giving her questions prior to the presidential debates? Did they lie about fixing the system against Senator Bernie Sanders so he couldn't get their nomination?

These investigations against Trump are just a continuation of the left's insidious shenanigans.

***

A Major Blow to Justice

I'm amazed that anyone in America can accept FBI Director James Comey's ruling on Hillary Clinton's e-mail case. Comey's ruling defies all logic. That said, he and Lynch struck a major blow to our justice system and rule in America.

During his address to the media, Comey admitted that Clinton sent or received 110 emails in fifty-two email chains that contained "classified material" at the time they were sent. Even so, there were probably many more. He told the media that it was "likely that there are other work-related emails that they did not produce ... that are now gone because they deleted all emails they did not return to State, and the lawyers cleaned their devices."

Based on Comey's comments, it appears that Clinton turned over to the FBI whatever she felt like turning over, and then she destroyed the rest of the evidence. How can she get away with this, and incredulously, still run for president of the United States?

I imagine that at some previous Bilderberg meeting, she was selected to be the next president of the United States. That means, come what may, that the global elitists, working behind and through our government, will do whatever it takes to get her the presidency. Never mind that she speaks in front of small crowds while Sanders and Trump speak before multitudes. There's a criminal element that's behind her.

Manipulation, deceit, and corruption radiates from/through our government. America is in great need of prayer. Christians, please pray.

***

Shame on Democrats

President Trump had a phone call with President Zelensky and released the transcript for all to see. President Zelensky said there was no quid pro quo. He said that he was not pressured by President Trump, and he got the aid without doing any investigations. He certainly got more aid than President Obama gave him, and again, without doing any required investigation into Burisma. No bribery, extortion, or abuse of power in evidence.

President Trump willingly released the transcript, but these are things that he didn't do:

- Order the I.R.S. to target political enemies
- Wiretap numerous reporters to spy on them

- Send assault weapons to Mexican drug cartels, which resulted in the deaths of dozens of Mexicans and at least two American law enforcement agents
- Go to sleep while an attack on a diplomatic compound in Libya raged, and an American ambassador was murdered
- Blatantly lie to the American people about Benghazi
- Give $1.7 billion to the world's leading nation that sponsors terrorism
- Send agents to Israel to try and defeat the current prime minister in a national election
- Eavesdrop on private conversations between American lawmakers and Israel
- Conduct mass surveillance against American citizens without a warrant in violation of Fourth Amendment
- Condone Hillary Clinton e-mail scandal and compromise of highly classified material
- Seize phone and e-mail records of reporter James Rosen

Shame on the Democrats for these corrupt politics.

***

Hearing of Decadence

This whole orchestration against Brett Kavanaugh had all the makings of a Deep State/Democrat plot against Kavanaugh. This is the same group of people who fabricated the Mueller investigation against President Trump for the false Russian collusion. The hearing process for Kavanaugh showed how decadent the global elitists and mainstream media have become and continue to be.

Based on Christine Ford's testimony, there are some serious considerations before one accuses Kavanaugh of attempted rape charges. Please consider:

– She does not remember how she got home that night but does remember getting a ride from someone. It seems this would have stuck in her mind if the event was so traumatic.
– Ford could not remember when she took the polygraph, only that it happened around the time of her grandmother's funeral. One would typically remember such a date.
– She claimed that she has a fear of flying; however, the prosecutor notes that Ford flies very often for work, vacation, hobbies, and even for the testimony itself.

- Ford initially contacted the Washington Post in order to get her accusations out, but could barely remember her interaction with the newspaper during the testimony.
- All three of Ford's witnesses refute her claims and/or recollections of the events entirely.
- She says her assault took place in the mid-80s and in other reports, the early-80s. Which is it?

It might be prudent to investigate Ford's medical condition and political activities/affiliation. In addition, America needs to see through this whole bogus ordeal.

***

Demonstrations Commonly Staged

I was a young navy lieutenant serving in the Middle East during the 1980s. I remember traveling to Damascus from Amman one October. While there, I had a conversation with an army major serving in that area. He conveyed to me how he got on a bus with some Syrians holding anti-America placards. These Syrians, apparently for slight compensation, were purposely being transported by the Syrian government to protest at a certain location against America. It was a staged demonstration where the cameras would film certain scenes and make certain points.

I learned something that day. Staged demonstrations, coupled with appropriate media coverage and spin, creates for propaganda dissemination. Demonstrations can be useful political tools to influence and deceive the masses.

Repeatedly, since President Trump's election, there have been reports of organized demonstrations against President Trump with people being compensated for their efforts. That said, it's no wonder that we've seen organized demonstrations in support of this impeachment scam. It's obvious the globalists are trying to influence public opinion in their coup attempt against President Trump. I wonder how many George Soros dollars have gone into these efforts?

My heart grieves over these insidious and ungrounded impeachment proceedings. These people have been trying to impeach Mr. Trump since his election. They planned a coup attempt with the Mueller investigation, but it didn't work out. Much of their deception, lies, and chicanery are now being revealed to the American public even though mainstream media fights against the total truth being revealed.

***

Cartels Thrive on Border Chaos

It's time to give our border control agents college credits for their résumés. How about three credit hours for daycare support, three credit hours for medical care against infectious diseases, and three credit hours for trying to provide security for America?

As drug cartels, human smugglers, criminals, gang members, potential terrorists, and global elitists attack our borders, many politicians yawn and say, "What's wrong with illegal immigrants trying to penetrate our borders?" They say, "Forget about the drugs. Forget about the infectious diseases, the crime, the potential terrorists. These people just want better lives." Many politicians care more about illegal immigrants than they do about their own citizens.

Why is "illegal immigration" illegal in the first place? Common sense dictates obvious and prudent answers. Laws of the land are to protect the people. That's why laws exist. A nation that doesn't enforce its laws will ultimately become a nation of chaos. A nation without borders will ultimately suffer increased crime, violence, and a decline in sovereignty.

Politicians such as Senator Chuck Schumer and Representative Nancy Pelosi have enabled drug cartels, human smugglers, gang members, and potential terrorists to successfully launch warfare against America. The cartels know our border control agents have become a daycare center and processing venue for thousands of migrants, and they seize the opportunity to run drugs and dangerous criminals through our border.

Many politicians really don't care about America.

***

Border Crisis Not Manufactured

It appears that the Democrats, liberals, and mainstream media believe the border crisis is manufactured. Maybe MS-13 is some kind of a game and not really a violent gang. Maybe illegal immigrants don't commit any crimes, murders, or need any taxpayer services. Maybe the drug cartels don't push drugs across our border anymore because they've now decided to be nice. What do you think?

Federal law enforcement, the Border Patrol, ICE, and the DEA tell us that there's a lot going on at the border with frightening consequences. They plead for immigration reform with a border wall. The border wall would also help them make better-targeted use of their resources. Maybe they're just fooling us. What do you think?

Democrats, liberals, and mainstream media apparently aren't concerned about the security of America, but instead, want to continue attention on things like socialistic health care, college student loans, and global warming. In reality, it's not the government's responsibility to run any of these programs, but it is the government's responsibility to provide security for America.

Why don't the Democrats, liberals, and mainstream media really want any effective immigration reform or border security? Why do they continue to support open borders? The answer is simple.

These are global elitist attitudes. They want control, power, and to take away our sovereignty while leading us down the socialist path. They want to make us a third-world nation and bring us under global governance. They want to smash capitalism and Judeo-Christian values. They want to destroy America as we know it.

***

Cooperate with Trump and Fix Immigration

It's common in America today to see sanctuary city leaders and liberals attempting to interfere with deportation of undocumented immigrants who have been ordered deported by a judge. In essence, these sanctuary city leaders and liberals are operating in defiant lawlessness.

These sanctuary city leaders and liberals give greater respect to people who are here illegally than they do to the ICE agents. ICE agents are only doing their jobs and trying to enforce the laws. The evidence of civil disobedience against the immigration laws is clear. These sanctuary leaders and liberals are wrong.

This lawlessness is disheartening, but what's even more disheartening is the behavior of the Democrats toward solving the border crisis. They want open borders and refuse to rectify the problem. Great strides would be significantly made if the Democrats would work with President Trump in modifying current immigration laws and improving border security. It's that easy.

***

Semi-automatic Weapons Should Not Be Banned

Criminals WILL ALWAYS have guns. Law-abiding citizens should not be penalized for having weapons to protect themselves, and that includes semi-automatic weapons.

Given how mainstream media and liberal influences continue to insti-gate/promote lawlessness or violence in our nation, this makes all the sense in the world for normal, law-abiding citizens.

Debates about homeowners having an AR-15 for defensive purposes is clearly supported when intruders entered a home in Glen St. Mary, Florida, during 2018. The intruders' group was made up of seven young men.

The first intruder wore a mask and shouted, "Sheriff's office!" from outside the mobile home before breaking down the front door in the early morning hours and shooting a round.

Upon hearing the break-in, one armed in the home with an AR-15, and another with a pistol, confronted the criminals with open fire in self-defense. In the exchange, one of the intruders was killed while two other intruders were wounded.

All this talk about homeowners not having the right to possess an AR-15 is wrong. In this case, several criminals entered into a home in the early morning hours. Given how gangs exist throughout our populace, having an AR-15 as a defensive weapon seems exceptionally prudent if things deteriorate.

Guns really aren't the issue in our society. Chicago has some of the nation's strictest gun laws but with little effect, as murders have been rampant.

It's a spiritual issue. You must change the spiritual condition in our society to see positive change. Change the spirit, change the man. Return to Judeo-Christian values.

***

Gay Choice Not a Civil Right

The gay movement is not like the civil rights movement in this nation. For the Obama administration to say that this case is similar is in error. It's certainly not. The Coalition of African American Pastors (CAAP) is cur-rently working to collect one million signatures to support the argument that same-sex sexuality is not a civil right that can be compared to what blacks have gone through in America.

Eric Holder has repeatedly circumvented established law to promote a particular type of sexual behavior and forced his own personal views on the states. He has violated his oath of office by attempting to impose same-sex "marriage" throughout the nation. This is blatantly wrong.

Same-sex sexuality is not a civil right.

Same-sex sexuality is not a civil right. What blacks have gone through in America is completely different. Equality as human beings in the eyes of God is biblical in context and most worthy of cause. Same-sex sexuality choice is not.

Some people who argue that same-sex sexuality is a civil right will also argue that partial-birth abortion is a civil right. Where does it stop? This was a nation founded on Judeo-Christian beliefs. Many of our laws were generated from the Ten Commandments. Moral direction for our nation was established early on with our Judeo-Christian heritage. True, all was not utopia, but biblical and positive direction was established from our roots as a country.

This is not about color or race. This is about individual choices one chooses to make.

***

Questions to Ponder

Would Islamic countries welcome millions of Christians?

Several wealthy Muslim countries refuse to take Syrian refugees, arguing that doing so would open them up to the risk of terrorism. Why would they say that?

Imagine a bowl of peanuts with 15 percent of them poisoned. Would you eat a handful? I wonder how this pertains to open borders?

I believe someone said that only 1 percent of Muslims are terrorists. Let's see, if there are 1.57 billion Muslims in the world, then 15.7 million would be terrorists. Now, is that really a threat?

Why do people lock their doors at night? I guess it doesn't mean that they hate the people outside their home, but it could be because they love the people inside their home. I wonder how this pertains to open borders?

Let's see, criminals don't care about gun laws and commonly get guns outside of stores. Don't you think that they want the politicians to keep focusing on the good guys?

President Obama and his administration were responsible for protecting America from Russian interference during the 2016 election; yet, President Trump is the only one who has to answer for it. What's wrong with this picture?

Why do people in Antifa wear masks? Wasn't it the KKK who wore masks? Does Antifa have something to hide? Are they bigots?

It has been said that criminals obey gun laws like many politicians follow their oaths of office. Why would they say that?

Ben Franklin once said, "We are all born ignorant, but one must work hard to remain stupid."

***

National ID Bill Threatens Liberty, Privacy

H.R. 4760 forces a new biometric National ID on every American citizen. This recently introduced bill is below the radar as mainstream media is not covering this. That tells you something. Privacy and liberty are under serious threat.

The Republican establishment is pushing a radical and longtime goal of a biometric National ID. If passed, what would this bill accomplish? It would provide control over all American citizens. Government would have extensive records on all citizens stored in a massive national database available for use in an instant. Subjects such as gun ownership, employment history, family and friends, purchasing habits, health records, travel, religious beliefs, past political contributions, and so forth would be under government scrutiny. Without this ID, one will not be able to legally hold a job, nor likely open a bank account, or even board an airplane.

The Obama administration even tried to pass legislation supporting this national ID-database scheme. Mainstream media is hiding this bill from public scrutiny by completely ignoring it. American citizens should seriously take note of this and not ignore this bill.

One may say that illegal immigrants would also be required to have this national ID for employment. Consider, however, that illegal immigrants are commonly paid under the table. This bill will do little in preventing unscrupulous employers from continuing to hire illegal immigrants off the books. This has little to do with border security. In reality, it's an assault on personal freedom and a significant step toward controlling American citizens.

Call your Congress representatives and oppose H.R. 4760.

***

Federal Reserve a Scam on Our Nation

America is often referred to as the richest nation on earth. Interesting, but both spouses today are commonly working in many households to make ends meet. Husbands and wives seek overtime hours just to pay interest on loans. Money doesn't seem to go as far as people think it should. Much of this can be attributed to America's current money system.

Article 1 of the Constitution states that Congress shall have the power to coin money and regulate the value thereof. Many Americans don't realize that Congress in 1913 literally "gave the nation's money-creating power" to private bankers who issue money they create out of nothing to buy bonds on which taxpayers have to pay interest. The U.S. was a prosperous, powerful, and growing nation prior to 1913. It was at peace with its neighbors and doing well. However, in 1913, Congress authorized the establishment of a Federal Reserve corporation, with a board of directors to run it, and America was divided into twelve Federal Reserve districts.

Basically, this action removed from Congress the power to create money or have control over its creation. Many in America still don't realize that the Federal Reserve Corporation is a private corporation controlled by bankers, and thus, is operated for financial gain from the people rather than necessarily for the good of the people. In reality, the word "Federal" is deceptive. The Federal Reserve has created tens of billions of dollars and credit since 1913, which, as their own personal property, they lend to our government and our people at interest.

One gets a better picture of this when one considers the need for money. Let's say the government has spent more than it has received from taxes in order to meet its needs. Since the Congress has given away its authority to create money, the government must go to the Federal Reserve. The Federal Reserve doesn't just give money away. A private corporation, the Federal Reserve prints up the money at a nominal fee to them and provides the money to the government in exchange for U.S. Treasury bonds authorized by Congress to be printed. The government has now indebted its citizens to the bankers with much interest added on. Imagine the inordinate amount of transactions that have transpired since 1913. Interest alone is staggering.

The U.S. bonds are assets of the Federal Reserve, which can also be used as "reserves" to "create" more "credit" to lend on. Thus, credit is further provided to states, municipalities, businesses, and individuals. Interest continues to accrue, and bankers continue to gain through almost unlimited usury.

In reality, government has been usurped by this banker-owned system. No doubt, the Federal Reserve has the true, current day power. Under the Constitutional way of creating money, Congress would spend much time and effort on the issuance of an adequate supply of stable money for the people. Based on increase requirements, Congress would authorize printing a determined amount. Bankers, of course, would cry foul and say that printing press money would soon become worthless or cause inflation, but not so. Inflation is actually caused as a result of immense usury charges on credit or debt.

Consider the Constitutional system approach to mammon. There would be no private banks to rob the people through usury. Government banks under the control of Congress would issue and control all money and credit. They would issue not only actual currency but could lend limited credit at no interest for the purpose of capital goods such as homes. A $100,000 loan would require only $100,000 repayment, not thousands more on interest.

Perhaps, this sounds too simplistic to some, but consider that American colonies did it in the 1700s and their wealth soon rivaled that of England's. The Saracen Empire forbade interest on money for 1,000 years, and its wealth was more impressive than even Saxon Europe. Mandarin China issued its own money, interest-free and debt-free, and historians consider those years as China's greatest time of wealth, culture, and peace. Money that doesn't have to be paid back in interest leaves it available for use in exchange of goods and services. Even the Mosaic law forbade charging interest to a fellow Israelite.

The Founding Fathers saw the importance of placing the power "to create money and the power to control it" only in the hands of Congress. These men believed that all citizens would benefit from an adequate and stable currency, and thus, the government must also be the controller of the value. The current Federal Reserve System is not what the Founding Fathers had in mind for this nation nor its people. I quote Thomas Jefferson, "If the American people ever allow private banks to control the issue of their money, first by inflation, and then by deflation, the banks and corporations that will grow up around them will deprive the people of their property until their children wake up homeless on the continent their fathers conquered."

I realize that this is a simplistic article and that much more could be written extensively on this subject; however, for the sake of brevity, I'll close with a statement made by Rep. Louis T. McFadden during the Great Depression. He said, "Mr. Chairman, we have in this country one of the most corrupt institutions the world has ever known. I refer to the Federal Reserve Board and the Federal Reserve Banks .... The Fed has cheated the government of the United States ... out of enough money to pay the Nation's debt."[12] Simply put, this debt-money system has greatly robbed the people of this nation.

One can see how America has gone from a prosperous debt-free nation in 1913 to an exceptionally debt-ridden nation today.

***

Federal Reserve Audit Reveals Bailouts

The first-ever Government Accountability Office audit of the Federal Reserve was carried out in the past few months due to Ron Paul, Alan Grayson Amendment to the Dodd-Frank bill. Bernanke, Greenspan, and various other bankers vehemently opposed the audit. Nevertheless, the first partial audit in the Federal Reserve's nearly 100-year history was carried out.

What was revealed? Sixteen trillion dollars had been secretly given to U.S. banks, corporations, and foreign banks everywhere from France to Scotland. The Federal Reserve likes to refer to these secret bailouts as an all-inclusive loan program, but virtually none of the money has been returned, and it was loaned out at zero percent interest. The American public should be outraged to find out that the Federal Reserve bailed out foreign banks while many Americans are unemployed and struggling to find jobs.

The Federal Reserve donated $2.5 trillion to Citigroup, $2.04 trillion to Morgan Stanley, while the Royal Bank of Scotland and Deutsche Bank, a German bank, split about a trillion. Numerous other banks received substantial portions of the $16 trillion.

There's nothing "federal" about the Federal Reserve. It's a group of professional bankers that creates money out of thin air and gives it to

---

[12]McFadden Remarks in Congress, "An Astounding Exposure," 1934, https://1ref.us/1ft (accessed November 4, 2020).

megabanks and super-corporations like water going over Niagara Falls while the middle class struggles to survive.

The Federal Reserve should have its trillion-dollar printing presses stopped. This organization is one of the biggest scams ever perpetrated on the American people, and reform should be unequivocally demanded by the American people.

***

More Oil Refineries Are Long Overdue

Why? Why? Do you realize that no new refinery has been built in the United States since 1976? This is largely due to outdated and exceedingly burdensome regulations, high taxes, imprudent policy direction, and law-suits. Thus, America continues to import expensive, refined oil products to meet its requisite demands. This defies logic. Bring in a major hurricane around the refineries in the Gulf, and my, watch the price of oil skyrocket because of a lack of prudent action by the American government and those who unscrupulously influence government decisions behind the scenes. The news media will then attribute high oil prices to an act of nature, but in reality, it would be largely due to over-regulation and lack of wise planning.

This is unfortunate also in respect to jobs. Not only does America continue to be substantially dependent on others for petroleum support when it does not have to be, but it continues to miss opportunities to develop jobs. Why? Why? Lack of action in these areas is not in America's best interest.

The world's energy demands will grow substantially in the foreseeable future. Make no mistake; this is very clear. If America built more refineries, it could not only better meet its needs but create jobs through export of refined petroleum products to other nations. The demand will be there, and someone will be there to supply the need. Obviously, this is also an opportunity to create jobs if America chooses to accept that opportunity.

***

Is Anyone in Washington Concerned About the National Debt?

A key concern for America that has been overlooked in recent months is the national debt. Any efforts that President Donald Trump can make in getting rid of the corruption in the FBI and intelligence agencies should be well applauded, but how is the national debt going to be dealt with is an exceptionally important question.

The national debt of this nation remains in high acceleration. Is federal debt still rising faster than the gross domestic product? Yes, and most significantly higher. Is this likely to change? Again, probably not. The number of true conservatives in Washington don't appear to be making much progress in this realm, and it's seriously questionable if forthcoming elections will change the mindset of Congress in the foreseeable future.

Federal deficits have been prevalent for many years now, but our current debt is staggering and almost unfathomable. Given the difficulty that Trump has had in dealing with Congress concerning immigration reform, it's an even more immense task for Trump to get Congress to shrink government and its spending.

Does the government really want to show spending restraint? When one considers the obstructionist Democrats and the RINOs (Republicans in name only), no. Trump might be able to sell limited government to a supportive populace at one of his big rallies, but selling this to Congress is another story.

Spending needs to be pulled in because America is on a train speeding toward national ruin. Pray for America to slow this train.

***

Operation COVID-19

There was a video, called "Plandemic," recently released over the Internet featuring virologist Dr. Judy Mikovits. That video has since been censored by YouTube. This pandemic of COVID-19 just didn't happen. There are indications that things are being orchestrated as an existential threat to America. It's clear that not everyone agrees with Dr. Anthony Fauci about this whole affair. There's something wrong about it all.

Dr. Mikovits, who once worked with Dr. Fauci, says during her interview that what Fauci is saying about COVID-19 is "absolutely propaganda." In the video, Dr. Mikovits contends the isolate-everyone policy is a big mistake, and claims officials have a financial incentive to implement vaccinations.

Mikovits claims she isolated HIV in patients in France, but Fauci was among the officials responsible for delaying research, allowing the HIV virus to spread, including Africa. She also claims that Fauci was among the top health officials who framed her and destroyed her career because of contrary views.

It's interesting that YouTube also recently removed videos of a press briefing in which two California doctors carefully laid out their case for ending lockdowns implemented in response to the coronavirus pandemic. The videos featured Dan Erickson and Artin Massihi, owners of Accelerated Urgent Care in Bakersfield, California, and presented their conclusions based on their testing of more than 5,000 patients for the coronavirus combined with public data.

There's a line in Hamlet that says, "Something is rotten in the state of Denmark." That can be equally said about this whole coronavirus situation. Some things just don't add up.

***

U.S. Heading down Dangerous Path

This is not about racism. This is not 1860, and America has made great strides forward since the Civil War in race relations. No, America is not a utopia, but no country is. Utopias don't exist. That said, America still gives all races a chance to succeed and provides great opportunity for all.

As long as there is a sin problem, there will still be situations that need to be dealt with within all races, not just white. Strive to make improvements in a prudent manner, but not to destroy the whole system. Antifa, Black Lives Matter, and the radical left seek the violent overthrow of our government in order to lead us to a Marxist state. Racism is nurtured and extremely abused as a tool used towards their objective. They purposely seek to cause division, hatred, and chaos throughout America.

> *As long as there is a sin problem, there will still be situations that need to be dealt with within all races.*

Prominent statues, including non-confederate statues, have been defaced, toppled, and removed. Recently, a Black Lives Matters leader called for tearing down statues of Jesus and churches. They want to dismantle the establishment and foundations of America.

Policemen and reporters have been attacked while governors, mayors, and journalists have defended the riots as "mostly peaceful." Blood is already spilling, with civilian defenders, bystanders, workers, and businesses being assaulted or destroyed by looters and rioters.

Anarchy must be stopped. Without a committed and targeted crack-down on this disorder and its leaders, targeted killings of their opponents and critics will come next.

That said, our foundations started to crack when the Supreme Court generated the bogus separation of church and state policy and took school prayer out of schools. The crack has widened since. As a nation turns from God, a nation goes the wrong direction. America, are you listening? The root of the problem is spiritual. Repent.

Chapter 6

News Media

Note: This chapter has 7 separate newspaper editorials and are not presented in a specific order of when written.

Why Media Hates Trump

Many politicians have been disliked throughout the years, but I don't know of any politician more hated than President Donald Trump. Why is Mr. Trump detested by the global elite, mainstream media, and liberals? It's because the globalists want a one-world government, a one-world economy, and a one-world religion. Unfortunately for them, but great for America, along came Donald Trump.

They hate Mr. Trump because he opposes the New World Order. Those in pursuit of the New World Order intend to unite the world under a single system of operation. They seek to impose their will on all humankind.

They'll use climate change, fake news, radical demonstrations, immorality, and other schemes to manipulate the people.

Mr. Trump is for America. Don't be misled by the deceitful mainstream media that has been continuous in its attacks on Mr. Trump. The mainstream media, which wants to turn the public against the president, believe in open borders, while Mr. Trump seeks to protect us. The media wants unbalanced trade deals to integrate nations into a single world economy, but Mr. Trump wants fair trade deals to benefit Americans. The media won't criticize Islam because Islam will be a key component of the one-world religion. Mr. Trump calls Islamic terrorists out and wants to protect America from those who seek us harm.

This explains the relentless opposition to Mr. Trump, who stands in the way of the mainstream press's "progress."

***

Journalism Is Dead

It appears that journalism has died. It has metamorphosed into theatrical entertainment. It's now part of Hollywood's shows for the season. Mainstream media and big-city newspapers are key participants. "Let me entertain you" seems to be their theme. Deception, lies, manipulation, and malice play daily parts in their broadcasts.

In many television shows or movies, people often figure out the plots. In this new theatrical entertainment that used to be known as journalism, many still haven't figured out the plots. Some get it, but many do not.

Entertainment is important because it helps ratings, but there's a greater purpose. The greater purpose is to destroy President Donald Trump at all costs. This entertainment has become known as propaganda to those who can figure it out.

Who's behind this propaganda? Someone has to foot the bill, someone powerful and wealthy. Although they don't want you to know it, this propaganda is being put out by the global elitists, establishment (Democrats and some Republicans), and leftists in efforts to move its New World Order, or globalist agenda, forward.

Trump is a stumbling block to their efforts. Therefore, they hate him and will do anything they can to block his success. Trump is for America. Barack Obama and Hillary Clinton didn't get this treatment because they're part of the establishment.

As a cancer attacks a living body, the global elitists and establishment are attacking the Constitution and soul of America. America is fighting for its life.

***

Mainstream Media Guilty of Treason

Mainstream media are guilty of treason. Media for months now have steadfastly conducted an exceptionally biased and daily assault on President Trump. They're doing everything they can to subvert this man and his presidency. It's insidious and grossly wrong. Media is not balanced; it's now propaganda filled with deception, lies, and fake news.

So who controls mainstream media? According to research, as of 2013, six corporations controlled the bulk of the media in America. They were Comcast, News Corp., Disney, Viacom, Time Warner, and CBS. Through a history of mergers and acquisitions, these companies have concentrated their control over what we see, hear, and read. Fifty companies controlled the media in 1983; however, since that time, things have vastly changed through consolidation. Programming, aptly named, is now in the hands of a few and powerful with deep ties to the establishment.

When you control what Americans watch, hear, and read, you gain a great deal of control over what they think. Fortunately, many more Americans are now starting to wake up and realize that mainstream media should not be trusted. It is social engineering in full operation.

I've heard it said that Vladimir Lenin once stated that a lie told often enough becomes the truth. Joseph Goebbels further stated that if you repeat a lie often enough, then it becomes truth.

That's what mainstream media have done with all this Russian collusion bunk. It's manufactured against Trump with no evidence. If they truly wanted a collusion story, they would investigate the Clinton and Russian uranium deal, or the Clinton Foundation.

***

Drawing Attention to Mind-Control Methods

Do: Use graphic images and focus on death. Shape events in accordance with political agenda. Use color photos of the dead, even when they were children. Subtly appeal to the emotions of the American people. Do this daily. Don't let up. You're psychologically affecting the American people. Now, couple this with calling the terrorists insurgents. This softens their image and helps justify their actions and make them seem more credible. Do this subtly, and the American public won't really pick up on these foreign criminals, murderers, and infiltrators who attack soft targets of women, children, and kidnap unarmed civilians and behead them for the world to see. Oh! And don't forget to focus on and magnify demonstrations even if isolated and small. They have great impact.

Do not: Ensure you do not focus on all the good being done. Do not show schools open, women being treated with more equal rights, roads being rebuilt, electrical grids being constructed with modern technology and equipment, pipelines and refineries being brought into usage, and water purification and distribution networks being rebuilt. Do not show joyful Afghan and Iraqi people even though there are literally thousands who hope we never leave.

Result: The American public will get the message: "Get Out!"

Note: The point of this letter is not to debate the war. It's to draw attention to the mind control methods of a one-sided media that shape the consciousness of this nation, regardless of truth or facts.

***

News Media Often Attacks Christianity

CNN reported that Anders Behring Breivik, the Norwegian mass murderer, was a "right-wing, Christian fundamentalist." If you recall, Timothy McVeigh was also said to be a Christian. He was not, and neither is Breivik. While McVeigh rejected God altogether, Breivik writes in his manifesto that he is not religious, has doubts about God's existence, and does not pray.

Eric Rudolf, the Olympic Park bomber, was also described as a Christian fundamentalist. Rudolf has stated he prefers Nietzsche to the Bible. Nietzsche is best known for the phrase "God is dead."

Conservative talk radio, Sarah Palin, and the Tea Party were blamed regarding Jared Loughner's shooting rampage in January. He has been identified as an atheist and a nihilist. An ardent atheist, Loughner has characterized people as sheep whose free will was being sapped by the government and the monotony of modern life.

Media are quick to demonize "right-wing Christian fundamentalism." Attack Christianity in as many ways possible. In reality, Christianity is the solution and not the problem in America.

America has become a nation desensitized to immorality. That's because America has rebelled against biblical direction. The humanistic media, by design, has enhanced and fostered this rebellion against God and is quick to take cheap, deceitful, and irresponsible shots at Christianity when and where opportunities present themselves. That's because some in Christianity stand up for what's right and point out the blatant and misguided direction that many in America are now pursuing as individuals and as a nation.

***

Media a Force for Globalist Agenda

The "Black Robe Regiment" was a group of patriot-preachers from virtually every Protestant denomination located throughout Colonial America at the time of America's fight for independence, who courageously preached the biblical principles of liberty and independence. The British viewed these pastors as a force and called them the "Black Robe Regiment."

They would preach the Word of God without fear or favor. These men of God would get in their pulpits, and they would basically tell people what or who they should and should not vote for because they understood that in order to have a great government, then you must have great citizens. The way that you have great citizens is by having them rooted in the Word of God. Week after week, they expounded upon the principles of the proper role of government, the proper role of individuals, all underneath the kingship of the Lord Jesus Christ.

As these pastors were a force against tyranny, so is the American media in support of the global elitist agenda. The media repeatedly back up the globalist agenda ushered through President Obama and our government.

Ferguson and Baltimore riots just didn't happen. Events are seemingly being orchestrated and staged behind the scenes in order to move us closer to a militarized police force. The media are walking hand-in-hand with what the government is doing in these pre-planned events (just waiting to act on the right incident). It's truly a tragedy.

May God move in the government, media, and populace of America.

***

"Outrage of the Week" Game Flourishes

The Deep State and mainstream media continue their current game of "outrage for the week." The Deep State, composed of global elitists, Democrats, liberals, and Republicans in name only, along with media, week after week, generate outrage over event after event to destroy President Trump.

No event is too small that cannot be made great in their eyes. Whether it's digging up dirt, like an old Stormy Daniels story, or generating fake news against Trump, they will beat their adversarial drums incessantly from week to week in order to generate outrage. They're quite adept at this, and the Deep State and media personally don't care what the public thinks about their game.

Some have diagnosed people outraged with Trump as having Trump Derangement Syndrome (TDS). How do people get it? The Deep State and media take pride in being a key reason. Their "outrage of the week" programs have greatly contributed in stirring up many against Trump, and subsequently, these people develop TDS. It is not obtained through bacteria, virus, or some germ. It's obtained through propaganda filled with deceptions, lies, and slander. Their propaganda is designed to ultimately develop triggers in people toward Trump. Just mention Trump's name, and those with the syndrome are automatically and emotionally triggered with irrational outrage.

Why do the Deep State and media play their outrage game? It's because Trump's for America's sovereignty and they're not. They have a globalist agenda to lead America into the New World Order. Trump has interfered with their agenda, fortunately for our nation.

Chapter 7

Globalism Policies

Note: This chapter has 33 separate newspaper editorials and are not presented in a specific order of when written.

Globalism: Promotes regional and global government; promotes one-world economic system of trade; global corporations, and their elite control government policies and directives; and globalism sets itself against national sovereignty, closed borders, and trade tariffs.

***

Globalism: Deception in America

It's interesting to see how citizens blame different political parties for the loss of jobs in this nation. Actually, in reference to jobs, it doesn't matter what party has the balance of power. You see, loss of jobs is part of a bigger scheme that multitudes have no insight into what is really going on. More people should begin to wonder "why and who" is trying to break down the middle class of this nation.

The North American Free Trade Agreement (NAFTA) is just part of the big picture to bring this nation's standard of living and influence down. NAFTA, along with the other measure, has caused innumerable jobs to be shipped out of this country. Breaking the industrial base of America will significantly help toward the efforts of globalization.

Before he left office, President Clinton signed numerous executive orders that locked up many acres of federal land containing natural resources. This, coupled with breaking the industrial base, created a great control over the public area. Locking up of public lands supported the United Nations agenda. Allow me to summarize this as a no-brainer; locking up of natural resources and breaking the industrial base sends poor and devastating signals to the future of the economy.

Illegal immigration also contributes toward globalization efforts. Putting more agents along the borders makes for some good newsprint, but it's not getting the job done. Why, because there are those behind the scenes who do not want it to work. I believe this is done by design. If you really wanted it to work, then you would develop choke or screen points at different processing locations, e.g., social security administration, driver license bureau, etc. Then, you would enforce the law. There are

> *There are thousands of illegal immigrants on Social Security who haven't worked a day in this country.*

thousands of illegal immigrants on Social Security who haven't worked a day in this country. The current handling of illegal immigration is costing this nation extensively.

What about foreign oil? Why is America so dependent on foreign oil when, in reality, it does not need to be? It's because of America's effort to send oil development out of this country through taxes, environmental decisions, and poor policy. Keeping Americans dependent on foreign oil serves the interests of the globalists. It takes more dollars out of the family budget on an ongoing basis. Why? It's because the standard of living must be lessened, along with American influence in the world.

Take a walk in Walmart or another department store. Now, start picking up items and check out the labels. Notice where the bulk of these products are made. America has progressively become a debtor nation. You can puff up the economy as strong in the news as much as you want, but in reality, America's economy has become a house of cards, and careful those cards don't fall because this structure has become quite fragile.

It wasn't too long ago that one spouse of the family could work and support his family. Today, it often takes both spouses working just to make ends meets. Even in this, it's still a struggle for some. Over time, the middle class has been attacked with design and purpose. The ultimate objective is to bring this nation down without the people knowing the true motives behind actions taken.

Notice the sly gun control initiatives. Second Amendment rights are strategically targeted bit by bit. Put out enough press to make man feel unsafe, and he'll become more conducive in giving up some liberties. Highlight crime, instill fear in the masses, and gun control initiatives sound better all the time. Please take note: this applies to terrorism as well.

There are international bankers and others behind the scenes with ultra-deep pockets influencing political and social decisions toward globalism. Controlling the money supply and keeping people in debt enables one to execute power and dominion.

Many people don't realize that Congress in 1913 literally "gave the nation's money-creating power" to private bankers who issue money they create out of nothing to buy bonds on which taxpayers have to pay interest. These international bankers make beaucoup dollars during wars. I think that's one key reason the Vietnam War was purposely extended. By the way, these bankers are doing quite well as a result of the current situation in Afghanistan and Iraq, thank you very much.

Have you noticed how many conflicts the United States has been in during the last few decades? We've had conflicts in Vietnam, Grenada, Libya, Panama, Somalia, Bosnia, Afghanistan, and now Iraq twice. Where to next? It sounds like we've become a militaristic nation. Have we gone to war for all the right reasons, or are there reasons hidden from the public's view? These bankers always make a lot of money during war situations, and each war drains the American economy and burdens the average citizen.

In recent years, have you listened to political speeches by elected and other well-known officials? The slant, spin, and screening of news media coverage often give clues toward globalism. The phrase "New World Order" was in vogue during the last decade. Now, I think they're trying to be a bit slyer on their phraseology, but the gist is still there if you listen closely. America is being "sensitized to adjust to oneness" within the scope of the world. Ultimately, this course will cost Americans their liberties and standard of living.

The globalists must bring America down. These international bankers, and others on their team, are powerfully manipulating the masses and influencing political decisions in profound ways most do not comprehend. I imagine their sphere of influence over many politicians is quite extensive because of policy direction.

What do these globalists want from all this? They're already ultra-rich. Global leadership will be required in the New World Order, and they intend to be heavily involved in that leadership. Power begets power.

***

Communism Is Alive and Well

Communism is not dead. It's alive and well. Globalists have stealthily been using communistic strategy to move its agenda forward for some time now. For example, in America, it's using socialism, progressive thought, and social justice to gradually change America.

Cleon Skousen authored the book *The Naked Communist* in 1958. In his book, Skousen cited forty-five declared goals of the Communist party to destroy the United States from within. Included in these goals were:

- Permit free trade between all nations regardless of Communist affiliation and regardless of whether or not items could be used for war.
- Provide American aid to all nations regardless of Communist domination.
- Grant recognition of Red China. Admission of Red China to the U.N.
- Promote the U.N. as the only hope for mankind. If its charter is rewritten, demand that it be set up as a one-world government with its own independent armed forces.
- Capture one or both of the political parties in the United States.
- Use technical decisions of the courts to weaken basic American institutions by claiming their activities violate civil rights.
- Get control of the schools. Use them as transmission belts for socialism and current Communist propaganda. Soften the curriculum. Get control of teachers' associations.

- Infiltrate the press. Get control of book-review assignments, editorial writing, and policy-making positions.
- Gain control of key positions in radio, TV, and motion pictures.
- Continue discrediting American culture by degrading all forms of artistic expression.
- Eliminate all laws governing obscenity by calling them "censorship" and a violation of free speech and free press.
- Infiltrate the churches and replace revealed religion with "social" religion. Discredit the Bible and emphasize the need for intellectual maturity, which does not need a "religious crutch."
- Eliminate prayer or any phase of religious expression in the schools on the ground that it violates the principle of "separation of church and state."
- Discredit the American Constitution by calling it inadequate, old-fashioned, out of step with modern needs, a hindrance to cooperation between nations on a worldwide basis.
- Discredit the American Founding Fathers. Present them as selfish aristocrats who had no concern for the "common man."

There is an agenda in this nation, make no mistake. Call it liberalism, humanism, socialism, progressive thought, political correctness, or whatever you desire, but there clearly is an agenda to change this nation from the great republic that it once was. Joseph Stalin once said, "America is like a healthy body, and its resistance is threefold: its patriotism, its morality, and its spiritual life. If we can undermine these three areas, America will collapse from within."

People should not wonder why biblical Judeo-Christian beliefs are now challenged and openly attacked. People should not wonder why the family unit is being destroyed. People should not wonder why government debt is out of control. People should not wonder why social programs are being used to destroy capitalism. People should not wonder why this country was purposely de-industrialized. People should not wonder how the environmental movement is being used to destroy business and capitalism.

President Obama ran on the platform of "change." They're now trying to move "change" forward at a quicker pace, and it's a tragedy to witness this vile transformation of America. Many politicians in Congress support this radical change. Their actions are becoming bolder and more defiant all the time.

America is being hijacked. Pressure and substantial dollars are being used by ultra-rich people behind the scenes to bring about their insidious global agenda, and America has been a prime target in their crosshairs for some time now.

***

New World Order Seeks Major Change

I think back to a speech given by President George Bush, Sr. in 1991, and I remember his words "New World Order." In reality, the pursuit of the "New World Order," or global government, was in effect for many decades before that speech.

The globalist agenda, by design, has targeted many facets of society without society knowing its ulterior motives. It has consistently been active in creating a new mindset. One area targeted has been the traditional family and its values. Through sex education programs, alternative life-styles, euthanasia pursuits, and abortions on demand, the globalist agenda has sought to undermine and modify morality in the home and society.

It has sought to restructure education and revise history. The education system has gradually and systematically changed significantly over time. History and school books have been rewritten to cleverly convey the values of secular humanism. It has led to a radical agenda in public education.

Please notice in today's society how things are termed in political correctness. Through control of the media, the globalists have created this philosophy as one means to destabilize Judeo-Christian ethics. Language is not used in this philosophy to affirm truth. Instead, political correctness is a sly way to attack moral absolutes that must be eliminated in the globalist agenda. That's why labeling the gay lifestyle as inappropriate is considered politically incorrect.

Sovereignty must be replaced with a global village government. That's why the United States has been dealt with, internally and externally, over the years by the globalists. Today, the U.S. Constitution is being interpreted for social democracy versus constitutional republic. It's not the way the Founding Fathers intended it to be. Notice how international law over the years has systematically crept into the United States judicial process.

The free enterprise system has been undermined. Part of the globalist agenda is redistribution of the world's wealth. Property has been taken from private citizens, not to mention a vast amount of land seized by the federal government. The North American Union was well planned before many Americans ever heard of the concept. NAFTA, by design, was just a cleverly disguised steppingstone to the North American Union.

Many environmental treaties are based on bogus or suspect scientific data in order for ecological fraud to be perpetrated on an unknowing world through controlled media. Global warming programs, again by design, are deceptively being used to bring people under the globalist hypnotic spell. Masses of people are being deceived. "Nature" has now become known as "Mother Earth."

Globalists ultimately intend one church for the New World Order. That's why true Christianity as a religion has been targeted. While others in society have latitude of speech, Christians are much more scrutinized. Truth will be muddled with mysticism in this new world religion as other figures are given parity with Jesus Christ. Christians know better, and that's why Christian expression, speech, and values are seriously being dealt with and oppressed in America today.

Rights must be taken away. Thus, terrorism was generated in order to create fear. Fear allows for the takeaway of rights through the provision of security measures, e.g., the Patriot Act and Homeland Security. Chaos and key events are staged, and wars are purposely planned, for the end result justifies the means in the globalist mindset.

Globalism will ultimately lead to tyranny and increased human suffering in America.

***

It's About Globalism

The Central American caravans have gained much attention, and rightly so. Some of the group include murderers, rapists, and gang members. Proper processing through legal immigration procedures would be prudent. That said, the global elitists and leftists have ulterior motives and really don't care about the rule of law.

Their motives include the destruction of Christianity and western culture, as most know it. Open borders is about globalism. That means making America a third world country that functions as a socialist state. They pretentiously smile and pretend their actions are for the good of the people, as they slyly try to destroy capitalism and Judeo-Christian values.

It's time to bring Michael Jackson back, and let's all sing along to a group rendition of "We Are The World." My, it certainly sounds good, but it's not. It's full of unscrupulous and insidious activity to control people from the top. It's really about power for the global elitists. Many are ultra-rich with deep pockets, and they don't want you to know who they are. They want power and control over the people, and it's inspired by the fires of hell.

The spirit behind their actions is one of lawlessness and antichrist. Global warming, illegal immigration, and LGBT policies are just tools used to destroy our culture. They use guerrilla-like tactics, mass psychology, and mainstream media in pursuit of their globalist obsession.

They'll shout at border agents for using tear gas against a few children, while equally shouting for the abortions of thousands of Hispanic children. There's a goal in mind.

***

Global Warming Is a Scam, Not a Crisis

Global warming is a scam. I'm not the only one of this opinion. John Coleman, Weather Channel founder and meteorologist, has repeatedly gone on record blasting this bogus doctrine.

More recently, speakers at the 2009 International Conference on Climate Change in New York City have drawn attention to this charade. Many were making a case that global warming is politically motivated and has nothing to do with science. More than seventy scientists, representing the views of tens of thousands of their colleagues, made the argument that media and environmental advocacy groups have it all wrong, that global warming is not a crisis. I could not agree with them more.

One of the prominent speakers was European Union and Czech Republic President Václav Klaus. President Klaus is an outspoken critic of human-made global warming doctrine in Europe. He compared the global warming hysteria to the communists of old Europe. Global warming treats people as if they're naive, uninformed, and confused. Communists treated people in a similar manner. It's not about climate change; it's about a mechanism to control and manipulate.

Another keynote speaker was Dr. Richard Lindzen, who has been Alfred P. Sloan Professor of Meteorology at MIT for more than twenty-five years. Dr. Lindzen acknowledged that it took him a while to realize that global warming was a highly organized political movement, and that opposing it was an uphill battle. He said that it has nothing to do with science.

Dr. Lindzen, one of the world's most respected atmospheric physicists, said that many of his good friends and colleagues have supported global warming out of fear for their jobs, or as a means to get funding for scientific projects. He also referenced the use of supposed "climate models." He contends that climate models are being fed erroneous data in order to get the results that the global warming alarmists desire.

Dr. Michael Coffman, CEO of Sovereignty International, led a multimillion-dollar research effort on global warming during the 1980s and early 1990s. He found that the data collected just did not support the hypothesis that man was causing global warming. He came to the conclusion that money being thrown at fixing the alleged problem is a waste. Dr. Coffman warned that politicians are moving towards having an international tribunal established that will regulate carbon emissions.

This, in reality, is all part of the globalist movement. Politicians are deceitfully using global warming to take America, along with other Western nations, further down the globalist path. Look for taxes to support this scam, and those dollars will come from already overtaxed American citizens. These policies will also cripple businesses who have to pay to meet increased government regulation standards.

The influence and sovereignty of America must significantly decline for globalism to be successful. This is all part of a methodical plan, as was NAFTA and the scam of 9/11, which was used to create the war on terror and take away your rights while putting America further into debt.

***

Global Warming Is a Scam

The Midwest has had some frigid arctic air temperatures this winter, and that made me ponder the outrageous global warming claims of Al Gore and the rest of his liberal supporters.

Time magazine's January 31, 1977, cover featured a story, "How to Survive The Coming Ice Age." It included "facts," such as scientists predicting that Earth's so-called average temperature could drop by twenty degrees Fahrenheit due to human-made global cooling. Dr. Murray Mitchell of the National Oceanic and Atmospheric Administration warned readers that "the drop in temperature between 1945 and 1968 had taken us one-sixth of the way to the next Ice Age temperature."

My, what a change we have today. The drum now beats for global warming. Interestingly, physicist Dr. William Happer, then director of energy research at the Department of Energy, testified before Congress in 1993 that scientific data did not support the hypothesis of human-made global warming.

Global warming is a scam. Yet, mainstream media will say global warming is backed by scientists. Give me a break. Mainstream media has lost all its credibility, and don't believe their so-called scientific data.

> **Mainstream media's reason for existence isn't for news anymore; it's for propaganda.**

Mainstream media's reason for existence isn't for news anymore; it's for propaganda. Propaganda is used to influence the masses to your way of thinking, and it's often full of falsities.

The global warming scheme is just one item of strategy being used to manipulate the masses and pass legislation to benefit their agenda.

***

Poisonous Globalist Agenda

It is amazing to me that so many people are unable to see through the scam of "climate change." This goes right along with the bogus Islamic immigration policies being pushed on Western nations. Such policies, clear as can be, are being pushed on Western countries by the global elitists. They want to destroy Western culture and capitalism as we know it. In addition, they want to bring on a one-world religion and blend Islam into the mix.

Former Energy Department Undersecretary Steven Koonin once told *The Wall Street Journal* that bureaucrats within former president Obama's administration spun scientific data to manipulate public opinion. Koonin said, referring to manipulation of climate data, "What you saw coming out of the press releases about climate data, climate analysis, was, I'd say, misleading, sometimes just wrong." Tell the public lies and more lies, and eventually, they believe them as truth. This is the case with climate change.

The mainstream press continues to promote the objectives of the global elitists. They've reinforced the rhetoric of climate change ad nauseam. (They also protect the data on rapes and remain silent on the many other crimes perpetrated by Muslims in Western nations.) Mainstream media is the propaganda arm of the global elitists.

The global elitists know that Sharia law and the Constitution don't mix, but they don't care. They're intent on using insidious and leftist polices in trying to move the world into a New World Order.

***

Globalism Promotes Ongoing Agenda

Many people don't truly understand some key features regarding globalism. Globalism promotes regional and global government. It promotes a one-world economic system of trade and sets itself against national sovereignty, closed borders, and trade tariffs. In essence, global corporations and their elite control government policies and directives.

Synonymous with the term globalism are the terms one-world government, global governance, New World Order, global village, and globalization. All these terms are used interchangeably and at different times to communicate to different audiences. Make no mistake—they basically mean the same thing.

The New World Order sounds good to many hearers, but it's deception in its truest definition. It's really being promoted by a group of satanic-inspired international elitists seeking to dominate, control, and manipulate governments, industry, and media organizations worldwide.

The Council on Foreign Relations, Bilderbergers, Trilateral Commission, United Nations, Club of Rome, World Bank, and International Monetary Fund are some of the organizations promoting globalism or New World Order efforts.

There is an agenda, and it has been ongoing for years but is now coming into full view. Cleon Skousen authored the book, *The Naked Communist* in 1958. In his book, Skousen cited forty-five declared goals of the Communist Party to destroy the United States from within. Many of these goals have come to pass.

Many of the laws currently being passed in the United States are totally absurd, lack common sense, and fall into the category of lunacy. They're being forced on the masses against their will for insidious reasons.

***

Global Warming a Religion

There's a new religion in the world. This one pervades the whole earth. It was developed by the global elitists as one means to start taking your rights.

Oh, it's very subtle how it's portrayed. They make it seem so real through the constant spread of propaganda. Deception and lies are repeated over and over again via mainstream media, and in grade school, colleges, and universities. Sometimes the words "scientific data" are thrown in to support its spread. Like most religions, it seeks to increase its following of believers. I'm referring to the "God of Global Warming."

Co-founder and former president of Greenpeace, Patrick Moore, says that climate change is a "complete hoax and scam," which has been "taking over science with superstition and a kind of toxic combination of religion and political ideology." The Greenpeace co-founder's message echoes that of John Coleman, the late Weather Channel founder who called global warming "the greatest scam in history."

Fear and guilt are used to promote the "God of Global Warming" as global elitists seek further control over people. It's one main tool used in pursuit of their agenda. In the 2007 Global Warming Petition project, 31,487 scientists (over 9,000 of whom have PhDs) signed a declaration debunking the climate consensus myth; yet, the global elitists continue to perpetrate this falsity disregarding the truth.

The "God of Global Warming" has many prophets. Some are well known, like Al Gore, Alexandra Ocasio-Cortez, and Greta Thunberg. Unfortunately, many people are naïve, believe their false rhetoric, and become faithful members of this false religion.

***

America Being Used as Globalist Pit Bull

Globalists are using America in the role of international policeman. That's right; put away the word "patriotism" for a while. Two key objectives are being accomplished by these efforts.

First, America is being drained of its resources and placed in serious debt. The international policeman role is seriously affecting America's economy as well as making substantial amounts of money for the international bankers and globalists. This has been a win-win situation for the globalists. Lower standard of living, attack sovereignty, and gain wealth from it.

Second, because of Desert Storm, the recent two pre-planned wars, and aggressive/imperialistic role/nature of America, terrorism has been extremely magnified and finally developed into a worldwide concern/crisis by the globalists. Globalists are using terrorism toward progression for one world government. America is now being used as the pit bull to fight this carefully developed and orchestrated war.

Both Republican and Democratic parties are under the globalist spell. There are probably a few earnest politicians, but the majority in Congress, in my perception, are either globalists or in the globalist grip. I imagine that there is a lot of pressure to play pool the globalist way or else suffer the consequences. Their grip within the American government is exceptionally strong. They have great wealth and powerful influence/control over all facets of society. Former president John Kennedy was not a team player, and he suffered the consequences. His silver certificate program did not go over well with the international bankers.

Yes, and by the way, Lee Harvey Oswald acted alone.

***

Global Elitists Have Hands in Both Parties

Let me entertain you. Is this what the Republican and Democrat debates are all about? Will there even be a presidential election? Will the global elitists keep their man in office since he's doing such a great job for them? Will they have Obama cancel the election since the destruction of America isn't quite there yet? One must admit that he has made great progress on the transformation of America since he ran on "change" in 2008. That said, there's still work to be done by the global elitists in this nation.

It's obvious that the global elitists have their hands in both political parties. If an outsider rises up from the Republican Party, will they risk a Hillary defeat? A Republican outsider might upend some of the things that they've worked diligently to alter. By causing, or drawing on an event, perhaps they'll cancel the next presidential election as they institute martial law. Things are already in place, so they can suspend the Constitution for five years in that scenario.

Consider how they've armed Homeland Security like a military force. Thousands of hollow-point ammunition rounds, many armored personnel carriers, and other military equipment have been obtained for Homeland Security. The global elitists plan to be prepared if civilians or militia groups rise up against Obama and their plans to transform America.

If you don't have picture by now, it's time to pray. Pray earnestly for America, and that there will be a presidential election with a godly Christian elected.

***

Trilateral Commission and Global Government

Prominent Trilateral Commission member Zbigniew Brzezinski once wrote in 1972 that, "nation-state as a fundamental unit of man's organized life has ceased to be the principal creative force: International banks and multinational corporations are acting and planning in terms that are far in advance of the political concepts of the nation-state."

The late Barry Goldwater had great insight to what Brzezinski was alluding to. In 1979, Goldwater wrote, "The Trilateral Commission is international and is intended to be the vehicle for multinational consolidation of the commercial and banking interests by (seizing control of the political government of the United States). The Trilateral Commission represents a skillful, coordinated effort to seize control and consolidate the four centers of power—political, monetary, intellectual, and ecclesiastical."

America has lost millions of prime manufacturing jobs to Mexico, India, and China, while our prime assets are being purchased by foreign investors. The strength of the dollar has been decimated throughout the world. America has further been confronted with serious banking, mortgage, and energy problems. All the aforementioned can be traced to policies set forth and executed by Trilateral Commission members.

The Trilateral Commission was founded in 1973 by David Rockefeller and Zbigniew Brzezinski. Rockefeller has long been a central member of the Council on Foreign Relations. Brzezinski has authored several books that have served as policy guidelines for the Trilateral Commission. One might put it this way—the Council on Foreign Relations fostered concepts of one-world idealism, and the Trilateral Commission is implementing them.

***

Global Elitists Adversarial to President Trump

Rothschild family-owned magazine, *The Economist*, branded President Trump a "present danger" to the "New World Order" and admitted that the globalist elitists that formed it are "spinning in their graves."

The global elitists have been working continuously behind the scenes to oppose Trump. Trump is the primary reason that the New World Order has been stymied. They're for global government while Trump is for America's sovereignty.

There are two kingdoms in the world if viewed from a Christian's perspective. There's the kingdom of darkness and the kingdom of light. Those who operate in the kingdom of darkness often do so in secret and privacy. In other words, they don't want others to see what they're doing. For example, many crimes are committed in darkness and away from public view. Criminals don't want you to see what they're doing.

Consider what they've been doing to Trump. They fabricated the Russian collusion hoax. They've attacked him with numerous smears and assaults, from the Stormy Daniels smear to the racist label, and now, to the current Ukraine impeachment scam. They control mainstream media and have used it incessantly to promulgate anti-Trump propaganda. Lies, deception, and altering of truth are commonly used in their anti-Trump attacks.

Notice how Adam Schiff has conducted his meetings with severe limitations to the Republicans. In essence, this is a coup attempt with no grounds for impeachment.

The New World Order is not in America's nor the world's best interests.

***

Beware the Left's Lies

Communism is all about power and the elites who govern the peons. It uses a system of controls that strangles the little guys while the top prospers in power and wealth. It kills economic prosperity and creativity and significantly dampens the morale of the masses. It controls all facets of society and is exceptionally strong once set in place. It uses deception, lies, and manipulation to advance its cause.

The Democrats and liberals are driving in that direction. They're using mainstream media to advance and support their agenda. Mainstream media is no longer journalistic; it is propagandist, and it doesn't care what the citizens think. It has an agenda, and day by day forces its propaganda down the throats of its listeners and viewers.

The Democrats and liberals will use misinformation and the creation of fear to deceive the American people. One scam that they've used successfully is the fear of global warming. They're instilling it into children and training the next generation in a bogus and false belief system in order to accomplish their agenda. If you tell lies often enough, then people start to believe them.

The Democrats, liberals, and mainstream media want others to jump on their bandwagon of subversion. They seek to destroy capitalism in America, give away our sovereignty to the globalists, take away guns from the good guys, and destroy Christianity.

If you're a true patriot, you'll resist their propaganda.

***

NASA Finds Fossil Fuels Cool Planet

Major theories about what causes temperatures to rise have been thrown into doubt after NASA found the earth has cooled in areas of heavy industrialization where more trees have been lost, and more fossil fuel burning takes place, according to an article by Jon Austin.

I was appalled when President Obama addressed a graduating class of one of the service academies this past year, telling them that climate control is the biggest problem we face. I thought how bogus, trying to tell these future and intelligent officers this junk. Then, just recently, he goes to Paris to ring the bell for climate control.

Climate change or global warming is a global elitist policy. The global elitists are riding this scam hard to lead nations into a New World Order.

He was placed in the presidency by the global elitists to purposely transform this nation into third-world status. His assignment was to destroy the United States as we know it.

Numerous scientists know the fallacies and deceptions of this subject. On the other hand, some scientists go along with this scam so they won't lose their jobs or grants. It's common knowledge that the government uses coercion to perpetrate false models and lies.

Climate control or global warming is a scam. It is being used in America as one tool to lead our nation into third-world nation status. Of course, Obama already knows this. He was placed in the presidency by the global elitists to purposely transform this nation into third-world status. His assignment was to destroy the United States as we know it. The global elitists, who control the media, back Obama all along the way.

***

Zoologist Says Polar Bears Are Thriving

Contrary to the predictions of many scientists, polar bears are actually thriving, according to a recent report. "Numbers are so high that Inuit leaders have been pleading with the Canadian government for more polar bear population control as violent attacks against native populations have dramatically risen in recent years," per Marc Morano of Climate Depot.

Susan Crockford, writing for the non-partisan Global Warming Policy Foundation, found that the polar bears are thriving. Crockford said the people of Nunavut "are not seeing starving, desperate bears—quite the opposite."

"Yet polar bear specialists are saying these bears are causing problems because they don't have enough sea ice to feed properly," she wrote. "The facts on the ground make their claims look silly, including the abundance of fat bears. Residents are pushing their government for a management policy that makes protection of human life the priority."

I don't think these residents would get much sympathy from America's Democrat Party for the protection of human life. I think the Democrat Party would still protect the polar bears since they won't protect born-alive babies as evidenced by their rejection of the Born-Alive Abortion Survivors Protection Act.

Anyway, the report shows that polar bear numbers have risen since 2005; yet, we've seen numerous photos of starving polar bears from mainstream media and sundry internet sources in recent years.

This begs the question why would mainstream media and miscellaneous internet sources consistently put out false information and starving photos of polar bears when they've been increasing since 2005?

Answer—It promotes their globalist agenda.

***

Conspiracy in America

As jobs leave America, I remind people that things are not always as they seem to be. This is by design. NAFTA and related actions were just the means to sell the program to a deceived nation.

The elite super-rich bankers and their associates have, for many years, schemed to manipulate this country into socialism while acquiring great wealth at America's expense. Their goal is eventually to control the world; thus, this meant that America's influence had to be lessened. This is why they slipped the Federal Reserve Bill through for passage in 1913. The creation of this centralized banking system has brought them great wealth at America's expense, while its citizens have lost thousands through this system of banking. As America's debt skyrockets under this system, these bankers collect enormous amounts from interest.

A progressive income tax was also imposed by design. Take more money from the common people. One would question this since these super-rich bankers and their associates would have to pay income taxes too, right? One has to understand that they created many loopholes in the tax system in order to beat their designed game toward socialism in America and the world.

Today, the Council on Foreign Relations, Trilateral Commission, and Bilderbergers are actively involved in planning toward a one-world government. Many things are manipulated behind the scenes, such as America's dependence on foreign oil and latitude of immigration over the years, which the public does not see.

***

Why Detention Camps?

A horrible provision exists in the Comprehensive Immigration Reform Act of 2006, which the public knows little about. The provision orders the construction of at least twenty detention facilities in the United States to hold not less than 20,000 people each, bringing the total capacity of these new detention camps to at least 400,000.

These detention camps are not for the estimated eleven million Hispanics currently living illegally in the United States since these new laws forbid their detention. Who are the future prisoners of these new detention camps? Americans will know in due time.

The American people, through American war efforts, have been used by powerful and ultra-rich people behind the scenes who influence and manipulate world developments in the direction they want the world to go. Sometimes events are deceitfully staged, such as 9/11, so that conditions may be developed in order to generate wars for their ulterior purposes.

America has served these people well, especially as one of its main aggressors in the world; however, America as a world power must be taken down so that full globalism and world domination may be brought into effect. Use America's force and deceitfully bring her down internally and externally. People will scoff at these comments, but in time they'll realize their validity.

***

Islamization: A Globalist Elitist Policy

Sadiq Khan, a man with extensive ties to jihadist and Islamic supremacists, was recently elected mayor of London. Muslims who voted for Khan did not reject his extremist ties and supremacist rhetoric. According to investigative journalist Soeren Kern, "In 2008, Khan gave a speech at the Global Peace and Unity Conference, an event organized by the Islam Channel, which has been censured repeatedly by British media regulators for extremism. Members of the audience were filmed flying the black flag of jihad while Khan was speaking." England, more and more, is becoming a de facto Islamic state.

This mass immigration policy of Muslims worldwide is a globalist elitist policy. Repeatedly, the common people in Sweden, Germany, England, France, United States, and other countries reject these mass Islamic immigrations into their countries. Even so, their governments continue to enforce these policies. Shouldn't this tell the common people something? These Islamic immigration policies are part of a bigger worldwide scheme. Destruction of western culture, along with Christianity, are the ultimate targets.

My personal experiences reinforce what I see happening in this nation and the world. The success of Arab Spring can be greatly attributed to America. Arab Spring was just another requisite step in the destabilization of the Middle East region. This just didn't happen by chance, but it was orchestrated. Let me explain with further dialogue.

I lived in the Sinai during 2007. While there, I observed how President Hosni Mubarak had to use strong force against the Muslim Brotherhood to maintain stability. Many may recall that the Muslim Brotherhood was affiliated with the group that assassinated Anwar Sadat in the fall of 1981.

Then in 2011, while living in Afghanistan, I saw how America was telling Mubarak to step down and allow Egypt to have presidential elections. Both the Executive Branch and the media were telling the

American citizens that the Muslim Brotherhood was a moderate group. I realized that the American people were being lied to. The Muslim Brotherhood is a radical group. They may not be as overt as al-Qaeda or ISIS, but they're at work behind the scenes with the same objectives. This is not a friendly group to nations with Judeo-Christian values, quite the contrary. They're hostile, but deliberate and shrewd in pursuit of their objectives.

Along comes Libya and America supported al-Qaeda-linked rebels against Muammar Gaddafi. Gaddafi seemingly had remained quiet since the Reagan years as he maintained stability throughout Libya. So why is America involved in the overthrow of Gaddafi since he was maintaining stability?

President Obama has appointed numerous Muslims affiliated with the Muslim Brotherhood to high-ranking positions in his administration. The Islamization of America has rapidly increased since 2008, with Muslim immigration substantially on the rise. The government will say it's humanitarian, but that's to cover what they're actually trying to achieve. There are ulterior motives.

The global elitists are attempting to pave the way for a New World Order or global government. This is just one of the many strategies that they're using to move toward their objectives. Global warming, the LGBT (lesbian, gay, bisexual, and transgender) movement, racist division, and other tactics are used in comparable manner while deceiving and lying to the common people of their true motives.

In similar situation to what is happening in England, the global elitists want Islamization in America and other western nations. It's planned by design in bringing us toward global government. That's also why the sovereignty of America must be significantly decreased.

***

U.S. Erred in Supporting Arab Spring

Having once lived in the Sinai and Cairo, I've been closely monitoring the turmoil currently going on in Egypt. I attribute much of what's going on directly to our government.

Our government, in essence, befriended and supported the Muslim Brotherhood against President Mubarak. Although our government and media clearly knew that the Muslim Brotherhood was radical, they stated it was moderate. President Mubarak kept things in order as he dealt hard with the Muslim Brotherhood. He had to deal hard with them because they're radical, and as such, he maintained stability in the region.

The whole Arab Spring support by our government was one of erroneous and wrong policy. Consider that President Gaddafi had been in check since the Reagan administration and how our government supported al-Qaeda-linked rebels in the recent overthrow. The government and media tried to spin it well as a humanitarian effort. That said, it's hard to sell a pig with mud all over it as a clean pig.

What's being achieved? Oil-rich nations are being destabilized. In time, what will this do to the price of oil? Oil prices, in time, will skyrocket. Please note that America has plenty of oil resources. There's no valid reason that we should be oil dependent on the Middle East, period.

We're dependent on foreign oil because of globalist policies implemented within the United States. One also needs to understand that the United States is being used by the globalists to assist them in the implementation of their worldwide policies; thus, Arab Spring.

***

Egypt and Libya Uprisings No Surprise

People should not be surprised when they hear news of uprisings in Libya or Egypt. Why do I say that? I ask people to look deeper and not just take the typical media rhetoric to heart.

I was serving in the Sinai during 2007. On a regular basis, I took note on how President Mubarak repeatedly suppressed, with a strong arm, the Muslim Brotherhood efforts toward instability and overthrow. Even so, Mubarak maintained peace and stability. That said, I was in Afghanistan last year and saw how our government was urging President Mubarak to step down. The government went further, and along with the media, told the American public how the Muslim Brotherhood was just a "moderate" organization. Excuse me; the Muslim Brotherhood is not moderate but radical.

In Libya we supported al-Qaeda linked rebels to overthrow Muammar Gaddafi, who had become less of threat since the Reagan years. He maintained stability. No, I'm not an advocate of Gadhafi, so don't misinterpret the comment, but he maintained stability while we were supporting his overthrow. Currently, we're supporting al-Qaeda-linked rebels for the overthrow of Assad in Syria.

Based on my perceptions, I believe that the globalists are using the Muslim Brotherhood and related elements to move its agenda forward in that region. That said, the globalists continue to use the U.S. military as its globalist pit bull while continuing to put the U.S. in greater debt.

***

Obamacare: A Global Elitist Bill

Peggy Noonan, of The Wall Street Journal, recently stated that Obamacare has been nothing but a "huge, historic" mess, and I most certainly agree. The bill's biggest proponent, California Rep. Nancy Pelosi, was Democratic House speaker when she said, "that we have to pass the bill to find out what's in it." That was a "truthful" admission of ignorance that the politicians really didn't know what was in the bill.

Even though the politicians really didn't know what was in this bill, they passed it anyway based on global elitist directions, in my perception. In other words, the global elitist lawyers, in essence, prepared this bill through hours of diligent work and put before Congress for them to pass. Congress passed this bill because, in reality, they take their orders from the global elite and not the populace they're supposed to represent.

Time and time again, the populace sees legislation passed by Congress that does not agree with the desires of the majority. People in America then turn their heads and wonder how Congress could consistently do these things. It's because our government is being greatly influenced and managed by unscrupulous global elitists working in the shadows for their globalist objectives to be accomplished.

A republic elects representation that is supposed to carry out the desires of the people. That is not truly happening in our government today. People are being greatly deceived and manipulated through deceptive political rhetoric and media coverage.

Obamacare will be devastating to America if fully implemented.

***

Islamization

Many still don't get what's happening with the Islamic immigration policies worldwide. Again, they're purposely designed by the global elitists to help destroy Christianity and western culture. The populations of western nations reject these policies, but their governments enforce them against the will of the people.

With Mr. Obama in office, the drive toward the Islamization of America rapidly increased. There are strong indications that he's a closet Muslim. I know, I've seen him on television/video say that he's a Christian. I know, the media also says he's a Christian. That said, I also know that you can lie as a Muslim if it advances the cause of Allah. Look at what politicians do and not what they say.

There has been a consistent drive by our government to purposely bring/force Islam into our Judeo-Christian culture. Why do this when the Koran emphatically says for Muslims to take neither Jews nor Christians as their friends? The Koran says to subjugate the infidels. That's what ISIS, al-Qaeda, and other Islamic groups are trying to do. If you're not a Muslim, then you're an infidel. Muslim law (Sharia) and our Constitution are not congruous. Oil and water don't mix.

Eventually, with increased Islamization of America, it'll lead to a different culture. Chaos will increase. This will help lay further ground for the coming of the antichrist as they pursue their New World Order. Eventually, these global elitists will try to bring on scene a convoluted one-world religion, probably with blending of Judaism, Christianity, and Islam. It's apostasy.

***

Islamic Immigration Policies Defy Logic

What's going on with more terror attacks recently taking place in Minnesota, New York, and New Jersey? Thousands of Somalis, Syrians, Afghans, and others continue to be resettled in America from radical Islamic states. Further, Hillary Clinton has vowed to bring substantially more thousands of these so-called refugees into America if she's elected president. It's seems to me that it's pretty logical to conclude what's really happening.

This massive Islamic immigration is part of the globalist elitist policy to destroy the fabric of this nation, along with other western nations. Our Islamic immigration policies are so ludicrous that they could only be done if purposely planned. One with any common sense could not possibly do these plans otherwise.

Please realize that the populations of Germany, Sweden, England, France, and the United States reject their governmental policies of

Islamic immigration. Yet, their governments enforce these globalist policies.

Why settle all these Islamic immigrants in western nations versus Islamic nations? Other Islamic nations share comparable beliefs, while western nations do not. These are not racist comments by any means, just logical deductions.

In America, Sharia law does not mix with our Constitution. Islam and Christianity have vast differences. The Koran clearly states not to take Christians or Jews as your friends. Based on this verbiage alone, there are already keen concerns.

It is the current Democrat leadership and those Republican Party leaders who follow along, who have purposely brought these destructive policies upon America.

***

Islamic Immigrants Protected

Her name is Morgan Evenson. She was walking home in Minneapolis on the evening of December 13, 2017, when a black man got out of his car, chased her down, and stabbed her repeatedly. Her attacker was described as a Somali man. Evenson suffered fourteen stab wounds with a lacerated kidney. Where was the media in its coverage? I guess they were still blaming President Trump for Russian collusion while also still trying to protect Islamic immigration policies.

> *The Islamic immigration policies are part of the global elitist strategy to destroy western societies, and that's why the Islamic immigrants are protected.*

It appears that Somali crimes might be covered up. This is a theme picked up in England. Cover up or downplay the crimes of the Islamic immigrants. America seems to have learned well from the British in this charade of justice. It also appears that no police response was recorded in the stabbing attack on Evenson. Are the police protecting the Islamic immigrants at the expense of American citizens?

Residents of the Linden Hills neighborhood in Minneapolis were terrorized by more than a dozen Somali men in June 2016. Several of the men threatened to rape a female resident of the community, saying it was their right under Sharia law, while others drove their cars over lawns shouting "jihad." The Minneapolis police were repeatedly called, but every time, they responded too late to make any arrests.

There are a number of other cases that could be cited; however, here's the key thought—the Islamic immigration policies are part of the global elitist strategy to destroy western societies, and that's why the Islamic immigrants are protected.

***

Open Borders a Globalist Policy

The reason for open borders is to destroy Christianity, our culture, and America's sovereignty. It's really not about humanitarianism. The globalist agenda is to bring about global governance. Open borders will accomplish all three. The Democrats, liberals, and mainstream media are being politically used in these endeavors.

The global elitists seek to control and govern the masses. They want to do away with citizenship, and they're trying to do that step by step. Their government will function under Socialism and be secularistic. Secularism, as defined in the Merriam-Webster dictionary, is the "indifference to, or rejection or exclusion of, religion and religious considerations."

I surmise that they'll develop a one-world religion by combining a composite of Judaism, Christianity, and Islam, but that'll be just a tool to placate and control the masses. The essential teachings of Christianity will be compromised because its teachings are a hindrance to their agenda. They're godless at their core.

Global governance will put vice-like controls in place and make the people totally dependent upon their leadership. Once they do that, they'll have people conditioned to do as they direct.

People under this system will wonder what happened to America and its values. Many will then realize that they had been greatly deceived and long for the way America used to be. They'll have realized that they drank the pink Kool-Aid agenda of the global elitists, Democrats, and liberals. Then it'll be too late.

***

Political Correctness a Globalist Policy

Political correctness, a policy generated years ago by the globalists, certainly shows its true colors when compared with truth. Truth is absolute and always proves its course, while political correctness is so often a protective shadow to lies.

I was recently reading about Muslim child-rape gangs in England. Many young girls are being raped callously, viciously, and violently in parts of this nation. Many cases are now being investigated by police. Typically, Muslim groups will accuse British authorities of "racism" and "Islamophobia."

I was reading where British police had known for more than a decade that Muslim rape gangs were targeting young girls in England, but they ignored evidence of rapes and failed to act because they were afraid of being accused of "racism."

I read of one case concerning five victims—the youngest was thirteen when the abuse began—who were plied with alcohol, drugs, and gifts so they could be "passed around" among a group of men aged between twenty-four and fifty-nine for sex in apartments, houses, cars, taxis, and kebab shops.

It's wrong that these Muslim child-rape gangs have been allowed to function with prior impunity under the protection of political correctness.

Racism and Islamophobia are also buzz words in America. Political correctness is being used to silence the moral majority and allow policies of the globalists to move forward with little resistance. Islamic actions will become more evident as time proceeds, and expect to hear racism or Islamophobia in their strong defense.

***

One World Religion

Although it wasn't significantly covered by mainstream media, an interfaith historic agreement was recently signed in the Middle East by Pope Francis, leader of the world's Catholics, and Sheikh Ahmed al-Tayeb, Grand Imam of Sunni Islam. According to a British news source, the signing of this covenant was done "in front of a global audience of religious leaders from Christianity, Islam, Judaism, and other faiths." In other words, there was a concerted effort to make sure that all the religions of the world were represented at this gathering.

This document encourages believers from all religions "to shake hands, embrace one another, kiss one another, and even pray" with one another. In essence, the document conveyed it's the will of God that there are hundreds of different religions in the world and that they're all acceptable in His sight. There's a lot of verbiage in this document advocating peace, but there's something that must be seriously noted. It repeatedly uses the word "God" to simultaneously identify Allah and the God of Christianity.

Why is this serious? It's serious because Allah and Jehovah are not the same deities. Religion would have you believe as such, but there are vast differences and principles between the Koran and the Bible. The characteristics of the two deities are extremely different. Let me say it this way—Allah is not Jehovah.

What you have here are processional efforts towards development of a one-world religion by the global elitists. It sounds nice, but it's inspired from hell, and it's part of the globalist agenda.

***

Geoengineering of Weather?

There probably is no greater act of defiance against the *New World Order* (NWO) agenda than President Trump's decision to pull out of the Paris Climate Accord. Trump is not a global elitist and doesn't support the NWO agenda. He's for America's sovereignty, and that's why the global elitists, daily and vigorously, oppose him.

Per State of the Nation, full-scale weather war is being waged against North America. Many do not understand how superstorms can be created and then carefully guided to their predetermined destinations. Highly advanced scientific techniques and applied technology are now routinely used within the realm of geoengineering.

Many believe that America and other areas are under direct assault from the geoengineers who are being used by the globalists to manipulate weather and create climate chaos and horrendous storms.

In just a span of one month, North America has seen the formation of major Hurricanes Harvey, Irma, Jose, and Maria. There were others that never made landfall. Could it be that the globalists don't care if they have to devastate whole islands or destroy major cities to impose their will on the planet?

These storms are not the result of global warming. Global warming is a scam. Nevertheless, it's plausible that the global elitists are using manufactured storms to reinforce their agenda of trying to influence people and nations to believe that it's a result of global warming. Thus, pressure for Trump to get into their camp or suffer the consequences.

Even so, sincere and continuous prayer is requisite against the insidious globalist agenda. It's anti-American.

***

Is Weather Being Manipulated?

Operation Popeye was a highly classified weather modification program in Southeast Asia. According to Wikipedia, the cloud seeding operation during the Vietnam War ran from 1967 until 1972 in an attempt to extend the monsoon season, specifically over areas of the Ho Chi Minh Trail.

The goal was to increase rainfall in carefully selected areas to deny Vietnamese military supply trucks the use of roads by softening road surfaces, by causing landslides along roadways, by washing out river crossings, and by maintaining saturated soil conditions beyond the normal time span.

Fast forward to the highly secretive HAARP (High-frequency Active Auroral Research Program), which was a military defense project that generated quite a bit of controversy over its alleged weather control capabilities, and much more. Some, over time, have claimed that HAARP technologies have been and continue to be used for weather control, to cause earthquakes, hurricanes, tsunamis, to disrupt global communications systems, and more.

If 1960s weather control technology allowed for Operation Popeye to be used successfully during the Vietnam War, then what would HAARP technologies allow for more than forty years later?

Given that the global elitists and Deep State continually pound the drum for climate change and global warming, could they be influencing the weather patterns through unscrupulous efforts? Even so, when severe storms occur, they quickly point the finger at climate change and global warming as the reasons.

The global elitist agenda seeks to control the masses. Could weather control and manipulation be just one more tactic deceitfully used in their arsenal of strategies?

***

Swine Flu Paranoia Clamors for Vaccine

Step up to the plate Baxter®, Novavax®, Roche®, and GlaxoSmithKline®. You are about to make billions from untested and unproven H1N1 vaccines. By the way, legal immunity has already been granted to you by the American government. It sounds like a pretty good deal.

Generate fear around the world, and this will help the effort. Magnify the paranoia. Have any tough questions really been asked about the swine flu situation? Instead, it seems that there has been great effort to declare swine flu a world catastrophe and force immunization vaccine shots on millions of unsuspecting people.

Some deaths have been directly attributed to swine flu, but in many of those cases, there were other circumstances that created complications. Further, there have been some cases reported where it was difficult to determine one virus from another.

I want to quote Dr. Russell Blaylock, who stated, "This virus continues to be an enigma for virologists. In the April 30, 2009, issue of Nature, a virologist was quoted as saying, 'Where the hell it got all these genes from we don't know.' Extensive analysis of the virus found that it contained the original 1918 H1N1 flu virus, the avian flu virus (bird flu), and two new H3N2 virus genes from Eurasia. Debate continues over the possibility that swine flu is a genetically engineered virus."

Baxter Labs® filed a patent for its H1N1 vaccine on August 28, 2008. That was months before the first known swine flu outbreak.

***

Operation Tyranny versus Freedom

Operation Tyranny's objective is to put freedom in chains. Although it started well before President Trump, it accelerated once he ran for president. Thus, let's pick up from there. These boxes have already been checked:

- Spy on him and his administration early to gather any possible dirt.
- Try to get his tax returns and find something to take him down with.
- Provide ongoing leaks to the media on phone calls and virtually anything he tries to do for the American people, and adversely twist information.
- Bring a video on-scene from his past to try and take him out.
- Destroy one of President Trump's selected Supreme Court justices with lies and slander.
- Fabricate lies and generate the false Mueller investigation to take him out.
- Attempt to impeach him on a normal phone call.

Now, let's pick it up with the coronavirus, violent demonstrations, and looting. They go together. First, develop the coronavirus, and release it into the world. Although it was developed in a lab, tell the American people it came from somewhere else. Feed Trump all sorts of pandemic death information so country can be shut down. Once America is shut down, prolong it to destroy economy, and ensure his non-reelection. Once he tries to get country back to normalization, wait for (or create) opportune time to release the violent demonstrations and looting. Cause chaos and use racism and division as tools in developing "useful idiots" in accordance with Comrade Lenin's verbiage. Bring in the well-trained anarchist groups, pay them well, and execute plans. Mainstream media will provide propaganda in all efforts.

Status of Operation: Ongoing.

***

What's Next for Anarchists?

Be assured the globalists and anarchists are already planning for the coming months. Will they initiate another round of COVID-19, or come out with a totally new virus from a laboratory? Will they increase the looting and violent demonstrations? Will America's adversaries continue to support these operations with supplies and monetary funds?

Expect all the above questions to be affirmative. It's exceptionally important for our government to move swiftly and aggressively against the leaders and infrastructure of the anarchist groups immediately. Unfortunately, many throughout the city, federal, and state governments support the globalists. That makes it challenging for the good guys in government, but this must be done.

The globalists and anarchists don't want President Trump reelected. Why? He impedes their new world order progress. They want to destroy America's sovereignty. They want global and socialistic government now, not later. It's not about racism; it's about destruction of America.

Come November, if Trump is reelected, things will be off the charts with increased looting and greater, more violent demonstrations if these anarchist organizations aren't stopped now. It will be horrendous as mainstream media will continue to stir strife and push the globalist agenda.

This is about life or death for America. These assaults are well-organized, and operations are well-planned. Not only must the government go after the leaders of these organizations, but the government must destroy their infrastructure and network of operations. This is already an insurgency. It's ongoing, and it must be stopped now.

In addition, Christians MUST pray fervently against the evil spirits behind these destructive operations, and for REPENTANCE in America.

Chapter 8

National Cover-ups

Note: This chapter has 19 separate newspaper editorials and are not presented in a specific order of when written.

Nation Has Been Deceived

All of these have something in common: the JFK, MLK, and RFK assassinations; Waco and Ruby Ridge incidents; World Trade Center carbombing; Oklahoma City bombing; TWA 800 incident; Vince Foster and Ron Brown cases; and 9/11. Truth has been hidden from the public in each instance. Study each of these cases, and you'll discover that all these cases have been enshrouded with disinformation and lies.

The American people are living in a bubble. They regularly accept what the government tells them on all matters. After all, this is the government of the red, white, and blue; however, there's an insidious and ultra-rich element interwoven within and behind the government, diligently working for global government and the demise of America.

As part of the globalist agenda, terrorism was planned and generated in order to create fear and take away rights. By creating fear, the government was allowed to pass the Patriot Act and establish Homeland Security. These measures will eventually allow for the use of martial law in the future.

Terrorism is a fabricated war; it's a planned mechanism to get to global government, and the sovereignty of the United States must be taken down in the process.

One is labeled a "conspiracy nut" to even mention something contrary to mainstream thought. I'm not a conspiracy nut, but I'm pro-American, and I want the best for this nation. That's why I'm trying to get people to become more sensitive to what's actually going on in the United States and the world.

> *Terrorism is a fabricated war; it's a planned mechanism to get to global government, and the sovereignty of the United States must be taken down in the process.*

***

Evidence of a 9/11 Cover-Up Is Overwhelming

Twin Towers: The jet impacts served as a diversion from the towers being demolished by insiders. A number of demolitions experts were confident that there were controlled demolitions used inside the structures. Suppressed accounts of numerous nearby firemen, released in August 2005, repeatedly describe loud bangs at the onset of the events.

Pennsylvania Crash: Eyewitness accounts and scattered debris contest the struggle story with the plane crashing vertically into the ground. A one-ton engine part was found far from the crash. Burning debris was seen falling from the sky. Clothing, books, and human remains were found miles away. An air traffic controller reports an F-16 near the airplane. Indications of a shoot-down exist.

Pentagon Crash: Based on eyewitness evidence, it's doubtful a jetliner would produce a sharp explosive concussion, emit the odor of cordite or result in explosions just before impact. There was significant lack of aircraft debris, and the area of impact was not conducive with size of damage an airliner would make.

Where there's smoke, there's often fire. Things are not as they appear to be. Forces are at work behind the scenes to bring about a New World Order. In the words of journalist H.L. Mencken, "The whole aim of practical politics is to keep the populace alarmed—and hence clamorous to be led to safety—and menacing it with an endless series of hobgoblins. All of them imaginary."

***

9/11 Was Total Deception

It's quite evident that 9/11 was a government cover-up when one objectively reviews the abundant evidence. Personally, I believe it was a CIA black covert operation. Why did this deception take place? I believe for oil profits, lucrative defense contracts, and the creation of terror in order to generate fear. Since the Taliban would not allow us to build an oil pipeline in Afghanistan from the Caspian Sea to the Arabian Sea, this nation needed a reason to take the Taliban out. 9/11 gave that reason. Thus, America subdues the Taliban, and an MOU was subsequently signed for a Trans-Afghanistan Gas Pipeline Project on May 30, 2002. Oil profits, lucrative defense contracts, and the perpetration of terror were also key to the attack on Iraq.

Of course, America has used deception before in going to war. It's common knowledge that the 1964 Gulf of Tonkin incident was fictitiously staged as a pretense to aggressively attack North Vietnam. In my view, that war was purposely extended so the international bankers and global elitists could make big dollars. What was achieved in the Vietnam War? Nothing, except extensive debt and a great loss of lives.

Global elitists, the real power brokers in and behind our government, are methodically driving this world toward a one-world government. By generating a terror threat, they are allowed to take rights away from the people. The Patriot Act could never have been done unless a terror threat had been created.[13]

***

---

[13]Please refer to following website for objective analysis: 9-11 Review, https://1ref.us/1fw (accessed November 5, 2020), and *Loose Change 9/11,* https://1ref.us/1fx (accessed November 5, 2020).

Gavel and Gage Present 9/11 Evidence

Former U.S. Sen. Mike Gravel, D-Alaska, and Richard Gage, founder of Architects & Engineers for 9/11 Truth, scheduled a press conference on September 9 to present hard evidence that all three World Trade Center skyscrapers on September 11, 2001, were destroyed by explosive-controlled demolitions.

Gravel notes, "Critically important evidence has come forward after the original government building reports were completed." A media-friendly summary of Gage's organization's findings, which was based on forensic evidence, as well as video and eyewitness testimony that was omitted from official reports, was to be presented. Evidence was to show that the WTC Twin Towers were not destroyed by jet plane impacts or fires, but by pre-set explosives and incendiaries.

Architects & Engineers for 9/11 Truth were also to call for a grand jury investigation of the government report. I really don't expect them to get too far because the nefarious element behind our government will stifle pursuit of the truth.

Even so, I'm still amazed that the American public bought into the government version of 9/11. Please think back to just the Pentagon news coverage alone. If a big Boeing aircraft crashed into the Pentagon, then where were the big turbine engines? I guess the huge turbine engines just burned up from the heat, or maybe rescue workers had the remains of the plane hauled away before the news media could possibly get any photos. Damage shown was more reminiscent of a missile strike vice huge aircraft with great wingspan. Ask yourselves, "Where was the plane after the hit?"

***

9/11 Anniversary Lingers

Many are reporting the fabricated Russian collusion story against President Trump as the greatest corruption ever perpetrated in American politics. Not so. Oh, there's corruption, alright. Extensive evidence supports that the Mueller investigation was a scam from the beginning. The global elitists are using unscrupulous tactics to try and take down Trump for sure.

That said, each year, we get the same story from our political leaders and all the news networks when the anniversary of 9/11 comes around. They address how Muslim terrorists attacked the World Trade Centers and Pentagon. I salute all the efforts of the firemen and rescue personnel, but I do not salute the fabricated story of these assaults. The 9/11 story remains the biggest scam ever perpetrated on the American people in recent history.

Hard evidence abounded, though stifled as conspiracy-related ideas, in support of 9/11 being a black CIA covert operation. Why? The global elitists needed to get things moving more quickly toward their objectives of a New World Order. As a result of 9/11, the worldwide war on terror was generated through a false flag operation, and the global elitists could now start taking away the rights of the people, e.g., the Patriot Act. They helped create this massive war on terror. It was lies and deception, as were Afghanistan and Iraq pre-planned wars.

In essence, substantial evidence supports that 9/11 was a false-flag operation that the global elitists blamed on the Muslims in order to move their agenda forward more expeditiously. The American people were purposely deceived and lied to.

***

USS Liberty Was a Cover-Up

On June 8, 1967, the USS Liberty was heavily attacked in international waters off the Sinai Peninsula by the air and naval forces of Israel, killing thirty-four American men.

Why would Israel, after hours of surveillance, attack the USS Liberty with the U.S. flag flying high in the breeze and clearly visible by the Israeli forces? Why did the Johnson administration not seek prosecution of the guilty parties? Why has the truth been hidden and covered up?

This was not a case of mistaken identity. Israel attacked the USS Liberty using unmarked aircraft. This further proves Israel knew exactly what they were doing. Israel intended to sink the USS Liberty, but why?

The men on the USS Liberty were betrayed by our government. Two aircraft carriers were in the Mediterranean at this time. The USS Liberty called for U.S. military assistance but received none. U.S. military aircraft were recalled through the direct intervention by President Johnson and Secretary of Defense McNamara. To me, this was disgraceful, but why?

Here's the reason. It was arranged with Israel that if Israel sank the USS Liberty, then the attack could have been blamed on Egypt. That would give President Johnson the chance to come into the war and control the Middle East area. The USS Liberty was placed exactly where it was supposed to be.

This was a false flag operation. This technique is not new. More recently, America used it during the 9/11 incident to create the war on terror.

***

Panama Canal: Trilateral Giveaway

The Panama Canal was built exclusively by the United States after acquiring the land with the Hay-Bunau Varilla Treaty of 1903. Even so, the Trilateral Commission, along with its international bankers and global elite, was directly responsible for the giveaway of the Panama Canal.

Panama owed certain international bankers well over $2 billion in loans and was in jeopardy of default. There was no economic solution; thus, the political arena was vigorously pursued. A scheme was devised to turn over the Panama Canal so that Panama could generate funds from passage fees, and thus, service its debt payments to the international bankers. Never mind that the Panama Canal was U.S. sovereign property and the most strategic military and economic asset held by the U.S. in this hemisphere.

President Carter chose fellow Trilateral Commission member Sol Linowitz to negotiate the Torrijos-Carter- Treaty. Linowitz, a director of Marine Midland Bank, stood to lose a bundle if Panama defaulted on its loans.

Here again, politicians, many Trilateral Commission members, prove that many do not give a hoot what the populace thinks. Something like 76 percent opposed the Panama Canal giveaway. I thought this was a nation by the people and for the people.

President Clinton, Trilateral Commission member, oversaw transfer of title to Panama on December 31, 1999. Shortly after turnover, Hutchinson Whampoa, a Chinese company, was given long-term port management contracts by Panama. A sovereign asset of the U.S. was turned over strictly for private gains without any concern of U.S. national security.

***

The Public Has Been Deceived

Retired Maj. Gen. Paul Vallely, the chief of Stand Up America, stated the "Certificate of Live Birth" released in April by the White House as "proof positive" of President Obama's Hawaiian birth is a forgery, but the FBI is covering the fraud, and no one in Congress is willing to tackle the situation because of fears of a "black backlash" if the failings of the nation's first black president are revealed. Vallely further stated, "We've had three CIA agents, retired, and some of their analytical associates look at it, and all came to the same conclusion, that even the long-form was a forged document."

Most in America don't want to hear something of this nature. They are of the opinion that anything the government says is right on. It's the same with 9/11. It's interesting that in 1962, the CIA had a project known as "Operation Northwoods." That project included U.S. government operations killing its own citizens and covertly blaming the attacks on Cuba. Covert operations are intended to deceive and hide from blame.

Study each of the following incidents: JFK/RFK/MLK assassinations; USS Liberty attack; TWA 800 flight; Vince Foster case; Ron Brown case; Oklahoma City Bombing; Gulf of Tonkin incidents; Panama Canal giveaway; and 9/11, and you'll see indications of cover-up after cover-up.

Many of you remain blind to the truth and never question information provided to you by the government. Truth is, the public has been deceived on many occasions while remaining oblivious to what's truly happening around them.

***

Evidence of Cover-Ups

In response to Jerry L. Hodson's critique of a Charles B. Smith *Viewpoint* article, I believe Hodson is misinformed about the truth of the Oklahoma bombing incident and the TWA Flight 800 explosion. The press can be used to mislead and does not always give us the whole truth. There certainly appears to be substantial evidence that the government covered up both of these cases if one cares to do some research.

Smith stated there were clear indications of a Middle East connection, possibly Iraq, involved in the Oklahoma bombing. He also stated that there was substantial evidence ignored during the TWA flight investigation. He appears to be right on both counts.

Former Arkansas State Representative Charles Key, founder and director of the Oklahoma Bombing Committee, has spoken out boldly, confidently, and extensively about that investigation from start to finish. Craig Roberts, also involved in the investigation, has spoken out boldly about this whole affair. Both of these men have reputable backgrounds and merit recognition. Incidentally, even the initial local Oklahoma news broadcasts were mysteriously changed or stifled as reporting progressed. It was not by accident.

As for the Flight 800 explosion, I recommend people review the eye-witness accounts of Michael Wire, Richard Goss, and Dwight Brumley, a retired Navy electronics expert, before making any final conclusions. Retired Admiral Thomas Moorer, former Chairman of the Joints Chiefs of Staff, once stated, "It's clear and there is no doubt that this aircraft was shot down. It's time for the media to get off their backsides and for Congress to hold hearings and take action." Of course, the latter never occurred.

However, I don't think we should stop there. There are strong indications of two major cover-ups during the Clinton administration that, if I may borrow from Hodson, really "take the cake."

Consider the 1993 supposed suicide case of Deputy White House Counsel Vince Foster. Christopher Ruddy addressed this case for the *Pittsburgh Tribune-Review* through a series of reports from 1994 to 1998. He eventually wrote the book, *"The Strange Death of Vincent Foster (An Investigation)."*

This case should never have been treated as an open-and-shut suicide. It certainly appears the investigators were uninterested in considering evidence of any wrongdoing. It also appears that numerous people told the truth but were ignored.

Now, consider the 1996 mysterious airplane crash of Secretary of Commerce Ron Brown. Many may recall that Ron Brown was under criminal investigation by independent counsel Daniel Pearson at the time. Stunning information surfaced in the *Pittsburgh Tribune-Review* late in 1997 as a result of investigations by reporter Christopher Ruddy.

Interestingly, three military pathologists believe there was significant evidence that Brown may have suffered a gunshot wound to his head and that the cause of death as an accident could not be supported unless there was an autopsy. No autopsy was ever conducted on Brown.

Based on extensive data I have not shared in this limited space, I believe there is significant evidence of cover-up for each case. For those who disagree with me, you're probably in the category of those who believe that Lee Harvey Oswald was the lone gunman who assassinated President Kennedy. By the way, the History Channel did a five-tape video presentation covering the Kennedy assassination for those who would like to see some interesting material on the subject.

It's my understanding that one of the key reasons Bobby Kennedy ran for president was so that he could uncover the truth of his brother's death. He needed presidential office authority in order to uncover and reveal the truth. Bobby Kennedy knew something beyond the Warren Commission report, something beyond the official report, something beyond the media story.

> *One of the key reasons Bobby Kennedy ran for president was so that he could uncover the truth of his brother's death.*

***

Casting Doubts about the TWA Flight 800 Probe

TWA flight 800 crashed off the coast of Long Island and killed 230 passengers on July 17, 1996. After four years of investigation from the Justice Department and National Transportation Safety Board, the government would have people believe that this crash was caused by a fuel tank explosion. Is this the truth, or has the government deliberately covered it up?

According to former Navy Commissioner W.S. Donaldson, chief air crash investigator of the Associated Retired Aviation Professionals, the following pertains:

- 755 witnesses, most which saw supersonic streaks of light and one which described a missile impact on the aircraft wing root, were ignored.
- FBI and Suffolk County Marine Police memorandum from their most qualified agents in the field that specified the precise off-shore point of two missiles were ignored.
- Radar evidence of a left-to-right missile impact through the aircraft and the establishment of a separate missile debris field was ignored.
- A Department of Defense report prepared by U.S. Navy missile experts requesting shoulder-fired weapons be fired at 747 ring root fuel tanks was ignored.
- The Ram hydraulic over-pressure of the entire left wing tank system was ignored.
- The explosion and total destruction of the left wing root fuel tank, which was the initialized point, was ignored.
- The failure and separation of the entire left wing at its strongest point was ignored.

- None of the appropriate metal testing to determine which fuel tank exploded first was done.

Three of the 755 witnesses were Michael Wire, Dwight Brumley, and Richard Goss. Michael Wire was standing on a drawbridge on the south shore of Long Island, gazing out over the water when he saw what he described at first as a "cheap firework" rising from behind a house not far away that was blocking his view of the horizon. According to Michael Wire, when it got high in the sky, it leveled out and sped out to sea. He lost sight of it momentarily, then, when there was an explosion so strong that when the shock wave hit several seconds later, it shook the seventy-ton bridge. He then saw a fireball that fell toward the ocean.

Dwight Brumley, a retired Navy electronics warfare expert, was a passenger in a northbound airliner that was about 7,000 feet above TWA 800 when it blew up. According to Dwight Brumley, he was looking out his window on the right side of the plane when he caught sight of a bright light below that was moving north at a high rate of speed. He said that as it peaked and pitched over, he saw two explosions, one after the other, followed by a fireball that elongated as it fell into the sea. Mr. Nugent, a passenger in the seat behind Dwight Brumley, told him that he had seen the cabin lights of an airliner before it blew up.

According to Richard Goss, who was on the porch of the Westhampton Yacht Club gazing over the ocean, he saw what he thought was a firework going straight up. It was very bright and arched over and went south out to the sea, but then it made a sharp left turn. Two explosions followed.

Folks, these are only three of a multitude of witnesses that have been ignored by the government's investigation. Paul Angelides, Major Frederick Meyer, William Gallagher, and a host of others have equally impressive testimonies most pertinent to this incident.

Has evidence been altered by the government to support its conclusions and discredit eyewitness accounts? This is worth truly pondering in light of a multitude of witnesses that have been virtually ignored. According to retired Admiral Thomas Moorer, former chairman of the Joints Chiefs of Staff, "It's clear and there is no doubt this aircraft was shot down. It's time for the media to get off their backsides and for Congress to hold hearings and take action."

It appears to me that this whole affair calls for a congressional investigation. The families of those who died and the American public deserve to know the truth.

***

Arkansas' Tainted Blood Scandal

Why hasn't the American media reported on a tainted blood scandal that may have infected about 2,000 Americans and killed hundreds of Canadian hemophiliacs? This insidious story goes back to Arkansas in the 1980s when Bill Clinton was governor.

According to an article by Gerald Jackson of *The New Australian* in February 1999, Health Management Associates (HMA) won a $3 million contract to provide medical services to Arkansas state prisons. The contract also allowed the company to collect blood from prisoners and sell it, but U.S. health regulations did not allow the sale of prisoners' blood within the country. Thus, HMA sold the blood outside the country. Critics claim that HMA ran a lucrative industry that knowingly sold blood plasma infected with AIDS, hepatitis, and other diseases to Canada.

Interestingly, according to Mr. Jackson, HMA had its license withdrawn by authorities because of poor medical practices; however, Bill Clinton publicly defended the company and used his authority as governor in 1985 to have its license renewed, even though the company was accused of using inmates to draw blood and had employed bogus doctors. HMA marketed the plasma all around the world, but much of it ended up in Canada, where a Toronto company used it to make a blood-clotting product called Factor VIII. That product was distributed by the Canadian Red Cross and eventually was used by unsuspecting Canadians.

The Christian Broadcast Network (CBN), based on a report by Dale Hurd, indicated that more than 1,000 Canadians are now expected to die from AIDS and hepatitis C because of blood received through the Arkansas prison program. Canadian Michael McCarthy is dying from hepatitis C as a result of the tainted blood. He said, "Somebody in the United States decided that for me it was OK to get hepatitis … that it was more important to provide prisoners with some cigarette money and have millions left over to go in the coffers of the state of Arkansas."

John Shock, a former inmate of Cummins State Prison in Arkansas, says HMA's blood safety tests were haphazard. He said, "Sometimes they would let you go two or three weeks without conducting blood tests. Other times, they'd be sticking you every time, testing you. Sometimes it would be two or three months before they'd test you again." Ultimately, Mr. Shock contracted hepatitis C, which ruined his first liver. Other witnesses at the prison also believed that the blood was collected under appalling conditions.

CBN further indicated that Dr. Michael Galster, an ex-employee of HMA at Cummins Prison, noticed that some of his diseased patients were frequently allowed to give blood in the prison's program. Dr. Galster, who questioned the safety of the blood shipments to Canada, accused Bill Clinton of personally withholding documentation describing how the Arkansas blood program was allowed to continue after the FDA had shut down the program.

Concerns about the Arkansas blood surfaced in 1995 when a commission headed by Canadian Justice Horace Krever determined certain blood in question had been purchased from HMA, according to comments made by James Carroll in *The Stuart News* (Stuart, FL.) on March 11, 1999. Shortly thereafter, the Royal Canadian Mounted Police began a criminal investigation, questioning the involvement of Arkansas officials and HMA associates. Since Canada launched an official investigation into Bill Clinton's possible involvement, several crimes have been committed to destroy files linked to the tainted blood program.

Surviving Canadian hemophiliacs have prepared a $5 billion lawsuit against those in the United States responsible for these operations. The FDA may also be sued, and the lead counsel for this group is also seeking a deposition from President Clinton on his role in the Arkansas prison blood program.

Two things immediately come to mind about this tragic affair. First, it appears that the U.S. Justice Department and media have turned their heads the other way. Why was there no criminal investigation on this nation's part? Second, whether Bill Clinton is found to be directly linked to the scandal or not, it taints this nation's image like tainted blood.

This horrific scandal does not speak well for the character of America.

Refer to the book *Blood Trail* by Michael Sullivan for more information on this subject. Dr. Michael Galster, using the pseudonym Michael Sullivan, wrote a fictionalized account of this whole affair and called it *Blood Trail*. He's the person actually responsible for exposing this scandal in the United States. Ceasing to fear repercussions, he eventually went public by revealing his true identity.

***

A Protected President

We still know little about Barack Obama's background. In his early presidential years, Obama's expensive lawyers built walls around various records, or simply made them disappear. It is estimated that Obama's legal team spent over a million dollars blocking access to common documents.

It's interesting that President Obama campaigned for a more "open government" and "full disclosure." As time would tell, it was quite the opposite.

Per former California State Assemblyman Steve Baldwin, he would not unseal his medical records, school records, birth records, or passport records. He would not release his Harvard records, Columbia College records, or Occidental College records. He would not even release his Columbia College thesis. All his legislative records from the Illinois State Senate were missing, and he claims his scheduling records during those State Senate years were lost as well. In addition, no one could find his elite prep school records.

Later on, according to Steve Baldwin, three document authentication experts declared the scanned "Certificate of Live Birth" for Obama was fake. That should give one pause for thought. As one looks at a plethora of other items, it seems things just don't add up.

Any documents revealing a foreign birth would have been of concern for Obama. Thus, it is not a coincidence that every document which contains information about his birth or citizenship is either missing, sealed, or has been altered.

It certainly appears that the global elitists and mainstream media deceived the American public, protected this man, and put him into office.

***

Questions Still Linger about President's Eligibility

Based on a recent and thorough investigation, Arizona Sheriff Joe Arpaio announced on March 1, 2012, that the White House-released Long Form Birth Certificate for President Barack Obama was most likely a forgery, probably produced on a computer. Additionally, the president's Selective Service card was also a computer-generated forgery.

To bring more confusion on President Obama's nativity, the Immigration and Naturalization Service cards filled out by airplane passengers arriving on international flights originating outside the United States in the month of August 1961, examined at the National Archives in Washington, D.C., are missing records for the week of Obama's reported birth, including the dates August 1–7, 1961.

Absent a copy of a birth certificate, a legitimate copy of a birth certificate, we do not have a single document that proves Mr. Obama's birth in Hawaii or anywhere else in the United States for that matter, a spokesman for the investigation team said. "We believe a full-blown investigation is warranted because the people of Maricopa County have been defrauded, and the people of Arizona have been defrauded."

The investigative team was made up of former law enforcement officers and lawyers with law enforcement experience. They examined dozens of witnesses and hundreds of documents, as well as taking numerous sworn statements from witnesses around the world.

There's distinct evidence that President Obama may not have been born in the United States. It's abundantly clear that the mainstream media are not interested in getting to the bottom of President Obama's background and eligibility.

***

Questions Asked on Connecticut Numbers

How can President Obama have a Connecticut Social Security number and yet has never lived in the state? The first three digits of President Obama's Social Security number are 042. That code falls within the range of numbers for someone with a Connecticut address, which according to the Social Security Administration, has been 040 through 049.

"There is obviously a case of fraud going on here," said private investigator Susan Daniels. "In fifteen years of having a private investigator's license in Ohio, I've never seen the Social Security Administration make a mistake of issuing a Connecticut Social Security number to a person who lived in Hawaii. There is no family connection that would appear to explain the anomaly."

Arizona Sheriff Joe Arpaio recently conducted a thorough investigation of Barack Obama's birth certificate and believes it's likely a forgery. Arpaio's probe also found probable cause that Obama's Selective Service registration card is a forgery.

What's bothersome about all this is that there has never been a congressional investigation into Barack Obama's background. Congress and the media are afraid to take it on. The American public deserves to know the truth, and yet Congress and the media ignore these issues.

I don't think Barack Obama will be doing any identity-theft commercials soon, that is, unless it's done with congressional and the media's blessing. It appears that the shadow government has told Congress and the media to lay down on this one, and they know from whom they take their orders.

***

Obama Was Given Permission to Lie

People were told by our current administration that there was a spontaneous uprising over an obscure video in Benghazi, Libya, on September 11, 2012, that caused the death of our ambassador, two Navy SEALs, and another American official.

Was it a spontaneous reaction to a video made in America? No, the Obama administration knew the answer from the start. They knew that it was a well-planned, professionally-executed military assault. When Mr. Romney stated and defended the freedom of speech we all have, he was strongly attacked by the media for a long period of time. The media completely ignored the facts and decidedly focused their attack on Romney.

The Obama administration continued to lie to the American people week after week, denying the facts that are now common knowledge. The whole thing was a cover. The attack was the work of al-Qaeda from the start.

Consider the "Fast and Furious" operation in Mexico. What Nixon did pales in comparison to this insidious and pre-planned operation that was clearly not in the best interest of all. The difference is that President Obama and his administration have been given a free pass by the media and Congress.

America, you've got serious problems. You've forsaken your God. You have a spiritual condition that requires immediate repentance, as a government and as a populace. It's time to get right with God, or dire circumstances will grip you like a thief in the night, and most assuredly, there will be weeping and gnashing of teeth throughout this land.

***

One Cooperates If There's Nothing to Hide

A House chairman probing the IRS scandal recently stated that President Obama has reneged on a promise to have his aides cooperate with the investigation, forcing the Ways and Means Committee to conduct a search for emails and documents needed to get to the truth.

Representative Dave Camp also revealed that federal agents conducting the investigation into the Internal Revenue Service's bid to punish Tea Party and conservative critics of the president have yet to talk to a single target of the scandal.

His committee has been frustrated with the administration's failure to provide emails from Lois Lerner, who ran the IRS department that blocked Tea Party groups from winning the typically quick approval of tax-exempt status. Lerner was at the Capitol recently, where she refused to testify before the House Committee on Oversight and Government Reform. Then, conveniently, it's revealed that pertinent emails have been lost after a year's time.

My, how could President Obama not honor his word on this? What's going on? Lois Lerner won't provide information. It seems to me one cooperates if one doesn't have anything to hide. Of course, President Obama didn't have to show his records. For that matter, he doesn't have to give details on Benghazi or Fast and Furious operations either. So there, take that, Congress.

Time and time again, President Obama defies Congress. The sad truth on all this is that Congress allows it. Where's the Congress that held Richard Nixon accountable for some tapes; yet, this president defiantly gets away with scandal after scandal.

***

Jeffrey Epstein: What Really Happened?

"Something is rotten in the state of Denmark" is a quote taken from Hamlet. Oh, how it so pertains to the case of alleged sex trafficker Jeffrey Epstein's apparent suicide. Once again, as often is the case with the government or mainstream media explanation, something doesn't add up.

Dr. Michael Baden, the noted forensic pathologist and former chief medical examiner for New York City, recently appeared on a Fox channel program to discuss this case. Baden has performed more than 20,000 autopsies, served as director of the Forensic Investigation Center of the New York State Police, was chairman of the Forensic Pathology Panel of Congress' Select Committee on Assassinations, which reinvestigated the deaths of President Kennedy and Martin Luther King Jr., and has held other extensive professional appointments.

Baden stated that the findings at autopsy were more consistent with "ligature homicidal strangulation." To further explain, the autopsy disclosed three fractures of the thyroid cartilage and the hyoid bone. According to Baden, such fractures "are very unusual for suicide and are more indicative of homicidal strangulation."

Baden further questioned where any DNA findings were, as well as some highly unusual breakdown of security occurrences during Epstein's supposed suicide. For example, two guards were allegedly asleep at the same time, a situation that Baden has never seen in more than fifty years of investigating prison deaths, and which he considers to be "extremely unlikely." He also questioned why all of the security cameras around Epstein's cell were inoperative.

It's interesting that many prominent and influential people stood to benefit from Epstein's death.

***

Possible Foul Play in Scalia Death?

Given all the subversive activity against President Trump, I revisit the death of Justice Scalia. The reports kept changing. First, we heard that he died of a heart attack. Second, we heard that no autopsy was performed and that his body was quickly embalmed, erasing any chances for the coroner to conduct toxicology tests.

Scalia was a strong conservative and tie-breaking voice on the Supreme Court, pushing back liberal policies. Timing of death was notable with the complete expectation that Hillary Clinton would be elected and appoint a liberal judge.

Reports were also heard of Scalia having a pillow over his head when he was found dead. Would a maid put the pillow over his head? Not likely. This was a strange report, and if true, should have led to some inner thinking.

Scalia was a strong conservative and tie-breaking voice on the Supreme Court, pushing back liberal policies. Timing of death was notable with the complete expectation that Hillary Clinton would be elected and appoint a liberal judge.

William Ritchie, former head of criminal investigations for Washington D.C. police, wrote that he was "stunned that no autopsy was ordered for Judge Scalia." "How can the Marshal say, without a thorough post mortem, that he was not injected with an illegal substance that would simulate a heart attack," asked Ritchie. "Did the U.S. Marshal check for petechial hemorrhage in his eyes or under his lips that would have suggested suffocation? Did the U.S. Marshal smell his breath for any unusual odor that might suggest poisoning? My gut tells me there is something fishy going on in Texas."

Something didn't add up, like in the cases of JFK, Vince Foster, and Ron Brown.

***

Pearl Harbor No Sneak Attack

On January 27, 1941, Joseph Grew, the U.S. ambassador to Japan, wired Washington that he had learned of the surprise attack Japan was preparing for Pearl Harbor. On September 24, a dispatch from Japanese Naval Intelligence to Japan's Consul General in Honolulu was deciphered. Surprisingly, Washington chose not to share this information with the officers at Pearl Harbor.

U.S. Naval Intelligence intercepted and translated many dispatches. Tokyo had sent numerous transmissions to the attack fleet before it reached Hawaii; however, information was withheld from the Pearl Harbor commanders.

On October 7, 1940, one of President Roosevelt's military advisers, Lt. Cmdr. Arthur McCollum, wrote a memorandum detailing an eight-step plan that would provoke Japan into attacking America. Over the next year, President Roosevelt implemented all eight of the recommendations. In the summer of 1941, America joined England in an oil embargo against Japan. Japan needed oil for its war with China, and had no remaining option but to invade the East Indies and Southeast Asia to get new resources. This required getting rid of the U.S. Pacific Fleet first.

It appears that President Roosevelt clearly allowed the attack on Pearl Harbor to happen and even helped Japan by making sure their attack was a surprise. As Rear Admiral Richmond Turner stated in 1941, "We were prepared to divert traffic when we believed war was imminent. We sent the traffic down via the Torres Strait so that the track of the Japanese task force would be clear of any traffic."

Chapter 9

Military

Note: This chapter has 10 separate newspaper editorials and are not presented in a specific order of when written.

Russia Re-Establishing Itself as Superpower

A Russian military vessel recently docked at a Havana naval base. According to Russia's defense minister, Sergei Shoigu, Russia is looking to build military bases in Vietnam, Cuba, Venezuela, Nicaragua, the Seychelles, Singapore, and several other countries. Some may suggest that the move to put military bases in Asia and Latin America is meant as retaliation against America for meddling in their affairs, but it goes much deeper than that.

Nicaragua and Cuba were Russian allies during the Cold War. What's the current motivation behind placing military bases in those countries?

In my opinion, Russia is re-establishing itself as a superpower again. She is increasing her influence in our Southern Hemisphere in a greater way for significant reasons.

While we've been spending billions on our pre-planned wars in Afghanistan and Iraq, and placing substantial and prolonged stress on our military forces and infrastructure, Russia has been steadfastly developing its forces under the radar. Russia is a strong nation and became much stronger over the last decade, although our media doesn't give this subject proper attention. Russia has even built large underground nuclear bunkers and weapons production facilities in the Ural Mountains, clearly intended to function during a nuclear war.

If there is no spiritual repentance unto the Lord Jesus Christ, don't be surprised, in time, when Russia, along with some of her allies, are on this soil and America is under foreign domination. Some will then ponder where was the protection of God?

***

Iraq: An Objective Analysis

Iraq has developed into an exceptionally challenging and dire situation. The population is in despair as there are as many as 3,000 citizens murdered each month. Three million Iraqis are internally displaced or have fled the country. Technical and educated elites are increasingly departing the country.

There is no function of government that operates effectively across Iraq. The Maliki government is despised by the Sunni populace as an Iranian surrogate and is perceived by the Kurds as being untrustworthy. The U.S. and allied forces are targeted extensively on an ongoing basis. The population is now terrorized by numerous criminal gangs. Please remember that Saddam Hussein released 80,000 criminal prisoners.

The Iraqi army, in reality, is too small and poorly equipped. Enemy insurgents or militia numbers may exceed 100,000, and obviously, as demonstrated, are capable of ongoing independent operations as they continue to be assisted by Iran and Syria. Casualties of U.S. forces, killed or wounded, now exceed 27,000, and the war costs America something like nine billion dollars monthly. Iraqi forces have also suffered more than 49,000 casualties in the last fourteen months.

The U.S. military forces are being stretched exceptionally thin. Stateside readiness ratings are seriously being affected, and equipment concerns are real. National Guard combat brigades continue to be called up for repeated tours of duty. The National Guard structure, which is important to America's domestic security, is being adversely affected. It was not designed for this kind of war effort. Further, the U.S. now has to use thousands of contractors in the Middle East to support its efforts in Iraq and other areas.

Typically, Iraq's neighbors are not part of the solution, with the possible exception of Saudi Arabia and Kuwait. These surrounding countries provide little economic or political support to the current government in Iraq. This is a problem.

Make no mistake; the U.S. military is working diligently to carry out objectives; however, it is a daunting task given the current situation. Military power alone cannot defeat this insurgency. Somehow and someway, there must be reconciliation between Shia and Sunni leadership. This means both groups must walk back from the line of an all-out civil war. Earnest and sincere efforts must be made to accomplish this reconciliation. This is essential.

If the U.S. is to withdraw in the near future, there must also be an effort to increase personnel numbers and adequately equip the Iraqi forces. This means helicopters, light armored vehicles, artillery, and C-130 aircraft. The Iraqi forces have already taken tremendous casualties. It would be extremely helpful if other nations would help bear this economic burden in order to accomplish this task.

The key objective in all this is to reestablish a governmental system where the Kurds, Shia, and Sunni agree about things, at least in a consensus and cooperative way. True, this is easier said than done, but it needs to be accomplished. If this is not accomplished, and the U.S. leaves Iraq as the situation currently exists, then there could be regional war in Iraq and the surrounding area for years to come.

If the Kurds, Shia, and Sunni factions cannot agree in a cooperative and consensus manner about government, then three distinct states should be considered as an alternative solution if the distribution of oil revenues can be worked out among the three. This is definitely a viable option and clearly would be a worthwhile effort, given the current situation.

***

War in Afghanistan Leaves U.S. in Serious Predicament

Russia was in Afghanistan from 1979 through 1989. Russia bordered Afghanistan and conducted warfare at a much closer proximity than

America. Eventually, Russia pulled out for a number of reasons while not being successful. Two key reasons are that the counterinsurgency was too challenging to overcome, and the war costs were too costly.

Guerilla warfare fights on its terms. It can hit, withdraw, and pick a better day to fight. It can lay low for a while and resurface, again, often on its terms. What this means is that war fought using guerilla tactics will typically prolong the war. For an occupying force from overseas, it can become quite expensive to support and maintain presence of longevity when opposing guerilla warfare.

Please notice how America was quite successful after the initial invasion of Afghanistan. Now, years later, see how the strength of the Taliban has resurfaced. Guerrilla warfare has a viable foundation if it has the populace support. Please note that Afghanistan has a number of different tribes, and ethnic tribe loyalties typically remain strong. The prominent tribe in Afghanistan is Pashtun, and the Taliban is primarily Pashtun. It's apparent that the Taliban has had some support, coupled with its ability to regress into Pakistan and return when convenient for them to do so.

America has now been in Afghanistan for close to the same period of time as Russia. It has faced numerous challenges while accumulating exorbitant debt and fighting this war from a much greater distance than Russia.

What's the current situation? Afghanistan remains poor, still lacks basic infrastructure, and is economically weak, even after all these years of American occupation. It has little to offer to the outside world. Numerous ethnic tribes exist with remaining complex and major differences. Government corruption remains strong. That said, Afghanistan has substantial ways to go in the advancement of its society.

It's to Afghanistan's benefit to keep international aid coming in. As such, Afghanistan has played various countries with vested interests against each other in order to keep the financial aid coming in. It appears to be doing that quite well and will continue to do so.

As a result of the policies that America has pursued over this past decade, it will have to deal with the adverse effects of its choices, probably in the not-too-distant future. It has accrued staggering debt as a result of its war efforts in Iraq and Afghanistan.

Where does this leave America? It leaves America in a serious predicament and situation. Debt will continue to accrue as these war efforts continue into the future.

One will quickly interject that action had to be taken after 9/11. For those that share this opinion, please carefully analyze and review the details of 9/11 for yourselves with an objective and open mind. Look past the deceptions of 9/11, and ask yourselves some serious questions after your personal research.

Wars are orchestrated, and Iraq and Afghanistan are no different. The war on terror had to be created, and the sovereignty of America brought down in order to facilitate the march toward globalism at a quicker pace. Many people cannot or refuse to see this.

Go back to the Gulf of Tonkin incident of August 4, 1964, as just one example of war orchestration. President Johnson went on television accusing North Vietnam of using patrol boats against two Navy destroyers. Based on various sources, those attacks appear to have never taken place; thus, it seems that President Johnson used a false flag operation to push America aggressively into the Vietnam War.

What was gained from this war? Absolutely nothing, except 58,000 American dead, substantial debt, higher inflation, and a multitude of Vietnamese killed. Oh, and by the way, international bankers make lots of money anytime we go to war.

***

America Disarms, While Russia and China Build

I understand that President Obama is seeking to abolish the Tomahawk and Hellfire missile programs that experts say have helped the Navy maintain military superiority for the past few decades. The Tomahawk missile program, known as "the world's most advanced cruise missile," is set to be cut by $128 million under Obama's 2015 budget proposal and completely eliminated by fiscal year 2016, according to budget documents released by the Navy.

As Obama continues to disarm and scale down our military armament and force in numerous areas, this should serve as an alarm to the citizens of America. He has even purged top military officers who have not supported his agenda. Retired Maj. Gen. Patrick Brady, U.S. Army, Medal of Honor recipient, stated, "There is no doubt Obama is intent on emasculating the military and will fire everyone who disagrees with him."

A strong military serves as a deterrent against aggression. Given the present conditions in the world, this is not the time to disarm by any means. Ronald Reagan knew this, but unfortunately, he's not our current commander-in-chief.

Russia and China continue to build and modernize while America disarms. Russia has been making ongoing submarine and aircraft incursions against America without the public knowing much about these events. The press yawns, and then returns to backing Obama and protecting his destructive agenda, instead of addressing and giving these incursions more attention and scrutiny.

The reason Russia is conducting these incursions is to test our responses. Can they do it without detection? How do our forces respond? All these events are being done with fixed purpose. All information gained will go into their war plans.

This policy of mutual destruction is antiquated. It won't happen like that. Russia is currently preparing and planning for a war on America when it takes the pre-emptive first strike. It'll be done by surprise, and it'll be done with submarines and long-range bombers being used in a coordinated effort. Russia is building, training, and modernizing its military at a rapid pace. They've developed extensive underground facilities to support their military efforts. Their preparations have been done under the radar while our press refuses to cover this subject more extensively.

Relations with Russia have soured immensely in recent years. America has provided some non-lethal assistance to Ukraine; however, if that assistance becomes lethal in military armament and munitions, then expect this to anger Russia that much more. Even the populace in Russia is beginning to view America more unfavorably than in the past.

I don't believe Putin has much respect for Obama, and he's certainly not afraid of him. Putin knows more about Obama than the American public knows. He knows (and so does Congress) about his shrouded background and global elitist agenda. If (or perhaps when) Russia attacks, it may think that it's doing the world a service by attacking America. Perception is in the eyes of the beholder.

Obama's leadership, unless there is a sincere repentance soon unto Almighty God, will lead this nation into ruin. God resists the proud. The arrogance that emanates from our government toward the things of God serves as a harbinger of things to come. This must change through repentance.

As I've stated before, I strongly urge Christian pastors to conduct prayer in their congregations for our nation on a designated and ongoing basis. I strongly urge Christians to intercede for America on an ongoing basis. The root of America's troubles is a spiritual one. That's why we have the government leadership we have today. We must cry out to God in earnestness for repentance and divine intervention in our nation. If no repentance, or divine intervention, disaster awaits.

***

Enemies of America: Red China and Russia

Let me see now. The media and political arena would have us think of North Korea and a few Middle Eastern countries as our enemies. I'm still amazed at how they refuse to acknowledge the significant threat of Red China and Russia. Supposedly, the Soviet Union has collapsed and is now considered a non-threat, and Red China, of course, is a friendly trading partner.

> *We have seen Red China grow from a third-rate military force to an exceptionally modern and well-equipped force ready to do battle anywhere in the world.*

We have seen Red China grow from a third-rate military force to an exceptionally modern and well-equipped force ready to do battle anywhere in the world. Red China has done this quietly as we have significantly helped them toward their goals. Here are few thoughts for consideration on how we have strengthened Red China and Russia militarily while weakening ourselves.

- We continue to abundantly buy their products.
- President Carter gave away the Panama Canal, and now China operates it. This means they control who uses it.
- President Clinton gave Red China "most favored" nation trading status. This has opened markets to cheap goods produced essentially by slave labor. This has destroyed many U.S. companies. It has cost us jobs by underselling markets with cheap products.
- President Clinton allowed Loral and Hughes to sell Red China important missile technology and guidance systems for communications satellites.
- Red Chinese spies were discovered at Los Alamos and other places during the President Clinton administration. Nuclear secrets were stolen.

- Our border along Mexico has been so porous that, in addition to Mexicans, Asians, Central Americans, and Middle Easterners commonly come across.
- The Chinese Ocean Shipping Co. has established a huge transshipment center in Freeport, Bahamas, off the Florida Coast. This is a great place to store Red Chinese pre-deployment equipment and supplies. Need I remind people of a few years ago when a sealift container was smuggled into Long Beach, California, that was loaded with AK-47 weapons?
- We've closed bases, reduced aircraft in air squadrons, reduced ships in our fleets, reduced war stocks, and have greatly overextended our reserve and National Guard forces overseas.
- Red China and Russia now share joint intelligence. They also conducted a joint military exercise within the last year. Border dispute days are over.
- Russia also has continued to develop selected areas militarily. Their submarines have become exceptionally quiet.

One thing America still has going for it is the right to bear arms. Both Red China and Russia would like to see Americans disarmed, but this has not happened yet, although there are forces behind the scenes trying to move America to this direction. Fighting an armed population in a guerilla-type war is very difficult to sustain unless one can win the hearts and minds of the people. You need the popular support of the people to be successful in a war of this nature. Currently, Red China and Russia do not have this.

Red China and Russia are enemies of America, even though many in America do not truly realize this. If there's not a spiritual recrudescence unto Jesus Christ in the near future, look for Red China and Russia, along with other allies in time, to lead a surprise limited nuclear attack against this nation. America will not see it coming. It will be a total surprise. Look for this to take place after a series of natural disasters and/or internal strife.

Many in America ignore natural disasters as an extension of spirit of the spiritual realm. I recall how King David went to God concerning a famine in Israel. He cried out to God on why the famine was taking place. God revealed that the famine came about as a result of something that King Saul had set in motion years before.

Russia will come on the East Coast and Red China on the West Coast and through Mexico. Let me say that the Red Chinese will be ruthless and that Red China and Russia will not be afraid to drill in a nineteen-square-mile area of Alaska for its oil. Why would anyone want to be dependent on OPEC or foreign oil when one does not have to be?

***

We Need Anti-Missile Defense

Dialogue between Russia and the United States over U.S. anti-missile defenses has not impressed me. Russia has firmly opposed any development of U.S. anti-missile defenses, while the United States is attempting to get Russia's approval to amend the 1972 arms treaty between the former Soviet Union and the United States that did not allow for development of national missile-defense systems.

First, the treaty signed in 1972 is outdated in light of current realities. Proliferation of ballistic missile technology has spread to numerous rogue nations, such as North Korea, Iraq, Iran, Libya, and Syria. These nations did not sign the treaty and bear serious watching. Second, the Soviet Union no longer exists.

Russia contends that an amendment to the treaty would commence a new arms race and upset the strategic military balance. Red China, of course, supports this position. Perhaps this sounds good to some ears, but in reality, Russian and Red China have never abandoned their race for arms superiority. Don't be fooled otherwise.

Washington has ignored that Russia already has a missile-defense system in place while the United States has virtually none. The Russian System was completed years before the Soviet Union signed the treaty in 1972. Many believe that U.S. politicians bartered away the future national defenses of this nation while the Soviet Union sacrificed very little.

According to Colonel Stanislav Lunev, who defected from Russia to the United States in 1992, shortly after Boris Yeltsin came to power, the Soviet Union created its system against both missile and air attack with both active and passive measures. Per Colonel Lunev, the following pertains:

- Active measures included design and deployment of ground, air, and space anti-missile weapons, and battle-management target-tracking radars. Active measures were designed for the destruction of incoming missiles and aircraft in the event of a surprise attack.
- Passive measures included construction of underground bunkers, which could protect the Soviet top echelon from hostile missile strikes,

underground and air-based command posts for the Soviet military, and super-secret underground systems for evacuation of leaders from their peacetime locations.

- The Politburo of the Communist Party ordered the completion of the anti-ballistic missile system for Moscow by 1967, but due to technical problems, it didn't become operational until after the treaty was signed in 1972.
- In total, the Soviet Union deployed two generations of national defense systems, consisting of eighteen large radars and 12,000 interceptors at 280 complexes.
- In 1992 and 1995, Russia upgraded its SA-10s, including retrofitting them with new missiles and electronics with improved performance against strategic missiles and added capability to intercept tactical missiles with low radar cross-sections.

I don't think the American public is aware of the massive development of bunkers and underground communication systems within Russia. Underground construction has continued throughout the last decade at extremely costly figures. The underground city in Yamantau in the Ural Mountains alone is about the size of Washington, D.C. Do you really think all the Western dollars put into Russia went into just the economy?

It's time for America to quit snoozing. Russia has consistently pursued an anti-ballistic program. To get to the point, Russia has never considered abandonment of its own missile-defense system, so why shouldn't the United States get serious about the welfare of its people. Rogue states have ballistic-missile technology and seek increase. Is the United States blind to what's really going on? Put me on record—this is one citizen who favors development of the anti-ballistic-missile defense system with no serious concessions. It should have started seventeen years ago during the Reagan administration.

One may argue that development of this system would be extremely costly. True, but consider the consequences. Peace is maintained through strength. That includes identifying one's significant weaknesses and rectifying them. To delay is to play into the hands of one's enemies, for weakness invites provocation. Continued appeasement towards Russia and Red China will not work in America's favor. Pragmatically speaking, stakes are high on this issue, and later may be too late.

***

U.S. Security System Needs Tightening

Many in America have a false security about our nation today. This is something I've known all along, but it was further corroborated in my reading about the "bipartisan" Cox Report and its revelations through a summary by Senator James Inhofe of Oklahoma. It appears a serious security scandal and possible cover-up have occurred during this current presidential administration. Many in the American public may not be aware of the following points.

- Sixteen of the seventeen most significant nuclear-related security breaches revealed in the Cox Report were discovered during the Clinton administration. Loss of information on the advanced W-88 warhead was discovered in 1995.
- Top officials, including the secretary of energy, the attorney general, the FBI director, and the deputy National Security adviser, were briefed on the W-88 breach well before the 1996 election. The news media reported that the White House chief of staff, the CIA director, and the president's National Security adviser were also informed in 1995.
- Numerous instances of China's proliferation of prohibited military technologies to countries like Pakistan, Iran, North Korea, Syria, Libya, and Egypt were either ignored or downplayed during the current administration.
- In 1993, the Clinton administration put an end to the Coordinating Committee for Multilateral Export Controls, which had worked to assure U.S. allies of a unified approach to the export of security-sensitive high technology items to countries like China. This caused a mad scramble to sell technology to China without regard to security. More than 600 U.S. supercomputers were sold to China, some of which are now being used in military-related applications.
- The Clinton administration consistently relaxed security-based trade restrictions on military-related high technology. Easing of restrictions on satellite transfers occurred. China used technology gained from two U.S. aerospace companies, Loral and Hughes, to improve the accuracy and reliability of its military rockets, many of which are currently aimed at America.
- The Cox Report includes numerous instances in which it reports that information and evidence on specific matters are being withheld from public view. This can be attributed to the Clinton administration's unilateral decision that the material should not be made public, not

because the bipartisanship committee saw a need to protect those items.

What did President Clinton know, and when did he know it? The bipartisan committee revealed the White House could not produce an independently verifiable, straight answer. I don't want to focus on that point, although it could be interesting to pursue. Instead, I want to focus on security. Our government must seriously examine what has happened, execute immediate and aggressive damage control, and take keen measures to prevent further breaches of security from happening in the future.

Blow off the political and patronizing rhetoric. Security, especially nuclear-related, must be taken seriously. Staying ahead of one's adversaries in military warfare is especially important in this modernistic and technological age we live in. The government must seriously protect and advance any advantages the United States has. Let an enemy gain equal status, and you're getting on dangerous ground, especially with the kind of folks that are out there today. Many would love to harm America or see her fall from global influence. Tightening the belt on security is not only prudent but essential to the well-being of this nation.

***

U.S. Should Not Ignore Cyber Security

Pulse attacks with nuclear weapons detonated at high altitude and cyber warfare can enable adversaries to deliver a crippling blow far greater than many believe. Discussion on nuclear warfare typically focuses on a bomb being set off on the ground or at low altitude with a ballistic missile. Damage at this level would be extensive indeed, but detonating a nuclear weapon at high altitude could conceivably do more extensive or greater damage.

The explosion at high-altitude sets off what is called Electro-Magnetic Pulse (EMP). This can put out all electronic devices for hundreds or thousands of miles, depending upon where it happens. This threat is not fantasy. According to Dr. William Graham, chairman of the Congressional EMP Threat Commission and former science adviser to President Reagan, he stated, "I'd have to say that 70 to 90 percent of the population would not be sustainable after this kind of attack." He even goes on to indicate that life would be similar to life around the 1800s.

In a case like this, the country would not have the ability to support or sustain people like they've grown accustomed. An attack of this nature against America would also limit America's retaliatory capacity. Tracing the culprit in a scenario of this nature may be difficult, or at least limited.

Billions of dollars are being spent on the Afghanistan and Iraq wars, but what about the homeland itself? Protecting power grids and cybersecurity should not be ignored by Congress. Protecting the homeland should be given far greater attention.

***

Obama Erred on Military Policy

President Obama officially began his assault on Christian military members and their religious liberties in 2013 when it was announced in the military: "Religious proselytization is not permitted within the Department of Defense … Court martials will be decided on a case-by-case basis …" Unconstitutional as it was, these efforts to punish and silence Christian chaplains and service members were ungodly.

What did this mean? Christian chaplains and service members risked court-martial, prosecution, or even discharge if they talked about Jesus, quoted the Bible, or shared their faith with others. Under Obama's guidance, if an atheist, homosexual, or non-Christian was offended in any way, the Christian member could be punished. Obama's policies are still in effect today. It's time for them to be repealed.

Chaplains are forced against biblical teaching to facilitate same-sex marriage ceremonies. If they refuse, they suffer punitive consequences. Under Obama's policies, still in force, many chaplains have already faced ridicule and lost the ability to stand true to their beliefs. Numerous other service members have also suffered punitive measures for standing in their Christian beliefs.

Obama's actions were unprecedented in American history, wrong, immoral, and a grave threat to religious freedom.

Evil can only succeed if good men do nothing. America's Christian service members should be protected and not prosecuted for standing in their faith. Please contact your senators and representatives and recommend these leftist policies be rescinded.

***

America Needs to Repent

Many people have been duped about the Russian military and Russia itself. Many still believe that Russia is a sleeping bear. This is totally wrong.

Equally, many people have been duped about the American military. Many think that the American military is far superior to any and all forces. That being said, most of the world would have bet on Goliath when David went out to face him. Just like that, David took Goliath down quickly and efficiently while the rest of the Philistines stood by stunned at what they just saw.

Russia has been slowly building under the radar since we've been fighting for years now in Iraq and Afghanistan, accumulating great debt, and spending our resources. Russia also accumulated much debt from Afghanistan, but wisely got out in 1989 after ten years of warfare. Since that time, Russia has been transitioning into strength.

Russia has advanced technology that the mainstream media is not telling the public about.

Some may say that the Constitution made us a great nation, but in essence, that is not so. It was God who made us great. America has *America has been blessed by God, period.* been blessed by God, period. To walk away from God is stupidity; yet, that's what we've been doing as a nation for years now.

Make no mistake—Russia is formidable. America needs to repent and repent now.

Chapter 10

United Nations

Note: This chapter has 4 separate newspaper editorials and are not presented in a specific order of when written.

United Nations Is a Globalist Organization

The United Nations is a globalist organization being used to move the world toward the New World Order. Through an air of benevolence, the United Nations covers its key motives. Their use of propaganda and political correctness lulls the masses into a stupor. Consider just a few comments:

• Leon Panetta, Secretary of Defense, stated that the U.N.'s approval would be sought regarding declarations of war, as opposed to the approval of Congress.

- The U.N. has announced intentions to create a global environmental agency rife with crippling economic sanctions against any country that does not follow the Agenda 21 line.
- Through Codex Alimentarius, the U.N. is attempting to control the health of the world. By forcing GMO foods, removing our options, and requiring food modernization, the U.N. is removing the right for basic health freedom.
- The U.N. threatened to withdraw aid from countries that did not allow abortion for religious reasons. While the U.N. supports global blasphemy laws that protect Islam, they support efforts to have crosses removed from the exterior of buildings because the sight of crosses could incite violence.

The United Nations, along with its policies, is being used by the global elite to progressively accomplish their agenda. One might believe that the U.S. would strongly oppose being controlled by foreign interests, but one must consider how propaganda, the "false green movement," and Mr. Obama are being used to manipulate the people and give more control away from America to the U.N. on multi-levels.

***

United Nations: Global Taxation

Many Americans know that the U.S. contributes 22 percent of the United Nations' annual budget, even though the U.N. is an inept and mismanaged organization. Now, here's one for you. U.N. personnel have now proposed an international tax on aviation fuel, a tax on airline tickets, taxes on international currency transactions, carbon-use taxes, including a 4.8-cent tax on each gallon of gasoline, and other taxes on an extensive range of transactions, goods, and services.

The U.S. should oppose all efforts by the U.N. to create global taxation. Recently, the House of Representatives passed a bill, S3633 (Protection Against United Nations Taxation Act of 2006), that now awaits action in the Senate. Passage of this bill would stop payment of U.S. dues to the U.N. if it attempts to implement or impose any kind of tax on U.S. citizens. Even so, the U.S. contributes too much to the U.N. budget already.

This U.N. initiation of global taxation does not surprise me. True, it would generate funds for this corrupt organization, but it also, once again, points to the globalist agenda. Tie the world into one government domination. Have sovereign nations, including the United States, to incrementally give up their sovereignty. The United States should not relinquish any form of sovereignty to the United Nations, period. The United Nations, through the Earth Charter and some of its other bureaucratic efforts, is attempting to bring the world under its all-encompassing umbrella. "Globalism," in reality, is another name for "New World Order."

***

Locking up Public Lands

Many in America are not aware that the current presidential administration has designated millions of acres of federal land off-limits to multiple uses such as mining and seems to be attempting to lock up public land. This is all being done without consulting Congress or the public. What's the real reason this is all being done? Upon closer scrutiny, one notices the current administration is conforming the U.S. environmental policy to United Nations (UN) strategies.

Defendants shrug off criticism by saying designations affect only land that is already controlled by the federal government, but one best look deeper. Many are beginning to observe that the Clinton administration is not only interested in locking up federal land, but also private land as well through such programs as the Clean Water Action Plan and the Lands Legacy Initiative.

The Clean Water Action Plan dramatically expands the 1976 Clean Water Action Act by administratively shifting water protection from point source pollution to non-point source pollution over an entire watershed. This plan will extend federal land-use jurisdiction to all of the 2,100 watersheds in America when completed. Congress has taken no action to authorize such a dramatic change in national policy. This plan imposes buffer zones along two million miles of streams and rivers, a minimum of forty-eight million acres of private property.

The Land Legacy Initiative typically has been funded by Congress at $200-$300 million annually to buy private land. The president wants that increased to $1 billion yearly with perpetuity. What does this mean? It means that more than ten million acres of private land could be purchased over the next decade with "no congressional" oversight.

President Clinton once mentioned that locking up of land will provide a legacy for the children of America. Let's take a look at the Grand Staircase-Escalante National Monument situation when 1.7 million acres were locked in 1996. The president locked up the largest clean coal deposit in the world, forcing U.S. industry to go to foreign sources for clean coal in the future. A multitude of jobs were lost, and families across America are now paying more for electricity.

At this point, I think it good to examine UN Agenda 21 and the Convention on Biological Diversity. UN Agenda 21 focuses on reorganizing society around sustainable use and development of the planet. Based on socialist principles of equal sharing of all natural resources, UN Agenda 21 was developed to control all human activity to protect the Earth's ecosystems and biological diversity.

The International Union for the Conservation of Nature (IUCN) is an accredited scientific advisory body to the UN. Its members include 878 state and federal governmental agencies and non-governmental organizations in 181 countries. The IUCN's official mission is to influence, encourage, and assist societies throughout the world to conserve the integrity and diversity of nature and to ensure that any use of natural resources is equitable and ecologically sustainable. The IUCN has various U.S. federal agencies enlisted as members and touches virtually every environmental problem in America today.

Many believe that the IUCN's approach to conserving the integrity and diversity of nature is not based on facts but on religious ideas of conservation biology. In other words, they are rooted in pantheism—the belief that nature is god and thus knows best, and that all human activity leads to fragmentation of ecosystems, which in turn leads to a depletion of biodiversity.

President Clinton acknowledged UN goals during a speech to the UN General Assembly on September 22, 1997. It certainly appears U.S. policy has conformed to UN strategies since he took office. The influence and dictates of UN Agenda 21 and the Convention on Biological Diversity appear to be clearly evident in the president's actions of setting aside huge national landmarks, wilderness areas, and interconnecting river corridors via the Clean Water Action Plan.

The administration's actions represent a major threat to private property and the control of government over American citizens. Everything that we use and eat starts as a natural resource either on or under the land. We must not destroy the sector of our economy that provides the goods, services, and wealth of this nation.

It is not in this nation's best interest to support the global governance agenda of the UN if a legacy is truly to be left to America's children.

Congress and the public need to wake up, get the facts, and seek the best for this nation. Get to the roots of the president's actions and realize that UN Agenda 21 and the Convention on Biological Diversity are clearly in the background of this administration's lockup of all this land.

***

Treaty Threatens National Power

The Earth Charter Commission announced on March 15 a comprehensive document on new global ethical guidelines known as the Earth Charter. Ruud Lubbers, former Prime Minister of Holland, initiated the Earth Charter process. It was carried out under the direction of Mikhail Gorbachev and Maurice Strong, chairman of the Earth Council. The process took eight years of deliberation with a multitude of nations and global leaders involved in the environmental, business, political, religious, and education sectors of society.

According to Maurice Strong, "The Earth Charter will be presented to the United Nations, governments, businesses, schools, and nongovernmental organizations (NGOs) as the basis for new laws and codes of conduct." In other words, this is part of a plan to try and integrate humanity into a global whole.

So what about the principles of the Earth Charter? These principles are incorporated into global governance as defined in the United Nations (UN) Commission on Global Governance's 1995 report "Our Global Neighborhood." It must be noted that the Earth Charter provides pantheistic universal religious values that are fully harmonized with a pantheistic world government whose purpose is to protect the earth at all costs. Is man now to worship the creation versus the Creator? It certainly sounds like it.

I previously mentioned the International Union for the Conservation of Nature (IUCN), an accredited scientific advisory body to the UN, in a recent article I did about the locking up of land in America by the current presidential administration. I must not draw attention to the International Covenant on Environment and Development treaty written by this organization. This document serves to integrate world religion into world government and codify the goals of the Earth Charter into international law, which is tentatively scheduled for ratification in 2002.

What does this all mean? It means that once the Earth Charter is codified into law by the IUCN treaty that it will be used to execute control over all citizens, forcing adherence to pantheistic principles that put nature's needs above human needs and welfare. Be assured; churches will be affected by these pantheistic mandates. Both the Earth Charter and IUCN are threats to western civilization. People should not view these documents with apathy.

The new treaty will be administered, along with all environmental international treaties, by the UN Trusteeship Council. The UN Trusteeship Council, as outlined in "Our Global Neighborhood," will incorporate NGOs into its structure and serve as administrator over what kind of activities will be permitted concerning the earth.

The United States must be "exceptionally wary about signing any UN treaties" that would cede sovereignty. In fact, it must be vigilant about signing any international agreements that would do this. Unmistakably, "the UN has a global governance agenda," and the Earth Charter is part of it. Much of the UN rhetoric sounds good on the surface, but one must look beyond the seemingly impressive jargon. There's poison mixed in the solution, and America best not drink it.

To freely buy into these kinds of treaties is to incrementally give up the American way of life as one knows it today. America does not need the UN to govern it. That's why we have our current government and the Constitution. America's sovereignty was bought with great price. Let's be prudent in maintaining it. To cede sovereignty to some global organization is a blatant mistake.

Chapter 11

Israel

Note: This chapter has 6 separate newspaper editorials and are not presented in a specific order of when written.

Israelis Win Wars Through Leadership

Some factors must be considered when analyzing why the Israelis win their wars with the Arabs.

First, thinking outside the box is not typically encouraged in Arab militaries, and even doing so in public can damage a military career. Further, head-to-head competition among individuals is often avoided, at least openly, for it means someone wins and someone loses. This is part of the "save face" mentality in the Arab culture, which generates a certain amount of paranoia. Paranoia can easily stifle creativity and initiative.

Second, leadership is not given sufficient attention in the Arab system of training. Two things preclude this from being so. There is a class system and a lack of noncommissioned officer development. The noncommissioned officer bridges the gap between officers and enlisted in Western forces. Typically, this is not so in the Arab militaries.

Third, decisions are very centralized in the Arab militaries without much lateral communication. U.S. officers often experience much frustration when dealing with Arab counterparts because of this highly centralized system of decision-making. Authority is rarely delegated; thus, quick and decisive decisions can be slow in coming.

The Israelis empower and encourage their lower ranks in making decisions. This leads to creativity, decisiveness, and initiative on the battlefield. As an individual who has worked with both Arab and Israeli militaries, there is a stark difference in military approach.

Finally, but foremost, there's the Abrahamic Covenant. Translated—God watches over Israel because of covenant and the honor of His Word.

***

Israel Correct in Gaza Blockade

Israel has a right to protect itself against arms flow into Gaza. The world has aggressively criticized Israel's actions, but consider that rockets continue to pour into Israel out of Gaza. Let us not mince words; Hamas and Israel are at war with each other. Preventing arms flow into Gaza that will be used against Israel is prudent.

The world, and now the United States more so, continues to criticize and put pressure on Israel for their protective actions. What would America do if rockets continually were fired into America from Mexico? Would America do nothing, or would it take action to eliminate and/or mitigate the threat?

In regard to Israel, one also needs to understand the creed of its Islamic neighbors. Countries surround Israel that want Israel totally destroyed with Arab Muslims in possession of all the land. Enemies want Israel pushed into the sea, period. Get to the core of the ultimate objective.

Given the aforementioned, can one truly blame Israel in its efforts toward self-preservation? When making policy in the political arena, countries should consider the Abrahamic Covenant with close attention.

God stated clearly in the Old Testament that the Israelites would be disbursed throughout the world, but in the last days, God would bring

Israel back together again as a nation. That, people, is a miracle. The Jews retained their identity throughout time and were never totally assimilated into other cultures.

Nations of the world, watch how you treat Israel. God is watching you.

***

Send the Palestinians to Other Arab Nations

I had the opportunity to live or work in Egypt, Jordan, Israel, and in Southern Lebanon for short periods of time during a Middle Eastern tour of duty while on assignment with the United Nations. I have conducted liaison with the Palestinian Liberation Organization and Israeli Defense Force during this period and was substantially exposed to the political instability in this area.

I have concluded that there is no political solution when fundamental religion is involved, yet, politicians will continue to play the game as though there was a suitable answer for everyone.

The simplest solution is to assimilate the Palestinians into the other Arab countries. Consider that there's no distinct Palestinian culture or language. Palestinians are Arabs, indistinguishable from Jordanians, Syrians, Lebanese, Iraqis, and others. They could be easily assimilated into these other countries if Arab nations are truly interested in resolving this situation.

It will be a mistake if Israel gives up land to establish a Palestinian State. Prior to the 1967 Arab-Israeli War, there was no serious movement for a Palestinian homeland. Admittedly, that was before the Israelis seized the West Bank and Jerusalem. But Israel captured Judea, Samaria, and East Jerusalem from Jordan's King Hussein, not Yasser Arafat, who was born in Egypt.

Arabs control almost all the Middle Eastern lands. Israel controls a minuscule section. Why have the Palestinians suddenly discovered their national identity? The Arabs want all the land. That is what all the fighting is about in Israel. No matter how many land concessions Israel makes, it will never be enough.

Giving up land to establish a Palestinian state will not resolve this conflict. It will provide a base for the Palestinians to concentrate their efforts toward further aggression against Israel.

Is this really being fair to the Palestinians? According to Arab-American author Joseph Farah, Palestine has never existed as an autonomous nation. The first time the name Palestine was used was in 70 A.D. when the Romans committed genocide against the Jews, destroyed their temple, and declared that the land of Israel would no longer be. From then on, the Romans declared it would be known as Palestine.

Palestine, as a name, was derived from the word "Philistines," a people conquered by the Jews many years prior. It was a way for the Romans to rub salt into the Jewish wounds. The area was ruled alternately by Rome, Islamic and Christian crusaders, the Ottoman Empire, and briefly, by the British after World War I.

What about Islamic holy sites in Israel? Aren't the Al Aksa Mosque and Dome of the Rock in Jerusalem important Islamic sites? One might think so, but the Koran says nothing about Jerusalem, although Mecca and Medina are mentioned countless times. In reality, there's no historical evidence to indicate that Muhammad ever visited Jerusalem.

In reality, there's no historical evidence to indicate that Muhammad ever visited Jerusalem.

How did Jerusalem become important to Islam? According to Farah, Muslims today cite a vague passage in the Koran, in the 17th Surah, entitled "The Night Journey." It relates that in a dream or vision, Muhammad was carried by night "from the sacred temple to the temple that is most remote, whose precinct we have blessed, that we might show him our signs."

In the seventh century, some Muslims identified these temples as being in Mecca and Jerusalem. That's as close as Islam's connection to Jerusalem gets. On the other hand, Jews can unequivocally trace their roots back to the days of Abraham.

Why won't the other Arab nations assimilate the Palestinians? Some of the smaller nations, such as Jordan, fear the political clout of the Palestinians. Some have a fixed dislike of the Jews and would like to see the land subjugated under Islam. I'm sure different reasons exist, but assimilation would provide a viable solution to the current situation of war and turmoil. Are the Arab nations really interested in peace? They can have peace if they really want it.

***

Don't Force Israel to Give up Land

President Trump's visit to Saudi Arabia, Israel, and the Vatican is a significant one. All three locations represent bastions of Islam, Judaism, and Christianity. That said, I want to address an item of keen concern.

Trump believes in making good deals. He believes in bringing people together to discuss issues. One issue that has remained a problem in the Middle East is the creation of a Palestinian state. Trump may have good intentions on this issue, but caution must be greatly exercised.

Do not force Israel to give up land for the creation of a Palestinian state. The world may make celebration over a movement of this nature, but it could bring devastation to America. If America forces Israel to give up land, it will set us on a collision course with God.

John McTernan, in his book *As America Has Done to Israel*, chronicles massive national disasters against America. His book points out how there is a direct correlation between the alarming number of massive disasters striking America when our leaders have pressured Israel to surrender land for so-called peace. Forcing Israel to give up land could bring catastrophe to our nation.

In Christian circles, numerous prophecies have gone forth regarding this subject. In the mouth of two or three witnesses, let everything be established. These prophecies have highlighted devastation coming to America if we force Israel to give up land.

America's future will be greatly determined how it treats Israel. Do not force Israel to give up land.

***

Do Not Divide Jerusalem or Israel

President Trump just announced his Mideast Peace Plan. Personally, I think it was a big mistake. Many will disagree with my comments. Pragmatically, it sounds good on paper, but I'm approaching this with a spiritual perspective.

I would want nothing to do with dividing Jerusalem or Israel. God gave the Israelites certain land when they finally entered the Promised Land under the leadership of Joshua. Through the centuries, turmoil and wars ensued, and the Israelites were displaced; however, in 1948, Israel became a nation again.

There is much sympathy for the Palestinians to have a homeland. I know that this is a contentious issue. I also know that Judaism, Christianity, and Islam all consider Jerusalem important to their beliefs. Again, pragmatically, it would seem to make sense to try and please both the Palestinians and Israel. Trump has tried to do that.

Even so, Shane Warren, a minister from Louisiana, stated that he heard a booming voice speak from behind him, saying, "They have divided my land; now I will divide their land." In the vision Warren knew that God was speaking about Israel and specifically Jerusalem. Warren, along with other men of God, has seen a major earthquake divide America from the Great Lakes to the Gulf of Mexico because of our efforts in dividing Jerusalem and Israel.

I recall when we forced Israel to give up Gaza that Hurricane Katrina ripped the Gulf Coast about one week later. I don't believe this was a coincidence.

America—have nothing to do with dividing Jerusalem or Israel. Don't do it!

***

Oil to Be Discovered in Israel?

The Valley of Jezreel is located near Megiddo in Israel. It's a lush, green valley that has endured wars in the past and will host the greatest of wars in the future. You see, according to the Bible, this is the area where Armageddon will take place. As I think of this location, I ponder what will bring the forces of the world into this area.

Of course, many nations that surround Israel would like to see her cast into the sea, due to ethnic and religious reasons; however, there is another catalyst that many have failed to recognize. That catalyst is oil. Some oil has already been discovered in Israel; however, sooner than many think I expect, a much larger oil discovery is going to be found in Israel.

Consider the story of Sodom and Gomorrah. Could a tremendous explosion blowing tons of rock and dirt skyward, leaving a gaping hole with great width and depth, have caused the formation of the Dead Sea? Could it have been the ignition of a huge quantity of underground methane gas and oil? After all, this is in the area where formerly Sodom, Gomorrah, and the Valley of Siddim were located. Throughout this region there were numerous oil pockets and wells that were on ground level, which is proven both historically and biblically.

Genesis 14:10 says, "And the vale of Siddim was full of slimepits; and the kings of Sodom and Gomorrah fled, and fell there; and they that remained fled to the mountain." "'Slimepits" are also translated "bitumen" or "tar pits" in other translations.

Now, consider Ezekiel 16:53, "When I shall bring again their captivity, **the captivity of Sodom and her daughters**, and the captivity of Samaria and her daughters, then will I bring again the captivity of thy captives in the midst of them." "The captivity" is also translated "fortunes" in other translations.

In 1948, Israel became a nation again. I believe a greater discovery of oil is not far off. Most assuredly, the fortunes of Sodom weren't rocks, grains of sand, nor pebbles.

Much rock that is mined from the Dead Sea is apparently saturated with oil and could possibly be mined as shale oil. Deep ravines surround this area where oil seeps are quite noticeable. The indicators are there for a potential massive discovery.

The world's demand for oil is ever-growing. It's a precious commodity that nations fight wars over. Do you think that Desert Storm was just to protect Kuwait? America was also protecting oil interests. Could discovery of substantially more oil in Israel be further reasons for nations to converge on this tiny country?

I personally believe that this oil will be discovered in Israel in accordance with God's timetable. Look for it, ultimately, to become another catalyst toward the road to Armageddon.

Isaiah 45:3 further says, "And **I will give thee the treasures of darkness, and hidden riches of secret places**, that thou mayest know that I, the Lord, which call thee by thy name, am the God of Israel." Although this scripture was spoken to Cyrus, I don't believe the treasures of darkness are far behind for Israel in the form of oil.

Discovery of a vast supply of oil in Israel will have worldwide strategic, geopolitical, and economic implications. Be assured, major secular news and media organizations will quickly and pervasively broadcast this discovery. Although much of the secular world will not see God's hand in this whole affair, many will truly acknowledge the glory and honor of God, who keeps His covenant.

The world's demand for oil is ever-growing. It's a precious commodity that nations fight wars over. Do you think that Desert Storm was just to protect Kuwait? America was also protecting oil interests. Could discovery of oil in Israel be further reason for nations to converge on this tiny country?

I personally believe that oil will be discovered in Israel in accordance with God's timetable. Look for it, ultimately, to become another catalyst towards the road to Armageddon.

Chapter 12

Miscellaneous Commentaries

Note: This chapter has 11 separate newspaper editorials and are not presented in a specific order of when written.

Duduman's Message to America: Repent

Dumitru Duduman, a strong and committed man of God from Romania, smuggled over 300,000 Bibles into the former Soviet Union. Eventually, Romanian forces found Duduman and put him in jail. There they brutally persecuted and tortured him for months; however, he was strengthened by an angel throughout this whole ordeal and survived.

Duduman subsequently was told by the angel that he would be going to America on a certain date. The Romanian forces were not having success with Duduman giving them revelation about the Bible operations; thus, they eventually decided to exile him from Romania on July 22, 1984.

It happened to be on the exact date that the angel had previously told Duduman he would leave. God was sending Duduman to America with a message to tell her to repent.

After Duduman arrived in California, he realized that he was in a sinful country. An angel appeared to Duduman and showed him the future of America. He was shown scenes of Las Vegas, New York City, California, and Florida as he was told that America would burn. He was told that Russia, Cuba, Central America, Nicaragua, Mexico, and two other countries would attack America. He was told that Russia will bomb our nuclear missile sites. He was told that the fall of America would start with an internal revolution started by the communists. Some of the people would be fighting against the government. The U.S. government would be busy trying to handle the internal problems, and then adversarial forces would seize the opportunity and launch an attack. Then he more clearly understood why God had sent him here.

God loves America, but He does not love what America has become. Sin had reached the Most High as a stench, and God is not pleased with this nation. There is sin in the church and throughout America.

Message to America: **Repent. America must repent or suffer the consequences of its sin.**

Note: I've previously read Dumitru Duduman's book, *Through the Fire Without Burning*. I'm convinced that this was a genuine man of God. His story needs to be heard; therefore, I've included his message to America in this section.

***

Parallels Between Israel and the U.S.

Significant parallels exist between Israel and the United States. One only needs examine Israel's history to predict America's future. There are distinct warning signs for our nation, but America refuses to recognize them. Unmistakably, humanism and secularism have significantly affected the course of this nation.

God made it clear to Israel not to marry the heathen in the land. He told Israel to clear out the land of the heathen. However, we know through history that Israel ultimately allowed inter-marriage with the heathen. What did this bring? It brought in the worship of false gods and their practices. It affected their relationship with God.

Child sacrifice became a reality as a result of Israel's transgressions. Where's the parallel with America? It's quite obvious when one considers that abortion is, in reality, child sacrifice. Is there really a difference between a child sacrificed to Molech or one to the god of selfishness or hedonism? Many people have become apathetic and tired of hearing about the subject of abortion. Time for a yawn. Regardless, child sacrifice is abominable to God, whether one wants to hear it or not. It was wrong then, and it's wrong now.

God said not to have strange gods before them. However, once again, history shows how the influences of pagans gripped the heart of Israel. These influences caused Israel to go in the wrong direction. Things were allowed that shouldn't have been allowed. Things were done that shouldn't have been done. Oh, how the heart can slowly grow cold.

God brought Israel into a good land and established them. God established America. Take a look at the Mayflower Compact, Declaration of Independence, and the Constitution. Read them with the heart each was originally written, not with the heart of today's Washington interpretation.

This nation has allowed humanistic, secularist, and pagan influences to affect its walk and allegiance to God. What happens to nations of this sort? What happened to Israel?

In 586 B.C., history shows that Nebuchadnezzar stormed Jerusalem and took Israel into captivity. Oppressive armies continued to come in future years, even after Israel was restored. History could have been written differently for them. Follow their relationship with God during their periods of tribulation as you track their history. Distinct clues and reasons are given for causation of their problematic periods. America, with pen in hand, should take notes.

Our Judeo-Christian heritage has allowed us to serve the true and living God since this nation's inception. His guidance has been given to us through the Holy Bible. We need not pay homage to the guidance of other false gods since we serve the true and living God. Even so, this nation has done just that. The melting pot effect of false gods has tainted this nation's way of thinking and the direction it chooses to follow.

The guidance and laws of this nation must pay homage, first and foremost, to God if it's going to continue to prosper. It must not depart from its Judeo-Christian heritage. One might be an atheist, Buddhist, Muslim, or humanist, but the laws of this land must not appease the beliefs and religions of such. It must remain firmly grounded in Christianity if there is to be a future for America. It must eliminate this aberrant separation of church and state policy.

If America does not reverse the course she's on, she will face dire circumstances in the future. She will pay dearly. Expect to see increased storms or natural disasters, such as earthquakes. Expect to see foreign troops on this land. Expect to see Americans in chains on their own soil. Many in America will then cry out to the false gods they embraced, but their false gods won't answer. Why? False gods don't exist except in the deceptions and wiles used by Satan to draw this nation into sin, death, and chaos.

America must honor God again with a pure heart. Her heart must return to God from the top on down with repentance. For our government, here's a good and immediate start: restore school prayer, repeal Roe vs. Wade, allow monuments such as the Ten Commandments to be placed in government buildings, and lead in righteousness. Give honor and priority to the true and living God.

Let the words of Joshua 24:15 ring true for our government and nation, "But as for me and my house, we will serve the Lord." Those who honor God, God will honor.

***

U.S.A. May Face Judgment for a National Irreverence

Agnostics and atheists will probably not find this article very appealing and interesting; however, I hope anyone who has or has had a relationship with God, will strongly ponder these words.

It's becoming painfully obvious that America does not respect the holiness of God. Simply put, He is holy and deserves sincere reverence. America, in recent decades, has begun to show irreverence and a deep lack of respect for the Bible and things of God. And what point does God say, "It's enough"? Yes, God is merciful, but at what point does America cross the line?

Does the shedding of innocent blood cry out from the ground to God? It certainly did when Abel was slain by Cain. The Bible says God does not change. America has legalized the abortion of close to forty million babies since the tragic Roe vs. Wade Supreme Court decision. Israel even went astray during periods of apostasy when it sacrificed babies to the false gods of Molech and Baal. Today, children in America are sacrificed to the gods of materialism and selfishness. To say the least, blood is dripping from the claws of the eagle, and it's innocent blood.

God destroyed Sodom and Gomorrah for their lewdness and debauchery. The term "sodomite" was derived from the city of Sodom. Just last year, our leaders in Washington openly celebrated the assignment of a gay ambassador to Luxemburg. Vermont recently legalized gay civil unions. Gay rights parades are becoming commonplace as many in America are beginning to accept this as an acceptable lifestyle. Once again, God does not change. Is there an arrogance in America that says it doesn't matter what God thinks about this subject?

Is there a lust for pleasure? After all, one only goes around once in life. It's clear that many in America have centered themselves on the recreational pleasures of this finite world. "Live and be happy, for tomorrow one may die" has become a motto for many. If it feels good, then do it. Drugs, adultery, and fornication are commonplace. Divorce is rampant. Do all these things please God?

Society has become more desensitized as it continues to honor and soak in movies and music that preach lust, violence, and rebellion. Violence is regularly reported on the television screens and front pages of newspapers. It's now not unusual for teens to shoot fellow classmates. Random shootings by gang members are just another news item. Rapes are common occurrence. Do all these things please God?

Pornography is honored as a means of free expression. After all, a man has his rights. Young children today can get on the Internet and see all sorts of things that, ultimately, will not edify but negatively influence them. Does one really believe the availability and openness of pornography in America please God?

In recent years there have been severe earthquakes, floods, hurricanes, and tornadoes. Are these warnings to America that she needs to repent and reverse the irreverent course she has been on? Will she heed these warnings? Often, as shown in the Bible, God's ultimate judgment to a deviant and defiant nation came through force. Are oppression and war coming to America's soil?

Let me say this as clearly as I can say it: America is not as secure as many people believe it to be. Don't think for one moment that war could not take place on this soil. America has virtually no defense against ballistic missiles and would be vulnerable to surprise attack. Consider that Russia and China formed a strategic partnership in November 1998 and now share joint intelligence. Consider the spirits behind these governors.

Where is the outrage of the churches in America for what has been happening within this nation? Apathy must be replaced with prayerful and repentant hearts if America is to reverse course. It must start within the churches. Churches must recognize the times, and in unity, pray fervently for this nation. Setting special prayer times aside for this nation is in order for churches not already doing this. America needs prayer, and she needs it now.

Is judgment coming to America? God does not change. One may say that judgment is punishment, but in reality, it's the consequences of sin. America is not special in this regard. Once again, Christians need to fervently intercede for this nation and do it now.

***

Not-So-Civil Liberties Union

The American Civil Liberties Union (ACLU) was founded in 1920 by a group that included well-known Communists William Z. Foster, Elizabeth Gurley Flynn, and Harry Ward. Is sounds like a nice name for group that would stand for American civil liberties and moral values, but I believe quite the opposite is true. The ACLU has consistently worked to tear away the very foundation of true liberty, morality, and religion in America. Don't be fooled by the name.

Roger Baldwin was the ACLU's top official for more than fifty years until his death in 1981. According to the book *Valley of Decision* by Dr. Sterling Lacey, Roger Baldwin spelled out his own goals in 1935 as follows: "I am for socialism, disarmament, and ultimately for abolishing the State itself as an instrument of violence and compulsion. I seek the social ownership of property, the abolition of the propertied class, and sole control by those who produce wealth. Communism is the goal."[14]

Currently, the ACLU has a fifty-state network of staffed affiliate offices in most major cities, more than 300 chapters in smaller towns, and regional offices in Denver and Atlanta. Work is coordinated by a national office in New York, aided by a legislative office in Washington that lobbies Congress.

It has more than sixty staff attorneys, who collaborate with at least 2,000 volunteer attorneys in handling close to 6,000 cases annually—making them the largest public-interest law firm in the United States. The ACLU appears before the Supreme Court more than any other organization except the U.S. Department of Justice.

---

[14]"Talk: Roger Nash Baldwin," Wikiquote, https://1ref.us/1fy (accessed November 5, 2020).

The organization has consistently waged war against internal security laws, school prayer, restrictions against abortion, community nativity scenes and similar practices, and capital punishment for horrible crimes. Far from defending the moral values of this nation, the ACLU has spent extensive effort defending the interests of pornographers, homosexuals, drug pushers, and other elements of counter-culture in our society.

Nadine Strossen, president of the ACLU since 1991 and pornography defender, for example, believes that depictions of any and all sensual activities should be a protected form of expression under the First Amendment for anyone. By defending a supposed right such as pornography, the organization threatens the foundations of a moral America. In reality, the vast majority of Americans find themselves severely imposed upon and less free.

Anti-traditional views of Nadine Strauss and the ACLU that flow from the acceptance of pornography, due to breakdown of other social restraints, include:

- Recreational drugs should be legalized for all adults.
- Recreational drugs should be made available to children with parent's consent.
- Pornography should be available to mature children because minor females are old enough to get an abortion without parental consent.
- No random drug testing should be allowed, even for airline pilots.

There's a struggle going on in America against the common family. There's a struggle going on for the hearts and minds of its citizens. That's why it's so important to know what influential groups, such as the ACLU, really stand for. The Bill of Rights were written to protect the rights of its citizens. Unfortunately, the spirit that inspired the writing of these rights is not the same spirit of interpretation in select groups today.

President Calvin Coolidge once stated, "The foundations of our society and our government rest so much on the teachings of the Bible that it would be difficult to support them if faith in these teachings would cease to be practically universal in our country." Based on sustained performance, it's apparent that the ACLU does not share the same belief on this subject as President Coolidge. Be careful of wolves in sheep's clothing.

***

Youth Gangs on the Rise

Youth gangs throughout this country are on the rise. Sources vary on the exact number of them, but all appear to indicate that they are pervasive with vast numbers in membership. Youth growing up with little or no adult supervision clearly contributes to their increase. A child desires to feel secure, and when that security is not provided at home, then the child often seeks the security elsewhere. The void, in today's society, is commonly filled through gang membership. The gang becomes the child's surrogate family and provides a sense of identity, belonging, power, and protection.

It appears gangs are built from groups called "cliques" and are loosely organized, although many may have several leaders. It's not unusual for leadership responsibilities to be shared. It's also not unusual to find children as young as eight years old as members. From there, ages can easily exceed the teen years.

Gangs may be race/ethnic-oriented, economic-oriented, or territorial-oriented. Identity is depicted through colors, signs, symbols, and tattoos. Vocabulary is often peculiar, with code words being used as standard procedure. "Tagging" their territory through the use of graffiti is common practice. Extreme loyalty is expected and demanded.

A gang culture is much different than normalized society and projects different values. It confronts adult authority on a multitude of levels: dress, sex, power, love, education, language, and confrontational attitudes to mainline values. Partying and fighting are commonplace. Violence, abuse of women, and disrespect for authority are often evident.

Young people lacking values and a moral consciousness can easily be drawn into a gang lifestyle. Many children find themselves in hopeless situations at home. In so many cases, there aren't people there pointing them in the right direction and giving them self-esteem and encouragement. The decline of the nuclear family has exacerbated this problem.

Stopping young people from choosing a life of violence and crime is crucial for two key reasons as we turn to the next century. First, it's better for them. One reaps what one sows. Many will die early deaths or end up in prison. Second, violent crime will increase throughout the nation if it is not stopped. Violent crime by gang members can only increase as gangs grow and become more territorial. Many of these gangs are heavily armed with sophisticated weapons for those who have not noticed.

This leads us again to the importance of the nuclear family. Growing up in a balanced home where values are taught makes a difference. It makes a difference in quality of life for one's offspring and for the nation as a whole. Typically, a child raised with moral values and who has a good opinion of himself will not end up in a life of violent crime. Federal and state legislation to promote, support, and protect the nuclear family, as opposed to denigration of it, should be actively pursued by legislators.

Need I say more?

> *Growing up in a balanced home where values are taught makes a difference. It makes a difference in quality of life for one's offspring and for the nation as a whole.*

***

Halloween Traditions and Tales

Some thoughts on Halloween: How did Halloween come about? It appears that it actually evolved from the B.C. time period of the Celtic nations, during the holiday of Samhain, when summer officially ended on October 31. Apparently, the Celts believed that the veil between this world and the next was thinnest at this time of year. However, different versions exist on its evolvement from the Celtic people. Two versions are as follows:

- Disembodied spirits of all those who had died throughout the year would come back in search of living bodies to possess for the next year. It was believed to be their only hope for the afterlife. Of course, villagers do not want to be processed, so they would dress up in ghoulish costumes and noisily parade around the neighborhood, being destructive in order to frighten away the spirits.
- Souls of the dead returned to their former homes to be entertained by the living. Bonfires were built on top of hills so they could find their way. Suitable food and shelter were provided for these spirits, or else they would cast spells and cause havoc. The spirits demanded placating by receiving a type of worship or offering. Some believe "Trick or Treat" emulates this today.

Apparently, as time went on, the Catholic Church tried to eliminate this pagan celebration by offering All Saints Day as a substitute. All Saints Day is a Catholic day of observance in honor of saints on November 1.

Even so, a mixture of customs and traditions evolved into what is currently today known as Halloween.

Halloween was brought to America in the 1840s by Irish immigrants fleeing their country's potato famine. At that time, tipping over outhouses and unhinging fence gates were not uncommon in New England.

Along with the Irish immigrants came the tradition of the jack-o-lantern. Jack was an Irishman trickster, as the tale goes. He tricked Satan into climbing up an apple tree and then carved a cross symbol into the tree trunk. Although Satan was now trapped up the tree, Jack made a deal with Satan that, if he would never tempt him again, he would let Satan down.

As the tale goes, Jack died and was denied entrance into heaven because of his meanness. He was then denied access to hell because he had tricked Satan. Satan forced him to walk the earth endlessly but gave him a coal to light his path. Jack put it in a hollowed-out turnip to keep it glowing longer.

The Irish immigrants found that pumpkins were more plentiful in America than turnips. Although they had previously used turnips, the jack-o-lantern now became a hollowed-out pumpkin.

There are many other Halloween folk traditions. Three common ones associated with apples are as follows:

- Unmarried people would attempt to take a bite out of an apple bobbing in a pail of water or suspended on a string. The first person to take a bite would be the next to marry.
- Peeling an apple in front of a candle-lit mirror would show the image of one's future spouse.
- Producing a long unbroken peel was said to show longevity of years. The longer the peel, the longer the life.

People approach Halloween with different attitudes. Some see it as merely a vestige of some ancient pagan ritual, while others view it as something to totally avoid due to its pagan roots and practices.

It's acknowledged by Satanists as an important time on their calendar. Satanists practice horrible deeds and rituals of darkness on this time-honored day.

Many Christians point out that Halloween honors false gods or demonic spirits. Why allow one's child to dress up as a witch, hobgoblin, devil, or ghost? Although some may argue that Halloween is done only in fun, many Christians counter that its pagan roots and practices represent Satan and his domain. The Bible says to have nothing to do with the deeds of darkness. To emulate is to be on dangerous ground, and it does not honor God.

So now you have some background and thoughts on this holiday. What does Halloween mean to you? Pause and consider this question for a while. Everyone has an opinion. After all, this holiday is now upon us.

***

Harry Potter: A Cause for Concern

Harry Potter appears to be getting quite a bit of attention in the book and movie worlds. Harry Potter, a cute little boy, goes to witchcraft school to learn how to do witchcraft better. Although he's considered good, the entire theme should raise some serious questions and detailed scrutiny.

Webster's *New World Dictionary* defines witchcraft as "the power or practices of witches; sorcery." It further defines sorcery as "the supposed use of an evil supernatural power over people and their affairs; witchcraft." By definition, witchcraft uses evil supernatural power. It's nothing for young nor older minds to play with.

I confess I have not read a Harry Potter book nor have seen the movie, but merely on the surface of the aforementioned, I think I can make some valid conclusions. The Bible is clear about God's thoughts on witchcraft. To put it bluntly, divination, casting spells, witchcraft, and sorcery are detestable practices in the eyes of God. There's no ambiguity here, even as attractive and as inoffensive as Hollywood or well-written books can make them seem.

Sure the movie is entertaining. Would you expect anything less from Hollywood? It probably has some exceptional special effects. I expect the lighting, color, and animation features are probably outstanding, but remember, it's all designed to make it fun for the observer. Always remember one's eyes and ears are the key to one's heart or inner being.

Harry Potter is packaged nicely. As I understand it, many adults and children love the books and movie. Even so, one cannot separate evil spirits from the package and program. One cannot hide the fact that witchcraft and sorcery have to do with the demonic realm producing unnatural effects in the world.

Would Satan like people to watch this movie? You bet he would. To practice witchcraft is, in reality, serving Satan. Is it pleasing to God for people to entertain themselves by watching occult practices? Is it pleasing to God to have children cast spells or mix potions after reading a Harry Potter book or seeing a movie? No, it's not pleasing to him. There's nothing cute about it.

Just to imitate these practices is to begin to get on dangerous ground (fantasy or no fantasy).

Children will emulate their parents. Parents who compromise on godly values let their children know it's acceptable to compromise on them, too. A child will typically believe his parents when the parents say there's no harm in something. A parent who encourages reading of the Harry Potter books should consider what I'm saying. Children have impressionable minds. Is diligent reading about a cute little boy who practices wizardry, or in essence, the works of Satan, really what parents want their children feeding their hearts on?

The Internet gives people substantial access to numerous and varied subjects. I expect many young followers of Harry Potter probably check out different websites. Perhaps casting spells would be a good lead to some other interesting subjects like Ouija boards, tarot cards, or other occult items of possible interest. Don't underestimate the power of a young and inquisitive mind craftily pointed in a predetermined direction.

Some may still disagree with my comments and continue to insist that Harry Potter is just an innocent and entertaining story. That sounds good, but let's phrase it a little bit differently. It's acceptable and good to go to movies or read books that glorify Satan if there's an entertaining and compelling story involved. Always remember it's easy for one to justify oneself through secular rationalization.

***

Hurricanes with More to Come

I recall a story from the Old Testament that remains with me. David went to God because there was a great famine in the land. God revealed to him that it was caused by something Saul set in motion years before through his actions. Israel, as a nation, was reaping the negative results of its leadership.

Today, Roe v. Wade steadfastly continues since 1973. Abortion is a serious offense to God, whether people believe it or not. It is morally wrong. Innocent blood is shed through this infanticide policy; yet, America continues to follow this policy of legalized murder.

Pornography, homosexuality, and same-sex marriage issues continue to be given focus in our society. Christianity continues to be targeted, while religions with false gods are given greater latitude.

As I submit this, Hurricane Gustav is active in nearby waters off America. Yes, there have been hurricanes before, but I think America should perceive a message being sent its way. The number of storms with intensity appears to have increased around our shores in recent years. Tornadoes appear to have increased all over our nation in recent years.

I believe that many storms in previous years were lessened or impeded from reaching our shores, but I perceive that God's hand of protection is now lifting from America.

Demonic forces come to steal, kill, and destroy. America, once a great nation, has become wicked in God's sight. Without His hand of protection, America faces some serious days ahead.

***

Energy From Beneath Affects Weather Patterns

Earthquakes are the result of plate tectonics, of pressures forcing faults to rip apart. Magma activity may lead to volcanic eruptions, which often sets off harmonic tremors. Even so, one factor often missed by people in all this is energy.

Energy is generated from deep within the earth. Heavy metals are literally vaporized by intense heat and then compressed into a white-hot liquid by the weight of the earth pressing on it. Massive electromagnetic waves radiate upwards, and when it comes near the surface, those energy waves can, and do change weather patterns, often with much violence. Not only this but as the mantle is ripped apart, it releases a massive amount of this super-charged energy that moves with great speed, often resulting in a powerful earthquake.

As I've stated in previous submissions, the global-warming doctrine perpetrated on mankind is a scam, and the globalists behind this charade know it. The effect on weather has more to do with the rent in the earth's mantle than it does from man. Energy beneath the earth's surface is having more of an influence on the earth's climate and weather patterns more than most people realize.

This surging energy generates tremendous heat and appears to affect the atmosphere. Storms may be generated in the form of hurricanes, tornadoes, blizzards, and freezing cold.

As we proceed into this decade, look for earthquake activity to increase. In light of America's spiritual condition, look for it to hit America as well.

***

Let's Get Tough on Crime

America needs to get tough on crime. Crime costs the United States millions of dollars each year as thousands are killed or seriously injured. Many families have had loved ones greatly victimized. As society's misguided and neglected youth continue to grow up in our current-day society, look for crime to continue to increase if the current trend is not somehow reversed. As such, America better look hard at its anti-crime policies. What can be done to make them better? Where have current policies faltered? These are questions that must be closely examined and dealt with as we come into a new century.

Three areas that deserve close scrutiny are sentencing, criminal procedure, and enforcement.

First, let's take the subject of sentencing. Consider the following:

- Put serious, repeat felons away permanently.
- Keep violent criminals behind bars for their entire sentences. If the price they pay for crime is too low, then expect to see forthcoming violations on humanity when they get out.
- Try adolescents as adults and subject them to adult penalties if they commit adult crimes.
- Use restitution as punishment for less-serious offenses in order to relieve a highly burdened prison system.

Second, criminal procedure reforms need to be closely examined. Consider the following:

- Use and enforce the death penalty, affirmed by the Supreme Court in 1976, where justified. It should be noted that capital punishment was widely practiced in this country when the Constitution was drafted.
- Close legal loopholes that permit criminals to exploit the courts and eliminate the bureaucratic red tape. For example, Ted Bundy remained on death row for ten years after murdering more than fifty women. Procedures must be implemented to promote timely enforcement of sentencing if respect for the law is to be enhanced.
- Improve the exclusionary rule that was created by the courts to implement the Fourth Amendment (all persons have the right to be secure from unreasonable searches and seizures). This was to protect the public from law enforcement abuse, but the rule has been used unfairly to favor criminals.

- Allow the jury to ask questions if their questions aren't covered during the course of the trial.
- Inform the jury of the defendant's past criminal history, especially prior to sentence deliberations. Mitigating circumstances or a past record of incorrigible behavior may be important to know.

Third, enforcement must be aggressive. The following pertains:

- Ensure criminals are prosecuted.
- Increase the police force in areas were needed. This may mean hiring more policemen.
- Protect citizens from repeated sex felons. For example, "Megan's Law" amended the Violent Crime Control and Law Enforcement Act of 1994 and requires state governments to disclose information and notify communities about convicted sex offenders who are released from incarceration.

Examining our current crime policies only makes sense. People should be able to walk their streets and not live in fear. The average law-abiding citizens and victims have rights, too. Crime must be dealt with efficiently and effectively. Without sufficient deterrence and effective policies, there will be repeat violations on humanity from the same offenders.

I remember a conversation I had with an individual while I was on assignment in the Middle East during my military career. He had witnessed a public beheading in Saudi Arabia. He said it made quite an impression on those in observance. Crime is dealt with swiftly and with deterrence in mind in Saudi Arabia. Incidentally, their crime rate pales in comparison to America's. Strong deterrence, coupled with other effective policies, will make a difference.

***

Is Tipping an Obligation?

Tipping has become pervasive throughout the United States and many parts of the world. It covers a wide spectrum of areas, from food servers to porters to proprietors and numerous others. Notice that just a decade ago, it wasn't so common to brazenly solicit for counter service, but in today's coffeehouses or juice bars, tip jars are now even commonplace. In recent years, tipping had been considered an acronym for promptness and courteous service, but it has now evolved into standardization for figuring into payment of wages.

Many people consider tipping to be a muddled issue. Some realize that food servers and others count on tips as a real part of their salaries, while others may not view it as quite so important. After all, food servers get paid by the restaurants, don't they? Many do not realize that food servers commonly get $2.13 per hour and their tips. They also pay taxes on these tips. Get a couple of tables that don't leave tips, and a food server may be in big trouble for the day. Is this fair to a hardworking food server, or others that depend on tips in a similar manner to make a living?

Many in society believe that the public is expected to subsidize the tightness of their employers. Is this right? Should tipping be abolished as obligatory? After all, a recent survey indicated that 40 percent of Americans don't like to tip. I'm sure many diligent food servers, and others that depend on tips, have had their share of stingy customers that refuse to leave little or nothing, even if the service was excellent. Perhaps restaurants should be required to pay at least minimum wage and above to its food servers.

I expect there are many food servers and others who have had to quit their positions because they were not paid enough. After all, $2.13 an hour isn't much to lean on if tips aren't forthcoming. I imagine some weeks, some of them may feel like they've worked for pennies. They may be trying real hard, but if tips aren't there, then they're put into some cumbersome positions by this system of payment. One may say then let them quit, but one must also understand that they need a job. Receiving at least a minimum wage with the potential to make more would be advantageous to many of them placed into this situation of employment.

I imagine some of the restaurants would then say that they would have to raise meal prices if they paid their food servers more. Is this really true? Cafeteria and fast-food restaurants typically pay their employees at least minimum wage and above. A cafeteria gives meals comparable to many standard restaurants within similar price structure, and no tips are required. That's probably why many seniors go to a cafeteria because obligatory tipping significantly increases the price of a meal. I imagine many standard restaurants make some nice profit during the course of a year. Could they not properly pay their employees without raising the price of their meals? That would mean a bit less profit, but it would certainly be appreciated by many of their employees.

This leads to another perspective. Expectations of tipping vary in different countries. One may tip a bellman in America, but tipping a bellman in China is considered rude. One may tip in Europe for directions, but in America, it's not so expected. Thus, mores and traditions are dictated by one's particular culture and society. Perhaps this is paradigm thinking, but obligatory tipping could be done away with in America, and employees paid at least minimum salaries and above. This would accomplish the following:

- People would not feel obligatory toward tipping.
- Food servers and others would have dependable salaries.
- Tipping would not be such a muddled and unclear issue. Does one tip 15 percent, or is it now 20 percent? When and where is a tip expected? Who really dictates tip protocol?

This approach would not prevent a customer from leaving a tip for superb service if the customer desired to do so, but it would not be obligatory. It would then become the customer's prerogative and not thought of as some compelling requirement.

Conclusion

This book shared many opinions on the aspects of life. The common theme throughout the verbiage, in my viewpoint, was good versus evil. Now I want to get to the most important part of this book. **If there is any doubt as to your eternal destiny or salvation, then today, I urge you to consider the following Scriptures.**

"As it is written, There is none righteous, no, not one" (**Rom. 3:10**).

"For all have sinned, and come short of the glory of God" (**Rom. 3:23**).

"For the wages of sin is death; but the gift of God is eternal life through Jesus Christ our Lord" (**Rom. 6:23**).

"For there is one God, and one mediator between God and men, the man Christ Jesus" (**1 Tim. 2:5**).

"That if thou shalt confess with thy mouth the Lord Jesus, and shalt believe in thine heart that God hath raised him from the dead, thou shalt be saved. For with the heart man believeth unto righteousness; and with the mouth confession is made unto salvation" (**Rom. 10:9–10**).

Now, here's a Sinner's Prayer to receive Jesus as Lord and Savior. Please repeat the following prayer and mean it from your heart. You must be sincere, or they will only be words and mean nothing. If you are sincere, then God is sincere because God always honors His Word.

"Dear Heavenly Father, I come to You in the name of the Lord Jesus Christ. I ask You to forgive me of all my sins. I accept Jesus as my Lord and Savior and believe in my heart that He died on the cross for my sins and that You raised Him from the dead so that I could have right standing with You. I now repent and confess Jesus as my Lord and Savior. I thank You for giving me eternal salvation and ask that You would help me in my Christian walk."

I strongly encourage you to read your Bible daily to get to know the Lord better, talk to God daily in prayer, and find a church where the Bible is taught as the complete Word of God. I also encourage you to be water baptized.

About the Author

Commander Michael H. Imhof, U.S. Navy (ret.), and former Navy SEAL, was born in Fort Bragg, North Carolina and raised in Blasdell, New York. He attended the State University College of New York at Buffalo, where he received a Bachelor of Science Degree. He was commissioned in 1973. After completing Basic Underwater Demolition/SEAL training in Coronado, California, Commander Imhof was assigned to SEAL Team TWO, subsequent Naval Special Warfare commands, and other duty assignments.

Commander Imhof, possessing a Naval Special Warfare designator, has served throughout the world in numerous positions. Assignments include Platoon Commander, Training Officer, Operations Officer, Staff Officer, Executive Officer and Commanding Officer. A graduate of the U.S. Army Special Forces Officer Qualification Course, he also earned a Master's Degree in Administration from George Washington University and served as an instructor at the U.S. Naval Academy. He has numerous service awards.

He has lived in Egypt, Jordan, Israel, Panama, South Korea, Liberia, Sudan, Somalia, Sinai and Afghanistan besides serving in numerous other countries throughout the world. On December 17, 1981, he was hijacked in Southern Lebanon while on duty with the United Nations Truce Supervision Organization. He believes his later escape was truly a blessing of God. A military officer of strong Christian convictions, Commander Imhof is ready and willing to share his faith with all. He is convinced that the Bible is the authoritative and uncompromised Word of God and gives thanks for the wonderful blessings of God in his life. He is the author of seven other Christian books.

Additional Books by Author

• God's Word: Bulletproof

This 144-page book uses prophetic analysis, archeological evidence, and science and common sense reasoning to prove the Bible. The author draws from his many worldwide travels and personal experiences to lead people to logical conclusions in a concise, informative, insightful and easy-to-read book. This is a great book for anyone searching for the truth, or existence, of God, and for those who maintain reference books. **FIVE STAR READ.** Great book to have in your library, and for use in witnessing!

ISBN 978-1-4796-1347-2; Aspect Books; go to www.aspectbooks.com or www.amazon.com.

• Stand Up For God

This 66-page book discusses biblical principles learned in a military career. Travel with Commander Michael Imhof around the globe and learn about what it means to *Stand Up for God*. The former U.S. Navy SEAL shares his many experiences including Basic Underwater Demolition/SEAL training, being **HIJACKED** in Southern Lebanon, assignments at SEAL commands, and working with officers from the Soviet Union. These vivid stories, plus many more, will show the reader what it's like to be a fearless Christian in a sinful and selfish world. Material is written in simplicity and with clarity. It's outstanding reading and has something of interest for all.

If you have a friend or relative in the military, this is a great book to put in their hands. It's **Highly Recommended.**

ISBN 978-1-4796-0847-8; Aspect Books; go to www.aspectbooks. com or www.amazon.com.

• Supernatural Testimonies

This 152-page book has twenty-nine testimonies of people from a broad spectrum of different lifestyles.

Read about how the manifested love of God set people free from bondage, deception, and desperate situations.

The writer says, "The people in these testimonies came to realize that there was a void in their lives. So many times people look back over their lives and realize that God was tugging on their hearts all the time, but they wouldn't listen. Thus, people go their ways, make poor decisions, and plunge into sin. As a result, people often call out to God in desperate situations."

ISBN 1-933858-02-8; Evangel Press; go to www.amazon.com.

• Testimonies of Ex-Muslims

This 69-page book has eighteen testimonies of Muslims who left the Islamic faith and made their decision for Christianity. The content and style of these chapters has been presented the way the people have presented their testimonies. Read of how God moves on hearts who truly desire to know Him, regardless of the severe persecution and consequences.

The writer says, "I was living in Afghanistan when the idea came to me about putting together a small book of testimonies from ex-Muslims. Many people have been so misled by the religion of Islam. In many cases, Muslims are very sincere in their beliefs, but that does not make their beliefs correct. Truth, in reality, is more important than sincerity."

ISBN 1-933858-01-X; Evangel Press; go to www.amazon.com.

• Walking with God

This 188-page daily devotional in poetic form conveys truths of the Bible and how they apply to life in the area of successful everyday living.

The author says, "In reality, each daily reading provides distinct and positive direction, much like a small sermon. Value the truths of the Bible, for the Bible is a special gift to man. It always leads us to victory because God is a good God and only wants the best for us."

ISBN 1-57258-222-7; Aspect Books; go to www.aspectbooks.com or www.amazon.com.

• Lessons from Bible Characters

This 57-page book is a straightforward analysis of Biblical characters and situations that inspire both teens and adults.

The purpose of this book is to examine thirty-five situations where we can learn from Bible characters. In Chapter 28 titled "Faith Pays Off," the author writes about a specific Bible character then states, "Let us also not allow temporal circumstances, no matter what they are, prevent us from receiving from God. The storms of life or adversities say one thing, but the Word of God says victory."

ISBN 1-57258-019-4; TEACH Services, Inc.; go to www.teachservices. com, or www.amazon.com. (Also available in Spanish via author's website by request).

• More Lessons from Bible Characters

This 64-page book gives insightful analysis of Biblical characters and situations that bring encouragement both teens and adults.

The author writes, "Thirty-five situations are examined, and again, short summaries and simple conclusions are made for everyday living."

In Chapter 19 titled "Love Is An Action Word," the author analyzes a Bible character, then writes, "Love truly makes a difference in lives, for those in need of it and for those giving it. We're the better for it as we put love into action."

ISBN 1-57258-205-7; TEACH Services, Inc.; go to www.teachservices. com, or www.amazon.com. (Also available in Spanish via author's website by request).

CONTACT INFORMATION

EVANGELIST: Michael H. Imhof is an **EVANGELIST**. His goal is to speak before congregations where God opens the doors for him. That said, his background is unique versus most. He's a **retired U.S. Navy Commander and a former Navy SEAL**. He has lived and worked in a multitude of countries in the world on different continents, including Muslim countries.

He has spoken in numerous churches and different denominations throughout the United States and outside America on varied subjects over time. He speaks at men's events and also conducts revival meetings. He has a fervent heart for the things of God. He firmly believes that Jesus Christ is the way of salvation. If one does not find Jesus Christ in this lifetime as Lord and Savior, one will not find Him in the next.

A dynamic speaker, Commander Imhof, under the inspiration of the Holy Spirit, uses his unique background and many experiences in encouraging, edifying, and inspiring others in the things of God. Anytime he's behind the pulpit, he seeks for the Holy Spirit to speak through him. When he finishes ministering, he wants lives changed for God's glory. He gives God all the praise.

BASIC MISSION: Salvation of souls for God's kingdom and to assist/educate/encourage people in the things of God.

WEBSITE: www.michaelimhofministries.org.

SPEAKING ENGAGEMENTS: Feel free to contact Commander (Evangelist) Michael H. Imhof via website for speaking engagements.

We invite you to view the complete
selection of titles we publish at:
www.ASPECTBooks.com

We encourage you to write us
with your thoughts about this,
or any other book we publish at:
info@ASPECTBooks.com

ASPECT Books' titles may be purchased in
bulk quantities for educational, fund-raising,
business, or promotional use.
bulksales@ASPECTBooks.com

Finally, if you are interested in seeing
your own book in print, please contact us at:
publishing@ASPECTBooks.com

We are happy to review your manuscript at no charge.